MW00364687

C

A Dabhand Guide

Mark Burgess

DABS PRESS

C: A Dabhand Guide

© Mark Burgess 1988
ISBN 1-870336-16-X
First edition June 1988
Second edition January 1989

Editor: Shona McIsaac.
Typesetting: Bruce Smith and Janice Horrocks
Cover: Clare Atherton.
Internal Illustrations: Clare Atherton and David Price

Acornsoft is a trade mark of Acorn Computers Ltd, Fulbourn Road, Cherry Hinton, Cambridge England. MacAuthor is published by Icon Technology Ltd, Leicester England. All other trademarks and registered trademarks used are acknowledged.

Within this book the letters *BBC* refer to the British Broadcasting Corporation. The terms BBC micro, Master 128 and Master Compact refer to the computers manufactured by Acorn Computers Ltd under licence from the BBC.

All rights reserved. No part of this book (except brief passages quoted for critical purposes) or any of the computer programs to which it relates may be reproduced or translated in any form or by any means mechanical electronic or otherwise without the prior written consent of the copyright holder.

Disclaimer: Because neither Dabs Press nor the author have any control over the way the material in this book and accompanying programs disc is used, no warranty is given or should be implied as to the suitability of the advice or programs for any given application. No liability can be accepted for any consequential loss or damage, however caused, arising as a result of using the programs or advice printed in this book or on the accompanying programs disc.

Published by Dabs Press, 5 Victoria Lane, Whitefield, Manchester M25 6AL England. Tel. 061-766 8423 Telecom Gold 72:MAG11596, Prestel 942876210. Typeset in 10 on 11pt Palatino using the Acornsoft VIEW wordprocessor, MacAuthor, and an Apple Macintosh SE and Laserwriter.

Printed and bound in Great Britain by A.Wheaton & Co., Ltd, Exeter, Devon, a member of the BPCC Group.

Contents

Appendices

List of Figures

Preface

Every program is limited by the language which is used to write it.

C is a programmer's language. Unlike BASIC or Pascal, C was not written as a teaching aid, but as an implementation language. C is a computer language and a programming tool which has become popular because programmers like it! It is a tricky language, but a masterful one too. Sceptics have said that it is a language where everything which can go wrong, does go wrong. True, it does not do much hand-holding, but it also doesn't hold anything back. If you have come to C in the hope of finding a powerful language for writing everyday computer programs, then you will not be disappointed. C is ideally suited to modern computers and modern programming.

This book is a tutorial. Its aim is to teach C to the beginner, in a way which will not be outgrown as the years go by. It introduces basic concepts in a logical order and steadily progresses to more advanced topics. It isn't essential to follow the order of the chapters rigorously, but if you are a beginner, it is strongly recommended.

The example programs range from quick one-function programs, which do no more than illustrate the use of one simple feature, to complete application examples occupying several pages. In places these examples make use of features before they have been properly explained. These programs serve as a taster of things to come.

The final chapters concern current popular microcomputers which support C, with guidelines about how to get started on particular machines and the special facilities which those computers have to offer, such as graphics, windows, sound and so on.

Finally, computer languages have been in the hands of computer programmers for so long that a good deal of useless jargon has been injected into them. Unfortunately, it is not a good idea to ignore this entirely because it is the language that programmers speak! I have tried to point out the normal jargon wherever possible, but to avoid its use in the tutorial section as far as I can. There is a glossary at the end for quick and easy reference.

About this book

This book was written using the Scribble wordprocessor (Micro Systems Software), on the Commodore Amiga 1000. The finished text was transferred serially to a BBC micro using the author's own software.The index was generated and formatted using the index generator, written in C by the author, and the programs in book were developed primarily in Lattice C/Zorland C on the Amiga and the PC and optimised using the cross referencer listed in this book. The manuscript was edited using the VIEW wordprocessor and transfered to an Apple Macintosh. The text was then processed by MacAuthor, and output on an Apple LaserWriter Plus. The laser printed pages acted as camera ready copy for use by the printers.

Acknowledgements

I would like to extend my thanks to Metacomco UK Ltd. for providing me with their Lattice C compiler development system for the Atari ST. To the Lattice Corporation for swiftly answering a query about the Amiga compiler and to Acorn Computers for help and co-operation. A belated thanks goes to Sophus Software for help and information regarding the Amiga and for tolerating my impatience to know everything in a week! Look what happened! The idea that a computer program is like a 'society' is a paraphrase of Marvin Minsky.

Thanks especially to Bruce Smith and David Atherton for the tandoori ice cream and the prawn cocktail and for giving me the opportunity to do this book in the first place. I would also like to thank Tim Clacy for reading and liberally abusing the manuscript, and for helpful discussions and suggestions. Also, Andrew Leveridge, who discussed some of the initial graphic ideas, abandoning his wellingtons momentarily for my cause! I am, of course, solely responsible for ambiguities and errors which doubtless exist.

Mark Burgess, January 1988

Introduction

What is C?
What is it for?
Why is it Special?

Any kind of object, which is sufficiently complicated, can be thought of as having levels of detail. This means our perception of that object depends upon how closely it is examined, and the amount of detail which can be seen in a thing depends upon how closely the object is looked at. A computer falls easily into the category of highly complex objects and it can be thought of as working at many different levels. The terms *low-level* and *high-level* are often used to describe these onion-layers of complexity in computers.

Low-level is perhaps the easiest to understand: it describes a level of the computer which is buried down among the working parts of the machine. The low-level is the level at which the computer seems most primitive and machine-like. A higher level describes the same object, but with the detail left out. One might imagine stepping back from the complexity of the machine-level pieces and grouping together parts which work together, then covering up all the details. For instance in a car, a group of nuts, bolts and pistons can be grouped together to make up a new basic object – an engine. The computer then becomes a group of 'black boxes' which are thought of as being the basic components of the machine.

C is called a high-level, compiler language. The aim of any high-level computer language is to provide an easy and natural way of giving a programme of instructions to a computer. The language of the raw computer is a stream of number patterns called *machine code*. As you might expect, the action which results from a single machine code instruction is very primitive and many thousands of these are required to make up a program which does anything very useful. It is therefore the job of a high-level language to provide a new set of 'black box'

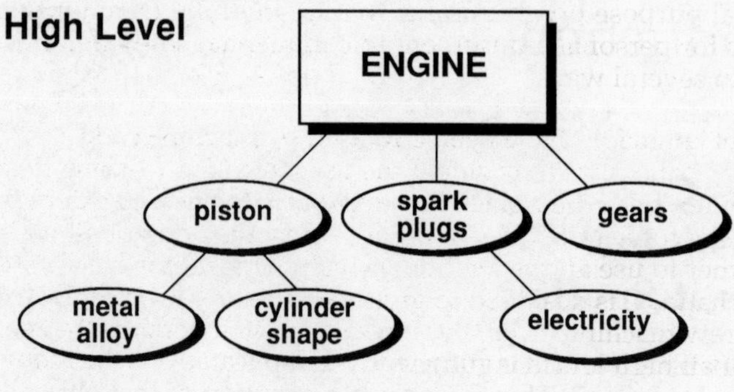

Levels of Complexity in an Engine.

Figure I.1. High-level and Low-level instructions.

instructions, which can be given to the computer without needing to see what happens inside them – and it is the job of a compiler to fill in the

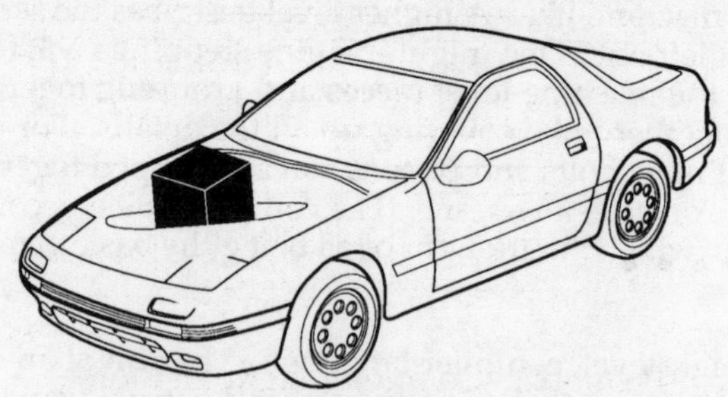

At the high level, an engine is just a black box.

details of these 'black boxes' so that the final product is a sequence of instructions in the language of the computer.

C is one of a large number of high-level languages which can be used for general purpose programming, that is, anything from writing small programs for personal amusement to commercial software. It is unusual in several ways.

High-level languages have been criticised by machine code programmers because they shield the user from the working details of the computer, with their black box approach, to such an extent that the languages become inflexible: in other words, they do not allow the programmer to use all the facilities which the machine has to offer. On the other hand, C is designed to give access to any level of the machine down to raw machine code. Because of this, it is perhaps the most flexible of all high level languages.

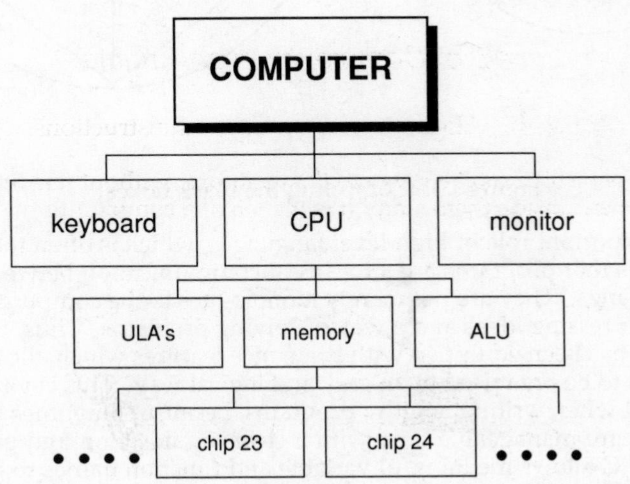

Figure I.2. Computer highs and lows.

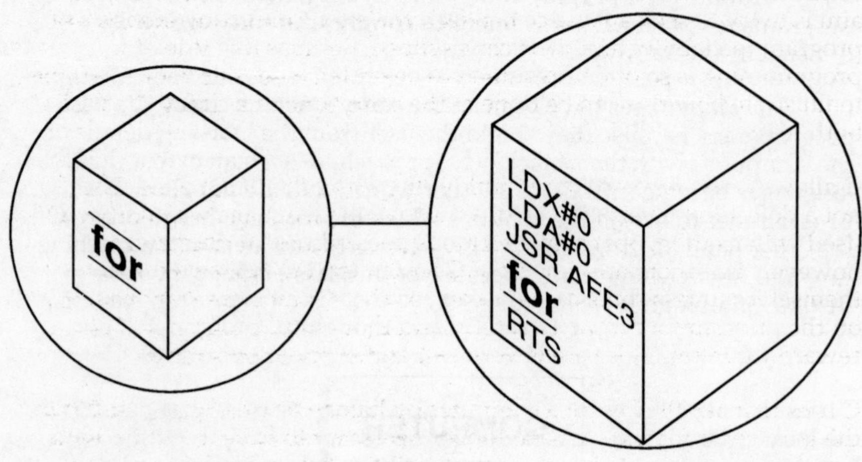

Figure I.3. Compiling the black boxes.

A very important role of high-level languages, which is often totally ignored, is that programs are a means of communication between human beings. They are not merely monologues to the computer, but a way of expressing ideas and a way of solving problems. Thus, the C language has been equipped with some nice features which allow programs to be organised in an easy and logical way. This is vitally important when writing lengthy programs, because sometimes whole problems are manageable only with a clear organisation and *program structure*. C allows meaningful variable and function names to be used in programs without any loss of efficiency. It gives a complete freedom of style – it has a set of very flexible loop constructions (for example: for, while, do) and neat ways of making decisions, providing an excellent basis for controlling the flow of programs.

Another unusual feature of C is the way it can express ideas very concisely. C gives the programmer the apparatus to build neat and compact programs. It does this by giving the programmer the freedom to do many things which are just plain illegal in many other languages!

At first, this sounds either like a great bonus for programmers or something a little suspect. Conciseness can be a mixed blessing – the aim is to try to seek a balance between the often conflicting interests of program readability and their conciseness. Because this side of programming is so often presumed to be understood, this book attempts to illustrate how this can be done at the same time as keeping the best of both features.

C allows activities which are frankly illegal in other languages. This is not a defect but a very powerful feature of the language which, when used with caution, opens up enormous possibilities. It does mean, however, that there are aspects of C which tend to run away with themselves unless some care is taken, so there is an extra responsibility on the programmer to write careful and thoughtful programs. The reward for taking this care is very fast and efficient programs.

C tries to make the best of a computer by linking as closely as possible to the local environment. It is no longer necessary to have to put up with hopelessly inadequate input/output facilities (a legacy of the timesharing/mainframe computer era). You can utilise everything that a computer has to offer. Above all, it is flexible. C is a very powerful language with the scope to write neat and efficient programs. Clearly no language can guarantee intrinsically good programs, there is always a responsibility on the programmer to ensure that a program is neat, logical and well organised, but it can give a framework in which it is easy to do so.

This book aims to convey some of the C philosophy in a practical way, and to provide a comprehensive introduction to the language through examples and by sticking to a strict structuring scheme. Hopefully, you will get a flavour of the kind of programming which C encourages.

1 : Basic Ideas

What to do with a Compiler

Using a compiler language is not the same as using an interpreted language like BASIC. It differs from interpreted languages in a number of ways. To begin with, a C program has to be created in two stages. These stages are as follows:

1) First, the program is written in the form of a number of text files using a screen editor. This form of the program is called the *source program* or *source file*. It is not possible to execute this file directly.

2) The completed source file is passed to a compiler. A compiler is a program which generates a new file containing a machine code translation of the source text. This file is called an *object file* or *executable file*. The executable file is said to have been *compiled* from the source text.

A major difference between compiler languages and BASIC-like languages is that compiler languages do not contain their own editor, nor do they have words like RUN with which to execute a finished program. A programmer uses a screen editor to create the words of a program, or program text, and runs the final program in its *object code* form in some way. This depends upon the operating system of the computer. It is normal just to type the name of the executable file.

Furthermore, C is different from many compiler languages in that it has something called a *pre-processor*. This is a tool which helps to keep programs tidy and readable, by allowing irrelevant details to be hidden away in dark places. A programmer can define his/her own words for making things simpler, and let external files be incorporated into programs as header files which expand the vocabulary of C.

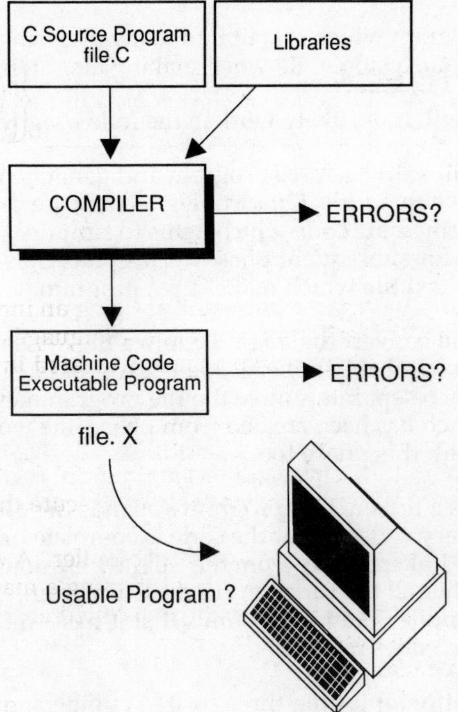

Figure 1.1. The stages of compilation.

The Compiler

A C program is made by running a program called a compiler, which takes a typed source program and converts it into something that the computer can execute.

It is common for a compiler program to come in the form of two or three separate programs or *phases*. (Sometimes the first two phases are amalgamated into one.) When this happens, each of these phases has to be executed, one after the other, in the correct order. The reason for taking this rather awkward approach is for portability of the compiler. For some programmers this approach also provides a more flexible way of compiling a program which is split into many files, since he/she then need only re-compile a single file when making alterations.

The three phases will most likely work in the following way:

1) Phase one will scan a source program and generate a compact code file known as a quad file. Quadruples, as they are called, are a compact intermediate code which helps to simplify the grammar of the language for subsequent phases. This phase has to be carried out for every text file which makes up a program.

2) Phase two will convert the quad file into a file of object code (though this is probably not executable). A separate object file is needed for each separate source file the programmer has used, so every file which has been created from phase one would have to be passed through this phase too.

3) Phase three is a linker. This program appends the object file with standard library code so that the code is complete or 'stand alone'. A C compiler linker suffers from the slightly arduous task of linking together all the functions in the C program. Even at this stage, the compiler can fail if it finds that it has a reference to a function which does not exist.

To avoid the irritation of typing three – often cumbersome – separate commands, it is usual to create a 'batch file' or 'exec file' to execute a compiler. This is a file of commands which are directed towards the operating system's interpreter. It is nothing to do with the program itself. The details of how to create such a file depend heavily upon the operating system and the computer under which the compiler runs, but the end result is that the whole compiler can be run from start to finish with a single command, which might look something like:

```
execute Ccompiler filename
```

or:

```
ex cc filename
```

or:

```
cc filename
```

or whatever... This file might already have been created for you, ready for use.

Errors

Errors are mistakes which programmers make. Compiler languages are not interactive in the sense that they do not usually register program errors while they are running, unlike BASIC which gives an error message and a line number when something goes wrong. There are two kinds of error in a compiler language. They are syntax errors and there are logical errors.

Errors in the syntax, or word structure, of a program are caught at compilation time by the compiler program and they are all listed in one go, with the line number in the text file at which the error occurred, and a message to say what was wrong. A program with syntax errors will cause a compiler program to abort its generation of machine code, so that no obviously incorrect program can be executed by the computer. An incorrect program can cause a machine to 'crash' or go out of control. A compiler will usually not stop at the first error it encounters, but will attempt to continue checking the syntax of a program right to the last line before aborting. It is common to submit a program for compilation only to receive a long and ungratifying list of errors from the compiler!

A shock which comes to everyone using a compiler for the first time is that, now and then, a single error will throw the compiler off course and result in a huge and confusing list of non-existent errors, following the true culprit. The situation looks much worse than it really is. This problem usually cures itself with experience, but it can be very disheartening at first.

If the compilation of a program is successful, then a new file (whose name depends upon the compiler) is created. This file will contain machine code which can be executed according to the rules of the computer's operating system.

The second type of error is far more serious, ie, program logic errors. These often can't be trapped by the compiler. The sort of errors which survive the scrutiny of the compiler are often fatal and cause the machine code program to do one of two things:

1) Terminate in some system-dependent way. This may be a detailed error message or simply a brief indication that something is wrong, depending on the particular compiler and the particular operating system of a machine.

2) Crash the system, ie, run wild and jam the normal operation of the computer.

When a programmer wants to make alterations and corrections to a C program, these have to be made in the source text file itself using a screen editor, so often the entire program must be recompiled when making an alteration.

Use of Upper and Lower Case

One of the reasons why the compiler can fail to produce the executable file for a program is that a function name has been mistyped, even through the careless use of upper and lower case characters. An important feature of the C language, is that it is 'case dependent'. The compiler distinguishes between small letters and capital letters in contrast to languages such as Pascal and some versions of BASIC, for instance. This is a potential source of quite trivial errors which can be very difficult to spot. If the case is wrongly typed, the compiler will complain and not produce an executable program.

Declarations

The vast majority of compiler languages require the programmer to make a list of the names and types of all variables which are going to be used in a program and information about where they are going to be used. This is called 'declaring' variables, and it is definitely a requirement of C. In fact it is not as bad as it sounds, the list is spread around the program and declaring variables quickly becomes second nature. It serves two purposes: first, it provides the compiler with a definitive list of the variables, enabling it to cross check typing errors and second, it informs the compiler how much space must be reserved for each variable at execution time, when the program is finally run. C supports a great variety of variable types (variables which hold different kinds of data) and allows one type to be converted into another, so the type of a variable is of great importance to the compiler.

Failing to declare a variable at all, or declaring it to be the wrong type, will result in a compilation error.

Questions:

1) What is a compiler?

2) How is a C program run?

3) How is a C program usually compiled?

4) Are upper and lower case equivalent in C?

5) What are the two different kinds of error which can be in a program?

2 : Reserved Words

Words with Special Significance

The basic instructions of C are built up using the set of words listed below. These words may not be used in just any way; C demands that they are only used for giving commands or making statements. They must not, for instance, be used to represent variables in a program and any attempt to do so would result in a compilation error. The words are listed mainly in alphabetical order so that they can be referred to easily. C requires all of these words to be in lower case. However, this does mean that, typed in upper case, the reserved words could be used as variable names, but this is not recommended.

The lower case 'd' after the word means that the word is used as part of a declaration. This will be discussed later.

auto	d
break	
case	
char	d
continue	
default	
do	
double	d
else	
entry	(This word is reserved for the future.)
extern	d
float	d
for	
goto	
if	
int	d
long	d
register	d

return	
short	d
sizeof	
static	d
struct	
switch	
typedef	d
union	d
unsigned	d
while	

Also in some implementations:

enum	d
void	d
const	d
signed	d
volatile	d

The last five words are not found in all implementations of C, but are being accepted in newer compilers. There is also, at the time of writing, a draft proposal for an ANSI standard version of C. These extra words are part of that proposal. They are covered in this book for completeness and for future accuracy. However, they are not assumed to exist in the reader's compiler.

This set of reserved words is used to build up the basic instructions of C. There doesn't appear to be many of these words, which is misleading. The reason for the small number of reserved words in C is that most of the facilities which C offers programmers are included in the form of *add on libraries*, added on to programs like plug-in expansion units. They are not strictly a part of the C language itself, though you never find a version of C without them! The contents of these libraries are covered in a later section in some detail, but it is worth pointing out here that when certain libraries have been included, new functions will have been defined implicitly. This means that the size of the language suddenly grows and that there will be further restrictions on choosing the names of functions and so on. If a variable, function or *macro* name has already been defined as something else, or it is a reserved word, the compiler will signal an error or a warning that it has already been used.

The print function

One invaluable function which is provided by the standard input/output library is called *printf,* or print-formatted. It is rather difficult to program without this function and it provides an extremely versatile way of printing text to a screen. The simplest way of using it, is to type in the following line:

```
printf ("..some string...");
```

Generally, variables can be inserted by using a *control sequence* inside the quotes and listing the variables after the string which then get inserted into the string in place of the control sequence. To print out an integer, %d is used as a control sequence, as follows:

```
printf ("Integer = %d",someinteger);
```

The variable 'someinteger' is then printed instead of %d. The printf function is described in full detail in the relevant chapter, but it will crop up in places from time to time. The example program below (listing 2.1) is a complete program. Try typing it in and compiling it.

Listing 2.1. A short poem.

```
/**********************************************************/
/*  Short Poem                                            */
/**********************************************************/

   #include <stdio.h>

/**********************************************************/
   main ()                      /* Poem */
   {
   printf ("Astronomy is %dderful \n",1);
   printf ("And interesting %d \n",2);
   printf ("The ear%d volves around the sun \n",3);
   printf ("And makes a year %d you \n",4);
   printf ("The moon affects the sur %d heard \n",5);
   printf ("By law of phy%d great \n",6);
   printf ("It %d when the stars so bright \n",7);
   printf ("Do nightly scintill%d \n",8);
   printf ("If watchful providence be%d \n",9);
   printf ("With good intentions fraught \n");
   printf ("Should not keep up her watch divine \n");
   printf ("We soon should come to %d \n",0);
   }
```

Output of listing 2.1

```
Astronomy is 1derful
And interesting 2
The ear3 volves around the sun
And makes a year 4 you
The moon affects the sur 5 heard
By law of phy6 great
It 7 when the stars so bright
Do nightly scintill8
If watchful providence be9
With good intentions fraught
Should not keep up her watch divine
We soon should come to 0
```

3 : Rival Languages

A Comparison with Pascal and BASIC

For the benefit of programmers who are already familiar with Pascal (Algol...etc) or BBC BASIC, the following table gives an extremely rough-and-ready indication of how the main words and symbols of the three languages relate to each other. Later chapters will cover detailed descriptions of C vocabulary.

C	Pascal	BASIC
=	:=	=
==	=	=
*,/	*,/	*,/
/,%	div, mod	DIV, MOD
printf ("...");	writeln ('...'); write ('...');	PRINT "..."
scanf ("...",a);	readln (a); read (a);	INPUT a

for (x = ..;...;)
{
}
	for x := ...to
	begin
	end;
		FOR x = ...
		
		NEXT x

while (...)
{
}
	while ...do
	begin
	end;
		N/A

do
{
}
while (...);
	N/A	N/A

	C	**Pascal**	**BASIC**
	N/A	repeat until (...)	REPEAT UNTIL ...
	if (..) ..; else ...;	if ... then ... else ....;	IF ... THEN... ELSE

	switch (...)
	{
	case :
	}
		case ... of
		
		end;
			N/A

Comment:	/* .... */	{ ..... }	REM ...
Pointer Symbol:	*		? ! $
	struct union	record N/A	N/A N/A

The conditional expressions 'if' and 'switch' are essentially identical to Pascal's own words 'if' and 'case', but there is no redundant 'then'. BASIC has no analogue of the 'switch' construction. However, the loop constructions of C are far superior to those of either BASIC or Pascal. Input and output in C is more flexible than Pascal, though correspondingly less robust in terms of program crashability. Input and output in C can match all of BASIC's string operations and provide more, though string variables can be awkward to deal with. You should refer to the main text for full accounts of the C vocabulary.

Questions:

1) Write a command to print out the message 'Wow big deal'.

2) Write a command to print out the number 22.

3) Write two different commands to print out 'The 3 Wise Men'.

4) Why are there only a few reserved command words in C?

4 : Systems & Environments

Where is a C Program Born? How is it Created?

The basic control of a computer rests with the operating system. This is a layer of software which provides the user with a comfortable environment in which to work with the computer. An operating system is usually thought of as having two main components: a command language and a filing system. The operating system is the route to all input and output, whether it be to a screen, a file or a disc. A language has to get at this input and output easily so that programs can send out and receive messages from the user. It also has to be in contact with the operating system in order to send out and receive these messages. In C the link between these two is very efficient.

Operating systems vary widely. On microcomputers they are usually very similar in concept, with just slightly different words for essentially the same commands. When most compiler languages were developed, they were intended for large mainframe computers which operated on a multi-user, time-sharing principle and were incapable of interactive, real-time communication with the user. Many compiler languages still retained this inadequacy when carried over to microcomputers, but C is an exception because of its unique design. Input and output are not actually defined as a fixed, unchanging part of the C language, instead there is a standard file which has to be included in programs. This defines the input/output commands which are supported by the language for a particular computer and operating system. This file is called a *standard C library*. (See the next chapter for more information.) The library is standard in the sense that it would not be very useful to have a different set of input/output commands on each computer, each with different words and commands. C has therefore developed a standard library of words and functions which are the same for all computers, but not all of which generally will be present in the library file. To find out which commands are allowed, check the manual for your compiler.

Files and Devices

The filing system is also a part of input/output. In many operating systems all routes in and out of the computer are treated by the operating system as if they were files (even the keyboard!). C does this implicitly. The file from which C normally gets its input from, is called 'stdin' or standard input file, and it is usually the keyboard. The corresponding route for output is called 'stdout', or standard output file, and is usually a monitor screen. Both of these are parts of 'stdio' or standard input/output. The keyboard and the monitor screen are not really files, of course, they are 'devices'. It is not possible to re-read what has been sent to the monitor, or write to the keyboard. Devices are represented by files with special names, so that the keyboard is treated as a read-only file and the monitor as a write-only file. The advantage of treating devices in this way is that you don't need to know how a particular device works, only that it exists somewhere, connected to the computer, and can be written to or read from. In other words, it is exactly the same to read or write from a device as it is to read or write from a file. This is a great simplification of input/output! The filenames of devices, often given the lofty title 'pseudo device names', will depend upon the particular operating system. For instance, the printer might be called 'PRN' or 'PRT'. When input is taken solely from the keyboard and output is always to the screen, then these details can be forgotten.

Filename Conventions

A convention is used by a compiler for the names of the program files which it uses and produces. In C this is probably the following:

A source program file:	filename.c
A quadruples file:	filename.q
An object file:	filename.o
An executable program:	filename.x
A header file:	libraryname.h

The endings 'dot something' identify the file contents for the compiler. The dotted endings mean that the compiler can generate an executable file with the same name as the original source, just a different ending.

The quad file and the object file are only working files and should be deleted by the compiler at the end of compilation. The '.c' suffix is to tell the compiler that the file contains a C source program, and similarly the other letters indicate non-source files in a convenient way. When executing a compiler, you are usually expected to type only the filename of a program itself, not the '.c' ending ie:

```
execute compiler filename
```

or:

```
cc filename
```

rather than :

```
execute compiler filename.c
```

or:

```
cc filename.c
```

The compiler checks for a file with the ending '.c'. A common error is to forget this and to type the '.c' as well as the filename. This results in an error message like this:

```
Can't find filename.c.c
```

Command Languages and Consoles

In order to do anything with a compiler, or an editor, it's essential to know something about the command language of the operating system. This means the instructions which can be given to the system itself, rather than the words which make up a C program. For example:

DIR
CAT
EXECUTE

In a large operating system (or even a relatively small one), it can be a major feat of recollection to know all of these commands! Fortunately, it is possible to get by with knowing just a handful of the most common ones, and having the system manual around to leaf through when absolutely necessary.

Another important object is the 'panic button' or BREAK key. Every system will have its own way of breaking the operation of a program or the execution of a command. This commonly involves two simultaneous key-presses, such as CTRL-Z, CTRL-A or CTRL-D and so on. It is worth finding the panic button before using a compiler!

Editors

Many operating systems provide their own editors for writing text. Often, they aren't very good! A language development system will almost certainly be provided with an editor if there isn't one already.

An editor must provide a simple way of altering the contents of a text file so that programs can be created, altered or corrected. Good computer program editors have some standard features. It is assumed here that all editors worthy of mention possess these features. Remember, a text editor is not at all like the BASIC line editor. Features to look out for are as follows:

1) A compiler always supplies the line number in a file at which an error occurred. An editor will therefore have some way of going straight to a particular line number.

2) A way of swapping all or selected instances of a particular string in the file, such as 'search and replace'

3) A way of inserting and deleting text.

It is amusing to learn that not all editors are lucky enough to be endowed with such features, and indeed some editors do not even have adequate ways of inserting or deleting text. These editors ought to be executed in the traditional sense of the word!

A good editor will also have a way of copying, deleting and moving whole blocks of text, either by placing markers around a block or, in modern systems, by painting over areas of text with a mouse.

It is worth learning how to manipulate an editor before trying to use it to write programs.

Questions:

1) What is an operating system for?

2) What is a pseudo device name?

3) If you had a C source program which you wanted to call 'accounts', what name would you save it under?

4) What would be the name of the file produced by the compiler of the program in question three?

5) How would this program be run?

5 : Libraries

Plug in C Expansions and Header Files

The special commands which C offers the programmer are almost entirely contained in the standard libraries. Standard libraries are files which are merged with a C program at compilation time, and contain functions and extra facilities called *macro definitions*. See the chapter on pre-processors which have a particular use. For example, there are libraries of mathematical functions, string handling functions and input/output functions. Why are they not all included in the first place? Why include them as files? The answer to these questions is that it would be a waste of time for the compiler to add on lots of code for maths functions, for example, if they weren't needed. When libraries are included in programs, they make the resulting object code longer. The use of libraries also implies that the facilities can depend, to some extent, upon the machine which is running the compiler. This is because certain libraries, like input/output, are machine dependent. They will not be the same for every computer.

When a library has been included, this has effectively added to the list of reserved words and commands in the language, because it is not possible to use the names of 'functions' or 'macros' which have already been defined.

The most commonly used library is the standard input/output library, whose header file is called 'stdio.h'. Libraries are accessed using the word:

```
#include
```

at the top of a program file, so that :

```
#include 'stdio.h'
```

or :

```
#include <stdio.h>
```

would allow the standard input/output (I/O) functions to be used in a file. Another name for the library file is a 'header file' because it is commonly placed at the head of a program. This is why these files end with '.h'. (The #include directive is actually a command to the C pre-processor, which is dealt with later.) Although some functions can be used without having to include library files, it is best to consult the compiler manual to be certain. The stdio.h file is always required, since it is hard to create useful programs without input and output! A very simple C program illustrates how this works:

```
#include <stdio.h>

main ()

{
printf ("C standard I/O file is included\n");
printf ("Hello world!");
}
```

A program wishing to use a mathematical function such as cos() would need to include a mathematics library header file. This would probably be called 'math.h':

```
#include <stdio.h>
#include <math.h>

main ()

{ double x,y;
y = sin (x);
printf ("Maths library ready");
}
```

A particular operating system might require its own special library for certain operations such as using a mouse or for opening windows in a WIMP environment, for example. These details will be found in the manual for a particular C compiler or operating system.

Although there is no limit, in principle, to the number of libraries which can be included in a program, there may be a practical limit: namely memory, since every library adds to the size of both source and object code. Libraries also add to the time it takes to compile a program.

It is difficult to know what names libraries will have in a particular implementation. It is certain that stdio.h will always be called stdio.h, but the names of other libraries or the distribution of functions within them might differ. The only way to make certain is to check it in the compiler manual.

Questions :

1) How is a library file incorporated into a C program?

2) Name the most common library file in C.

3) Is it possible to define new functions with the same names as standard library functions?

4) What is another name for a library file?

6 : Programming Style

The Shape of Programs to Come

An important aspect of programming, which is often ignored in computing texts, is that computer programs are not only a way of communicating instructions to a computer, they are also a means of communicating ideas between people. Try saying that all the programs printed in the pages of this book are not precisely for this purpose!

C is actually a free-format language. This means that there are no rules about how it must be typed, when to start new lines, where to place brackets or whatever. This has both advantages and dangers. The advantage is that the user is free to choose a style which best suits him or her, and there is freedom in the way in which a program can be structured. The disadvantage is that, unless a strict style is adopted, very sloppy programs can be the result. The reasons for choosing a well structured style are that:

1) Long programs are only manageable if those programs are properly organised.

2) Programs are only understandable if care is taken in choosing the names of variables and functions.

3) It is much easier to find parts of a program if a strict ordering convention is maintained.

No simple set of rules can ever provide the ultimate solution to writing good programs. In the end, experience and good judgement are the factors which decide whether a program is well written or not. The programs in this book are written according to a strict set of rules, which I believe are a good way of incorporating style into a program. They are explained in Appendix A.

Restrictions of memory size and of particular compilers often force restrictions upon style, making programs clustered and difficult. These pressures are recognised, but they are regrettable for the readability of programs. Most computers today are equipped with at least half a megabyte of free memory, so this should not be a problem. Books always assume that there are no pressures of this kind anyway, so this one will not be any different!

7 : Form of a C Program

What Goes into a C program? What Will it Look Like?

Unlike both BASIC and Pascal, a C program is entirely made up of building blocks which have a particular 'shape' or form and the form is the same everywhere in a program, whether it is the form of the main program or of a subroutine. A program is made up of instructions surrounded by curly brackets or braces { } and statements which are called declarations.

The basic building block in a C program is called a function. Every C program is a collection of one or more functions which are written in some arbitrary order. One, and only one, of these functions in the program must have the name 'main'. This function is always the starting point of a C program, so the simplest C program would be a single function definition as follows:

```
main ()

{
}
```

The brackets '()' which follow the name of the function must be included, even though they apparently serve no purpose. This is how C distinguishes functions from ordinary variables.

The function main() does not have to be at the top of a program, so a C program does not necessarily start at line one. It always starts where main() is. This is a new idea in C. Also, the function main() can't be called from any function. Only the operating system can call the function main(); this is how a C program starts.

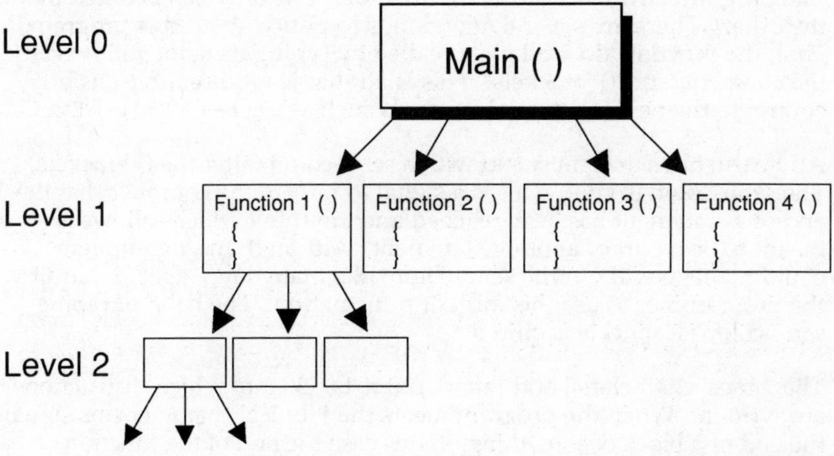

Figure 7.1. C Programs are built from functions.

Any function can be defined like the one on the previous page. The next most simple C program in listing 7.1 is perhaps a program which calls a function 'do_nothing' and then ends.

Listing 7.1. A 'do_nothing' program.

```
/******************************************************/
/* Program : do nothing                               */
/******************************************************/

    main ()          /* Main program */
    {
     do_nothing ();
    }

/******************************************************/

    do_nothing ()   /* Function called */
    {
    }
```

The program now consists of two functions, one of which is called by the other. There are several new things to notice about this program. First, the function 'do_nothing' is called by typing its name followed by the characteristic '()' brackets. This is all that is required to transfer control to the new function. No words such as CALL or PROC exist in C.

All instructions in C must end with a semi-colon (after the () brackets). The semi-colon is vital. This is a signal to inform the compiler that the end of a statement has been reached and anything which follows is meant to be a part of another statement. Although most compilers could manage without the semi-colon, like many languages, C requires the programmer to use this form of punctuation. The habit of typing semi-colons is quickly acquired.

The 'brace' characters { and } mark out a 'block' into which instructions are written. When the program meets the } 'brace' character this signals the end of a block of something, in this case the end of the function called do_nothing().

When the program meets the closing brace } it then transfers back to main() where it meets another } brace and the program ends. This is the simplest way in which control flows between functions in C.

All the functions have the same status as far as a program is concerned. The main() function is treated just as any other function. When a program is compiled, each function is compiled as a separate block and then at the end a 'linker' phase in the compiler attempts to sew them all together. These examples are obviously very simple. Hopefully, a C program will contain more than just empty functions!

There are some basic parts to a C program which are used to build up meaningful programs – these are listed below in the order they are generally required.

-) comments
-) pre-processor commands

1) functions
2) declarations
3) variables
4) statements

Neither comments nor preprocessor commands have a special place in this list – they do not have to be in any one particular place with respect to the others. The following skeleton plan of a program helps to show how the elements of a C program relate. The following chapters will then expand upon this as a kind of basic plan.

Listing 7.2. A Skeleton C Program.

```
/***********************************************************/
/*                                                         */
/* Skeleton program plan                                   */
/*                                                         */
/***********************************************************/

     #include <stdio.h>       /* Preprocessor defns */
     #include <myfile.c>

     #define scream          "arghhhhh"
     #define numofbones  123

/***********************************************************/

     main ()               /* Main program & start */

     { int a,b;
     function1();
     function2(a,b);
     }

/***********************************************************/

     function1 ()                          /* Purpose */
     {
     ....
     }

/***********************************************************/

     function2 (a,b)                       /* Purpose */

     int a,b;

     {
     ....
     }
```

Questions :

1) What is a block?

2) Name the six basic things which make up a C program.

3) Does a C program start at the beginning? Where is the beginning?

4) What happens when a program comes to a } character? What does this character signify?

5) What vital piece of punctuation goes at the end of every C statement?

8 : Comments

Annotated Programs

Comments are a way of inserting remarks and reminders into a program without affecting the program in any way.

Comments do not have a fixed place in a program – a compiler treats them as though they were 'white space' or blank characters, so they are ignored. One of the pleasant features of working with a compiled language, is that programs can contain any number of comments without losing speed. This is because comments are stripped out of a source program by the compiler when it converts the source program into machine code. This useful fact means that there are no restrictions upon the use of comments in programs. Typically, a program might have one or two comments for each function (at least one which describes what it does). However, it is not a good idea to go mad with comments. Some programmers, when finding themselves in the position of being able to comment a program without loss of efficiency, become wild and frenzied and spend half their tortured lives filling up their programs with comments which completely obscure their code! This is totally unnecessary, since C gives the programmer complete freedom to choose the meaningful variable names which should be used to make code self-explanatory!

Comments are marked out (or 'delimited' in the standard jargon) by the following pair of characters:

```
/* ...... comment ......*/
```

Because a comment is skipped over as though it were a single space, it can be placed anywhere where spaces are valid characters, even in the middle of a statement, though this is not to be encouraged.

Listing 8.1. How to use comments in C.

```
      main ()   /* The almost trivial program */
      {

/* This little line has no effect */
/* This little line has none */
/* This little line went all the way down  to the next line */
/* And so on ... */

      }
```

Listing 8.2. How to use comments in C.

```
      #include <stdio.h>        /* header file */
      #define  notfinished      0

/*********************************************/

   /* A bar like the one above can be used to   */
   /* separate functions visibly in a program   */

      main ()
      {    int i;                  /* declarations */

      do
           {
                /* Nothing !!! */
           }
      while (notfinished);

      }
```

Question:

1) What happens if a comment is not ended? That is, if the programmer types /* .. to start but forgets the ..*/ to close.

9 : Functions

Making Black Boxes
Solving Problems and Getting Results

A function is a module or block of program code which deals with a particular task and is isolated from other blocks of code by the programmer. Functions help to organise a program in a simple way; they are always written in the following form:

```
identifier (parameter1,parameter2,..)

        types of parameters

{ variable declarations
statements..
......
....
}
```

A function has a name or identifier by which it is referred to when called in a program. It can accept variables called parameters which it uses to receive information from the outside world. It also consists of a number of statements and declarations, enclosed by curly brackets { }, which make up the doing part of the object. The declarations and 'type of parameter' statements are formalities which will be described in good time. (They are a necessary but frankly irrelevant part of a program.)

The name of a function in C can be anything from a single letter to a word up to 31 characters long. The name of a function must begin with an alphabetic letter or the underscore '_' character. The other characters in the name can be chosen from the following groups:

a ... z (any letter from a to z)
A ... Z (any letter from A to Z)

0 ... 9 (any digit from zero to 9)
_ (the underscore character)

This means that sensible names can be chosen for functions which make a program easy to read.

A real example of a function is the following very simple example which adds together two integer numbers 'a' and 'b' and prints the result 'c'. All the variables are chosen to be integers to keep things simple and the result is printed out using the print-formatted function, printf, from the standard library, with a '%d' to indicate that it is printing an integer.

```
Add_Two_Numbers (a,b)    /* Add a and b */

int a,b;

{ int c;

c = a + b;
printf ("%d",c);

}
```

Notice the position of the function name and where brackets and semi-colons are placed. This is crucial. The details are quickly learnt with practice and experience.

This function is not very useful standing alone. It has to be called from some other function somewhere is a program, and this could well be the main program of a C source file. A function is 'called' (ie, control is passed to the function) by typing in its name and the usual brackets () to follow it, along with the values which are to be passed to the function:

```
main ()

{ int c,d;

c = 1;
d = 53;

Add_Two_Numbers (c,d);
Add_Two_Numbers (1,2);

}
```

The result of this program would be to print out the number 54 and then the number three, then stop. Listing 9.1 is a simple program which makes use of some functions in a playful way. The following structure diagram shows how this can be visualised and the significance of the program 'levels'. The idea is to illustrate the way in which functions connect together:

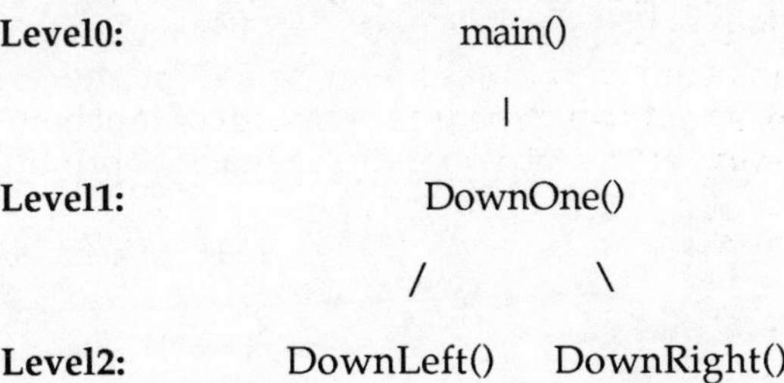

Listing 9.1. Making use of functions.

```
/*******************************************/
/*                                         */
/* Function Snakes & Ladders               */
/*                                         */
/*******************************************/

   #include <stdio.h>

/*******************************************/
/* Level 0                                 */
/*******************************************/

   main ()

   {
   printf ("This is level 0: the main program\n");
   printf ("About to go down a level          \n");

   DownOne ();
   printf ("Back at the end of the start!!\n");
   }

/********************************************/
/* Level 1                                  */
/********************************************/
```

```
    DownOne ()          "   /* Branch out! */
    {
    printf ("Down here at level 1, all is well\n");

    DownLeft (2);
    printf ("Through level 1....\n");
    DownRight (2);
    printf ("Going back up a level!\n);
    }

/*********************************************/
/* Level 2                                    */
/*********************************************/

    DownLeft (a)                    /* Left branch */

    int a;

    {
    printf ("This is deepest level %d\n",a);
    printf ("On the left branch of the picture\n");
    printf ("Going up!!");     }

/*********************************************/

    DownRight (a)                  /* Right branch */

    int a;

    {
    printf ("And level %d again!\n",a);
    }
```

Functions with Values

In other languages and in mathematics, a function is understood to be something which has a value or a number associated with its name. That is, the whole function is thought of as having a value. In C it is possible to choose whether or not a function will have a value. It is possible to make a function hand back a value to the place at which it was called. Take the following example:

```
    bill = CalculateBill (data...);
```

The variable 'bill' is assigned to a function. 'CalculateBill()' and 'data' are some data which are passed to the function. This statement makes it look as though CalculateBill() is a number. When this statement is executed in a program, control will be passed to the function CalculateBill() until it is finished whatever it does and this function will then hand back control and some value to the original statement. The value of the function is assigned to 'bill' and the program continues. Functions which work in this way are said to 'return' a value.

In C, returning a value is a simple matter. A very useful function called 'return()' is used to do this. 'return()' is defined by the C language on every implementation so it is not something that a user has to write personally. Consider the function CalculateBill() from the statement on the previous page:

```
CalculateBill (a,b,c)    /* Adds up a, b and c */

int a,b,c;

{ int total;

total = a + b + c;
return (total);

}
```

As soon as the return() function is met, CalculateBill() stops executing and assigns the value 'total' to the function. If there were no return() function, the program could not know which value it should associate with the name CalculateBill and so it would not be meaningful to speak of the function as having one value. Forgetting a return() statement can ruin a program. For instance if CalculateBill had just been:

```
CalculateBill (a,b,c)

int a,b,c;

{ int total;
total = a + b + c;
}
```

then the value 'bill' would be garbage, presuming that the compiler allowed this to be written at all. On the other hand, if the first version were used (the one which did use the return(total) statement) and furthermore no assignment were made:

```
main ()

{
CalculateBill (1,2,3);
}
```

then the value of the function would be discarded, quite legitimately. This is usually what is done with the input/output functions printf() and scanf() which actually return values. So a function in C can return a value but it does not have to be used. On the other hand, a value which has not been returned can't be used safely.

Note: Functions do not have to return integer types: they can usually return a value which is any data type at all. See the next chapter about this subject.

Breaking Out Early

Suppose that a program is in the middle of some awkward process in a function which is not main(), perhaps two or three loops working together, for example, and suddenly the function finds its answer. This is where the beauty of the return statement becomes clear. The program simply can call return(value) anywhere in the function and control will jump out of any number of loops, or whatever, and pass the value back to the calling statement without having to finish the function up to the closing brace, }. The result is immediate and it avoids using a much dreaded word in programming, 'go..', which is far less elegant. This is the first of several such facilities in C which banish the need for the terrible 'go...'!

```
function (a,b)      /* breaking out of functions early */
int a,b;

{
while (a < b)
        {
        if (a > b)
                {
                return (b);
                }
        a = a + 1;
        }
}
```

The example illustrates this. The function is entered with some values for a and b and, assuming that a is less than b, it starts to execute one of C's loops called 'while'. In that loop, is a single 'if' statement and a statement which increases a by one on each noop. If a becomes bigger than b at any point, the return(b) function gets executed and the function quits, without having to arrive at the end brace, }, and passes the value of b back to the place it was called.

The exit Function

Many C compilers will provide a function called exit() which can be used to quit a program at any point, no matter how many levels of function calls have been made. This is called with a return code, like the example below:

```
#define code  0
exit (code);
```

Functions and Types

All the variables and values used up to now have been integers. But what happens if a function is required to return a different kind of value such as a character? A statement like:

```
bill = CalculateBill (a,b,c);
```

can only make sense if the variable 'bill' and the value of the function CalculateBill() are the same kind of object. In other words, if CalculatBill() returns a floating point number, then 'bill' cannot be a character! Both sides of an assignment must match. In fact this is done by declaring functions to be of a particular type. So far no declarations have been needed because C assumes that all values are integers unless this is specifically changed. Declarations are covered in detail in the next chapter.

Questions:

1) Write a function which takes two values a and b and returns the value of (a*b).

2) Is there anything wrong with a function which returns no value?

3) What happens if a function returns a value but is not assigned to anything?

4) What happens if a function is assigned to an object but that function returns no value?

5) How can a function be made to quit early?

10 : Types & Declarations

Storing Data
Descriminating Types
Declaring Data

A variable is an area of memory with a name (or identifier). The name of a variable in C can be anything from a single letter to a word up to 32 characters long. The name of a variable must begin with an alphabetic letter or the underscore '_' character, but the other characters in the name can be chosen from the following groups:

a ... z (any letter from a to z)
A ... Z (any letter from A to Z)
0 ... 9 (any digit from zero to 9)
_ (the underscore character)

Some examples of valid variable names are:

a
total
Out_of_Memory
VAR
integer

In C, variables do not only have names, they also have types. This idea will be unfamiliar to users who are only familiar with BASIC. The variable 'type' conveys to the programmer and to the compiler what sort of data can be stored in it. In BASIC and in some older, largely obsolete languages, like PL/1, a special naming convention is used to determine the sort of data which can be held in particular variables. For example, the dollar symbol is commonly used in BASIC to mean that a variable is a string and the percentage symbol is used to indicate an integer. No such convention exists in C. Instead the programmer 'declares' the types of variables before they are used. This serves two distinct purposes:

a) It gives a compiler precise information about the amount of memory that will have to be given over to a variable when a program is finally run, and what sort of arithmetic will have to be used on it (eg, integer only or floating point or none).

b) It provides the compiler with a list of the variables in a convenient place so that it can cross-check names for any errors.

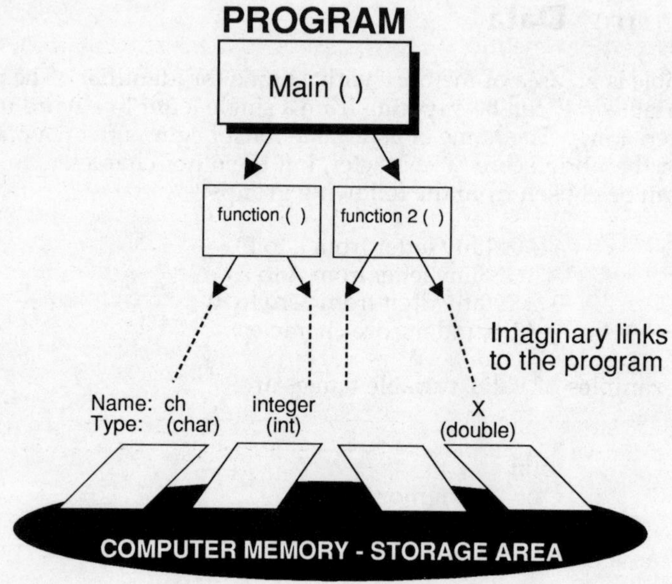

Figure 10.1. Variables are storage places used by a program.

There are a lot of different possible 'types' in C. In fact it is possible for the user to define his/her own, but luckily, for the beginner, there is no need to do this right away: there are some basic types which are provided by C ready for use. The names of these types are all reserved words in C and they are summarised as follows:

char	a single character
short	a short integer (usually 16-bits)
short int	a short integer

int	a standard integer (usually 32-bits)
long	a long integer
long int	a long integer (usually 32-bits)
float	a floating point or real number (short)
long float	a long floating point number
double	a long floating point number
void	}
enum	} these are discussed in Chapter 23.
volatile	}

There is a lot of repetition in these words. It is a historical quirk of the language that there are a lot of redundant words in C. In addition to the words above, the word 'unsigned' can also be placed in front of any of these types. Unsigned means that only positive or zero values can be used. That is there is no minus sign. The advantage of using this kind of variable is that storing a minus sign takes up some memory, so that if no minus sign is present, larger numbers can be stored in the same kind of variable. (The proposed ANSI standard mentioned earlier also allows the word 'signed' to be placed in front of any of these types, to indicate the opposite of unsigned. This word is completely redundant.)

Declarations

To declare a variable in a C program, the programmer simply writes the type of a variable followed by a list of variable names which are to be treated as being that type:

```
typename variablename1,..,..,variablenameN;
```

For example:

```
int i,j;
char ch;
double x,y,z,fred;
unsigned long int Name_of_Variable;
```

Failing to declare a variable is more risky than passing through customs and failing to declare villainous substances! A compiler is markedly more efficient than a customs officer: it will catch a missing declaration every time and will terminate a compiling session while complaining bitterly, often with a host of messages, one for each use of the undeclared variable.

As an aside: I once had the unusual pleasure of meeting a business executive of a large, well-known computing organisation who said: 'The way to write a program is to hammer out the basic idea, forgetting about all the details. Then run the compiler to see what you have to declare, then try to find all the bugs!' A word of advice – **Don't even think of it!** Computer programs should be thoughtful creations, not based on the philosophy that, if you hit something hard enough, it's bound to go a long way. The gentleman concerned admitted that programming took him a long time and that he didn't feel that he had quite grasped it to the full!

Where to Declare Things

There are two kinds of place in which declarations can be made. The implications of using the different options are discussed in Chapter 12. For now it will do to simply state what these places are.

a) One place is outside all of the functions. That is, in the space between function definitions. Underneath the #include <stdio.h> line, for instance. Variables declared here are called global variables. There are other names for them as well, such as static or external in special cases.

```
#include <stdio.h>

int globalinteger;                /* Here! outside {} */
float global_floating_point;

main ()
{
}
```

b) The other place where declarations can be made is following the opening brace of a block. Any block will do, as long as the declaration follows immediately after the opening brace. Variables of this kind only work inside their braces { } and are often called local variables. Another name which is sometimes used for them is automatic variables.

```
main ()

{ int a;
float x,y,z;
```

```
/* statements */
}
```

or:

```
function ()
{ int i;
/* .... */
while (i < 10)
    { char ch;
    int g;

    /* ... */
    }
}
```

Declarations and Initialisation

When a variable is declared in C, the language allows a neat piece of syntax which means that variables can be declared and assigned a value in one go. This is no more efficient than doing it in two stages, but it is sometimes tidier. The following lines:

```
int i = 0;
char ch = 'a';
```

are equivalent to the more longwinded :

```
int i;
char ch;

i = 0;
ch = 'a';
```

This is called 'initialisation' of the variables. C always allows the programmer to write declarations/initialisers in this way, but it is not always desirable to do so. If there are just one or two declarations, then this initialisation method can make a program neat and tidy. If there are a lot, then it is better to initialise separately, as in the second case. The reader may ask what is 'a lot'? The answer is, when it starts to look as though there are too many! It makes no odds to the compiler, nor (ideally) to the final code whether the first or second method is used. It is only for tidiness that this is allowed.

Individual Types

Characters

A character type is a variable which can store a single character. In C, single characters are written enclosed by single quotes! This is in contrast to strings of many characters which use double quotes. For instance, if 'ch' is the name of a character:

```
char ch;
ch = 'a';
```

would give ch the value of the character 'a'. The same effect can also be achieved by writing:

```
char ch = 'a';
```

A character can be any ASCII character, printable or not printable, from values -128 to 127. But only zero to 127 are used. Control characters, ie, non-printable characters, are put into programs by using a back-slash,\, and a special character or number. The characters and their meanings are as follows:

\b	backspace, BS
\f	form feed, FF (also clear screen)
\n	new line, NL (like pressing return)
\r	carriage return, CR (cursor to start of line)
\t	horizontal tab, HT
\v	vertical tab (not all versions)
\"	double quotes (not all versions)
\'	single quote character '
\\	back-slash character
\ddd	character ddd where ddd is an ASCII code given in octal or base 8. (See Appendix C.)

Listing 10.1. Special characters.

```
/****************************************************/
/*                                                  */
/* Special Characters                               */
```

```
/*                                              */
/************************************************/

      #include <stdio.h>

      main ()

      {
      printf ("Beep! \7 \n");
      printf ("ch = \'a\' \n");
      printf (" <- Start of this line!! \r");
      }
```

The output of this program is as follows:

```
Beep!
ch = 'a'
<- Start of this line!!
```

The bell will sound when Beep! is printed and the text cursor is left where the arrow points.

It is also possible to have the type:

```
unsigned char
```

This admits ASCII values from zero to 255, rather than -128 to 127.

Integers

There are two integer types in C and they are called 'long' and 'short'. The difference between the two is the size of the integer, where either can hold the amount of storage required for them. It can be seen from the list just mentioned that there are a handful of ways to declare integers. Fortunately, only two have to be remembered, the rest are just different ways of declaring the same thing. Most commonly, the two to remember are 'int' and 'short'. 'int' means a long integer and 'short' means a short one. On a typical 16-bit micro the size of these integers may be as follows:

Type	**Bits**	**Possible Values**
short	16	-32768 to 32767
unsigned short	16	zero to 65535
int	32	-2147483648 to 2147483647

long	32	(ditto)
unsigned int	32	zero to 4294967295

They are declared in the usual way:

```
int i,j;
i = j = 0;
```

or :

```
int i=0,j=0;
```

Floating Point

There are long and short floating point numbers in C. It is worth noting that all the mathematical functions which C can use require 'double' or 'long float' arguments, so it is common to use the type float for storage of small floating point numbers only, and to use double elsewhere. It is worth noting that this is not always true as the C 'cast' operator allows temporary conversions to be made. On a typical 16-bit implementation, the different types would be organised as follows:

Type	Bits	Possible Values
float	32	+/- 10E-37 to +/- 10E38
double	32	+/- 10E-307 to +/- 10E308
long float	32	(ditto)

Typical declarations:

```
float x,y,z;
x = 0.1;
y = 2.456E5
z = 0;

double bignum,smallnum;
bignum = 2.36E208;
smallnum = 3.2E-300;
```

Choosing Variables

The sort of procedure that a programmer would adopt when choosing variable names would probably be something like the following :

a) Decide what a variable is for and what type it needs to be.

b) Choose a sensible name for the variable.

c) Decide where the variable is allowed to exist.

d) Declare that name to be a variable of the chosen type.

Some local variables are only used temporarily, for controlling loops for instance. It is common to give these short names (single characters). A good habit to adopt is to keep to a consistent practice when using these variables. A common one, for instance is to use the letters:

```
int i,j,k;
```

For integer types. There is no particular reason why this should be, it is just common practice. Similarly, names like:

```
double x,y,z;
```

tend to make one think of floating point numbers.

Assigning Variables

Variables can be assigned to numbers:

```
var = 10;
```

and assigned to each other:

```
var1 = var2;
```

In either case the objects on either side of the '=' symbol must be of the same type. It is not possible, nor is it sensible, to assign a floating point number to a character, because there is just no single character which can be used to represent a floating point number! A compiler therefore forbids this. So:

```
        Int a, b = 1;
        a = b;
```

is a valid statement, but:

```
float x = 1.4;
char ch;
ch = x;
```

is wrong!

There is a single exception to this rule. Integers and characters will inter-convert because characters are stored by their ASCII codes (which are integers!) Thus the following will work:

```
int i;
char ch = 'A';
i = ch;
printf ("The ASCII code of %c is %d",ch,i);
```

The result of this would be:

```
The ASCII code of A is 65
```

Types and the Cast Operator

It is worth mentioning a very valuable operator in C. It is called the cast operator, and its function is to convert one type of value into another. For instance, it would convert a character into an integer:

```
int i;
char ch = '\n';

i = (int) ch;
```

The value of the integer would be the ASCII code for the character. This is the only integer which it would make any sense to talk about in connection with the character. Similarly, floating point and integer types can be inter-converted:

```
float x = 3.3;
int i;

i = (int) x;
```

The value of i would be three because an integer can't represent decimal points, so the cast operator rounds the number. There is no such problem the other way around.

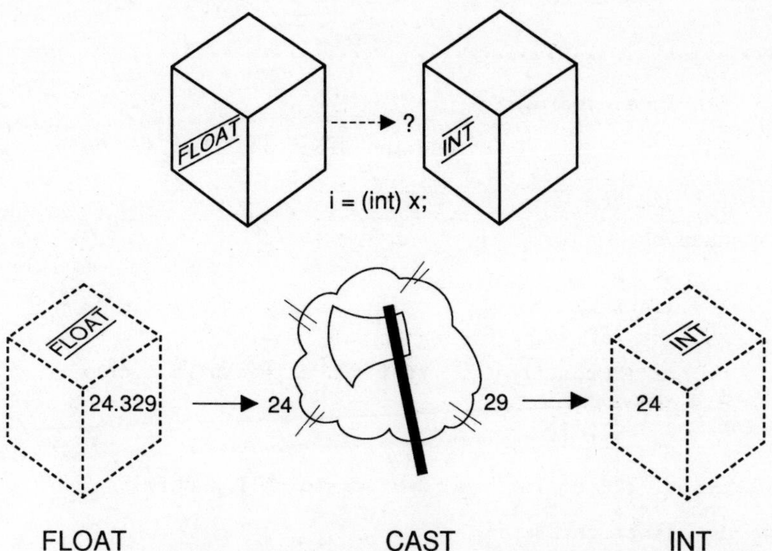

Figure 10.2. The cast operator in action.

For example :

```
float x;
int i = 12;
x = (float) i;
```

The general form of the cast operator is therefore:

```
(type) variable
```

It does not always make sense to convert types. This will be seen particularly with regard to structures and unions. Cast operators crop up in many areas of C. This is not the last time they will have to be explained.

Listing 10.2. Demo of cast operator.

```
/*******************************************************/
/*                                                     */
/* Demo of Cast operator                               */
```

```
/*                                                     */
/*******************************************************/

        #include <stdio.h>

        main ()             /* Use int float and char */

        { float x;
        int i;
        char ch;

        x = 2.345;
        i = (int) x;
        ch = (char) x;

        printf ("From float x =%f i =%d ch =%c\n",x,i,ch);
        i = 45;
        x = (float) i;
        ch = (char) i;

        printf ("From int i=%d x=%f ch=%c\n",i,x,ch);
        ch = '*';
        i = (int) ch;
        x = (float) ch;

        printf ("From char ch=%c i=%d x=%f\n",ch,i,x);

        }
```

Storage Classes:
Register, Static and Extern

Here are some remarks about advanced features of C. When it is critical that a program runs as fast as possible, variable declarations whose types are 'int' or 'char' can be preceded by the word 'register' which is a reserved word in C. The compiler takes this to mean that these variables will be heavily used and that storage should be found for them in registers, if at all possible. If the compiler is able to do this (and there is no guarantee that it will), then this should result in a noticeable increase in efficiency.

```
register int i;
register char ch;
```

Sometimes C programs are written in more than one text file. If this is the case then, on occasions, it will be necessary to get at variables which were defined in another file. If the word 'extern' is placed in front of a variable, then it can be referenced across files:

File one / **File two**

```
File one              File two

main ()               int i;

{
extern int i;         function ()
}                     {
                      }
```

In this example, the function main() in file one can use the variable i from the function main in file two.

A third class is called 'static'. The name static is given to variables which can hold their values between calls of a function. They are allocated once and once only and their values are preserved between any number of function calls. Space is allocated for static variables in the program code itself and it is never disposed of unless the whole program is. **Note**: Every global variable, defined *outside* functions automatically has the type *static* . The opposite of *static* is *auto*.

Functions, Types and Declarations

Functions do not always have to return values which are integers, despite the fact that this has been exclusively the case up to now. Unless something special is done to force a function to return a different kind of value, C will always assume that the type of a function is an integer.

If the programmer wants this to be different, then a function has to be declared to be a certain type, just as variables have to be. There are two places where this must be done:

a) The name of the function must be declared a certain type where the function is declared. For example a function which returns a float value must be declared as:

```
float function1 ()

{
return (1.229);
}
```

A function which returns a character:

```
char function2 ()

{
return ('*');
}
```

b) As well as declaring a function's identifier to be a certain type in the function definition, it (irritatingly) must be declared in the function in which it is called too! The reasons for this are related to the way in which C is compiled. So, if the two functions above were called from main(), they would have to declared in the variables section as follows:

```
main ()

{    char ch, function2 ();
     float x, function1 ();

x = function1 ();
ch = function2 ();
}
```

If a function whose type is not integer is not declared like this, then compilation errors will result! Notice also that the function must be declared inside every function which calls it, not just main().

Redundant Keywords

There are a number of reserved words which are seldom used and not really required by the language. These are included in C because the designers believed they can make code clearer. The following words are optional and are not used in this book. However, the reader may see them used elsewhere. They are:

auto Means an automatic variable. The name automatic is used because these variables are automatically allocated for the programmer when they are needed and disposed of afterwards. The opposite of auto is static, but all local variables are auto by default, so only the word 'static' is really required.

formal In some compilers this means a formal parameter.

signed Is an ANSI proposed standard and means all types are signed by default.

Questions:

1) What is an identifier?

2) Say which of the following are valid C identifiers:
   a) Ralph23
   b) 80shillings
   c) mission_control
   d) A%
   e) A$
   f) _off

3) Write a statement to declare two integers called i and j.

4) What is the difference between the types float and double?

5) What is the difference between the types int and unsigned int?

6) Write a statement which assigns 67 to the integer variable 'I'.

7) What type does a C function usually return?

8) A function has to be declared 'long float' in, at least, two places. Where are these?

9) Write a statement, using the cast operator, to print out the integer part of the number 23.1256.

10) Is it possible to have an automatic global variable?

11 : Parameters & Functions

Ways In and Out of Functions

Not all functions will be as simple as the ones we have come across so far. Functions are more useful if they can be given information to work with and if they can reach variables and data which are defined 'outside' of them. Examples of this have already been seen in a limited way. For instance the function CalculateBill accepted the three following values a, b and c.

```
CalculateBill (a,b,c)

int a,b,c;

{ int total;

total = a + b + c;
}
```

When variable values are handed to a function, by writing them inside a functions brackets like this, the function is said to *accept parameters*. In mathematics, a parameter is a variable which controls the behaviour of something. In C it is a variable which carries some special information. In CalculateBill the 'behaviour' is the addition process. In other words, the value of 'total' depends upon the starting values of a, b and c. Parameters are about communication between different program functions. They are like messengers which pass information to and from different places. They provide a way of getting information into a function, but they can also be used to get information back. Parameters are usually split into two categories: 'value' parameters and 'variable' parameters. Value parameters are a way of communicating by carrying information into a function from somewhere outside. Variable parameters are two-way.

Declaring Parameters

A function was defined as:

```
identifier (parameters...)
types of parameters
{
}
```

Parameters, like variables and functions, also have types which must be declared. For instance:

```
function1 (i,j,x,y)

int i,j;
float x,y;

{
}
```

or alternatively :

```
char function2 (x,ch)

double x;
char ch;

{ char ch2 = '*';

return (ch2);
}
```

Notice that they are declared outside the block braces { }. This is because they come from outside the function – from somewhere else in the program.

Value Parameters

A value parameter is the most common kind of parameter. All of the examples up to now have been examples of 'value' parameters . When a value parameter passes information to a function, its value is copied to a new place which is completely isolated from the place where that information came from. An example helps to show this. Consider a function which is called from main() whose purpose is to add together two numbers and to print out the result.

```
        #include <stdio.h>

        main ()

        {
        add (1,4);
        }

/*******************************************/

        add (a,b)

        int a,b;

        {
        printf ("%d", a+b);
        }
```

When this program is run, two new variables automatically are created by the language, called a and b. The value one is copied into a and the value four is copied into b. Obviously, if a and b were given new values in the function add(), then this could not change the values one and four in main(), because one is always one and four is always four. They are *constants*. However, if instead the program had been:

```
        main ()

        { int a = 1, b = 4;
        add (a,b);
        }

/**************************************/

        add (a,b)

        int a,b;

        {
        printf ("%d", a+b);
        }
```

then it is less clear what will happen. In fact exactly the same thing will happen:

1) When add() is called from main() two new variables, a and b, are created by the language (which have nothing to do with the variables a and b in main() and are completely isolated from those particular variables).

2) The value of a in main() is copied into the value of a in add()

3) The value of b in main() is copied into the value of b in add()

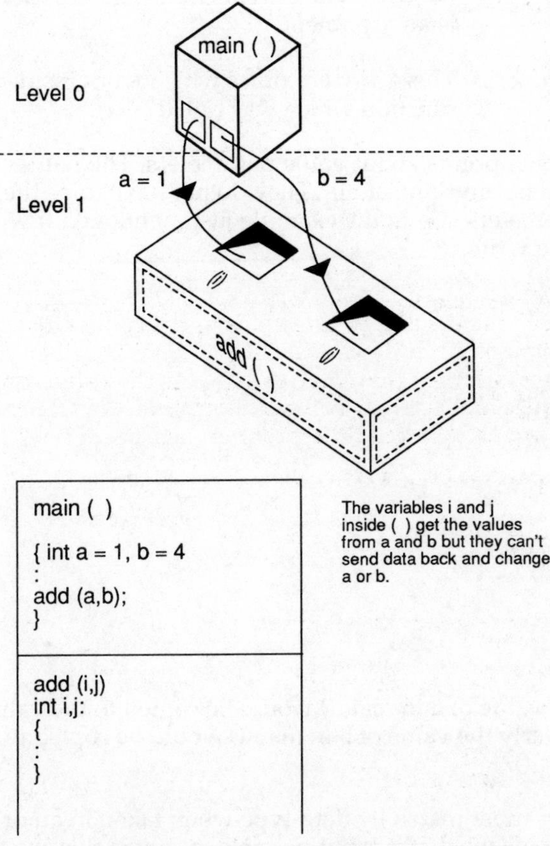

Figure 11.1. Value parameters in action.

Now, any reference to a and b within the function add() only refers to the two newly created variables and not to the original ones which appeared in main(). This means that if a and b are altered in add(), they will not affect a and b in main(). More advanced computing texts have names for the old and the new a and b:

Actual Parameters: These are the original variables which were handed over to a function. Another name for this is an argument.

Formal Parameters: These are the copies which work inside the function which was called.

Let's look at some points about value parameters. The names of formal parameters can be anything at all. They do not have to be the same as the actual parameters. So in the example just mentioned it would be equally valid to write:

```
#include <stdio.h>

main ()

{ int a = 1, b = 4;
add (a,b);
}

/*******************************************/

add (i,j)

int i,j;

{
printf ("%d", i+j);
}
```

In this case the value of a in main() would be copied to the value of i in add() and similarly the value of b in main() would be copied to the value of j in add().

The parameters must match by data-type when taken in an ordered sequence. This means that it is not possible to copy a floating point number into a character formal parameter. The compiler will spot this if it is done accidentally.

For example:

```
        main ()

        {
        function ('*',1.0);
        }

/******************************/

        function (ch,i)

        char ch;
        int i;

        {
        }
```

is wrong because 1.0 is a floating point value, not an integer. The parameters ought to, but need not necessarily match in number! This surprising fact is important because programs can go wrong because a formal parameter is missed out. If the number of actual parameters is more than the number of formal parameters and all the parameters match in type, then the extra values are just discarded. If the number of actual parameters is less than the number of formal parameters, then the compiler will assign some unknown value to the formal parameters. This will probably be garbage.

Functions as Actual Parameters

The value of a function can be used directly as a value parameter. It does not have to be assigned to a variable first. For instance:

```
        main ()

        {
        PrintOut (SomeValue ());
        }

/*****************************************/
        PrintOut (a)        /* Print the value */

        int a;

        {
        printf ("%d",a);
        }
```

```
/***********************************************/

      SomeValue () /* Return an arbitrary no */

      {
      return (42);
      }
```

This often gives a concise way of passing a value to a function.

Listing 11.1. Value parameters.

```
/**************************************************/
/*                                                */
/* Value Parameters                               */
/*                                                */
/**************************************************/
      /* Toying with value parameters */

      #include <stdio.h>

/**************************************************/
/* Level 0                                        */
/**************************************************/

      main ()     /* Example of value parameters */

           { int i,j;
           double x,x_plus_one();
           char ch;

      i = 0;
      x = 0;

      printf (" %f", x_plus_one(x));
      printf (" %f", x);
      j = resultof (i);
      printf (" %d",j);
      }

/**************************************************/
/* level 1                                        */
/**************************************************/
      double x_plus_one(x)      /* Add one to x ! */
      double x;

      {
      x = x + 1;
      return (x);
      }
```

```
/**************************************************/
      resultof (j)          /* Work out some result */

      int j;
      {
      return (2*j + 3);          /* why not... */
      }
```

Listing 11.2. More value parameters.

```
/****************************************************/
/*                                                  */
/* Program : More Value Parameters                  */
/*                                                  */
/****************************************************/
      /* Print out mock exam results etc */

      #include <stdio.h>

/****************************************************/

      main ()                 /* Print out exam results */

      {    int pupil1,pupil2,pupil3;
           int ppr1,ppr2,ppr3;
           float pen1,pen2,pen3;

      pupil1 = 87;
      pupil2 = 45;
      pupil3 = 12;

      ppr1 = 200;
      ppr2 = 230;
      ppr3 = 10;

      pen1 = 1;
      pen2 = 2;
      pen3 = 20;
      analyse (pupil1,pupil2,pupil3,ppr1,ppr2,
                  ppr3,pen1,pen2,pen3);

      }

/****************************************************/

      analyse (p1,p2,p3,w1,w2,w3,b1,b2,b3)

      int p1,p2,p3,w1,w2,w3;
```

```
        float b1,b2,b3;

        {
        printf ("Pupil 1 scored %d percent\n",p1);
        printf ("Pupil 2 scored %d percent\n",p2);
        printf ("Pupil 3 scored %d percent\n",p3);

        printf ("However: \n");
        printf ("Pupil1 wrote %d sides of paper\n",w1);
        printf ("Pupil2 wrote %d sides\n",w2);
        printf ("Pupil3 wrote %d sides\n",w3);

        if (w2 > w1)
            {
            printf ("Which just shows that quantity");
            printf (" does not imply quality\n");
            }

        printf ("Pupil1 used %f biros\n",b1);
        printf ("Pupil2 used %f \n",b2);
        printf ("Pupil3 used %f \n",b3);

        printf ("Total paper used = %d", total(w1,w2,w3));
        }

/****************************************************/

        total (a,b,c)                    /* add up total */

        int a,b,c;

        {
        return (a + b + c);
        }
```

Variable Parameters

A word of warning! First time readers may wish to omit this section until they have read about 'pointers and operators'. One way to hand information back is to use the return() function which was examined in Chapter 10. This function is slightly limited, however, in that it can only hand the value of one variable back at a time. There is another way of handing back values which is less restrictive, but more awkward than this. This is by using a special kind of parameter, often called a *variable parameter*.

It is most easily explained with the aid of an example:

```
#include <stdio.h>

main ()

{ int i,j;

GetValues (&i,&j);
printf ("i = %d and j = %d",i,j)
}

/**********************************************/

GetValues (p,q)

int *p,*q;

{
*p = 10;
*q = 20;
}
```

To fully understand what is going on, this program requires a knowledge of pointers and operators, which are covered in later chapters, but a brief explanation can be given here, so that the method can be used.

There are two new things to notice about this program: the symbols & and *. The ampersand symbol (&) should be read as 'the address of...'. The star symbol (*) should be read as 'the contents of the address...'. This is easily confused with the multiplication symbol (which is identical). The difference is only in the context in which the symbol is used. Fortunately, this is not ambiguous since multiplication always takes place between two numbers or variables, whereas the 'contents of a pointer' applies only to a single variable and the star precedes the variable name.

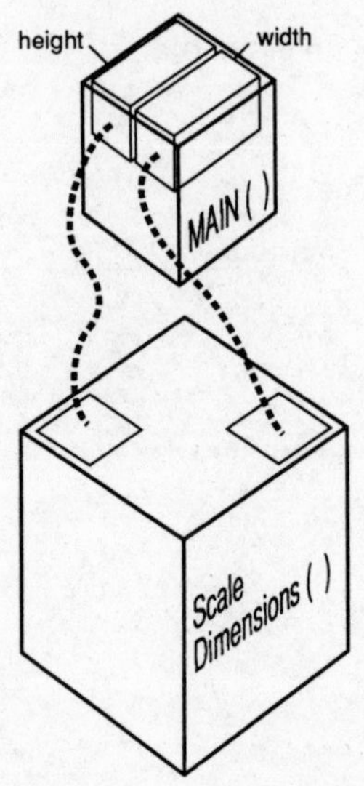

Values can go either way Scale Dimensions() is just connected to the variables in main() directly.

Figure 11.2.
Passing Variables.

So, in the program just mentioned, it is not the variables themselves which are being passed to the procedure but the addresses of the variables. In other words, information about where the variables are stored in the memory is passed to the function GetValues(). These addresses are copied into two new variables p and q, which are said to be pointers to i and j. So, with variable parameters, the function does not receive a copy of the variables themselves, but information about how to get at the original variable which was passed. This information can be used to alter the 'actual parameters' directly and this is done with the star operator:

```
*p = 10;
```

means make the contents of the address held in p are equal to 10. Recall that the address held in p is the address of the variable i, so this actually reads: make i equal to 10. Similarly:

```
*q = 20;
```

means make the contents of the address held in q equal to 20. Other operations are also possible (and these are detailed in the chapter on pointers) such as finding out the value of i and putting it into a new variable, say, a:

```
int a;
a = *p;    /* is equivalent to a = i */
```

Notice that the star symbol is required in the declaration of these parameters.

Listing 11.3. Variable parameters.

```
/**************************************************/
/*                                                */
/* Program : Variable Parameters                  */
/*                                                */
/**************************************************/
   /* Scale some measurements on a drawing, say */

      #include <stdio.h>

/**************************************************/

      main ()                     /* Scale measurements*/

      { int height,width;

      height = 4;
      width = 5;
      ScaleDimensions (&height,&width);
      printf ("Scaled height = %d\n",height);
      printf ("Scaled width = %d\n",width);
      }

/***************************************************/

      ScaleDimensions (h,w)/* return scaled values */

      int *h, *w;

      {    int hscale = 3;         /* scale factors */
           int wscale = 1;

      *h = *h * hscale;
      *w = *w * wscale;
      }
```

Questions:

1) Name two ways that values and results can be handed back from a function.

2) Where are parameters declared?

3) Can a function be used directly as a value parameter?

4) Does it mean anything to use a function directly as a variable parameter?

5) What do the symbols * and & mean when they are placed in front of an identifier?

6) Do actual and formal parameters need to have the same names?

12: Scope: Local & Global

Where a Program's Fingers can't Reach

From the computer's point of view, a C program is nothing more than a collection of functions and declarations. Functions can be thought of as sealed capsules of program code which float on a background of 'white space' (which might be called the 'global white space') and are connected together by means of function calls. 'White space' is the name given to the white of an imaginary piece of paper upon which a program is written, in other words the spaces and new line characters which are invisible to the eye. The 'global white space' is only the gaps between functions, not the gaps inside functions.

Thinking of functions as sealed capsules is a useful way of understanding the difference between *global* and *local* objects and the whole idea of 'scope' in a program.

Global Variables

Global variables are declared in the white space between functions. If every function is a ship floating in this sea of white space, then global variables are data storage areas which also float in this sea and can enter any ship and also enter anything inside any ship (see figure 12.1). Global variables are universal or 'global' (the meaning comes from the phrase 'true over the whole globe of the world').

Global variables are created when a program is started and are not destroyed until the program stops. They can be used anywhere in a program, there is no restriction about where they can be used.

Local Variables

Local variables are more interesting. They can't enter just any region of the program. This is because they are trapped inside blocks. To use the ship analogy again. Imagine that on board every ship (ie, inside every function), there is a large swimming pool on which many toy ships float, then local variables work anwhere in the swimming pool, (inside any

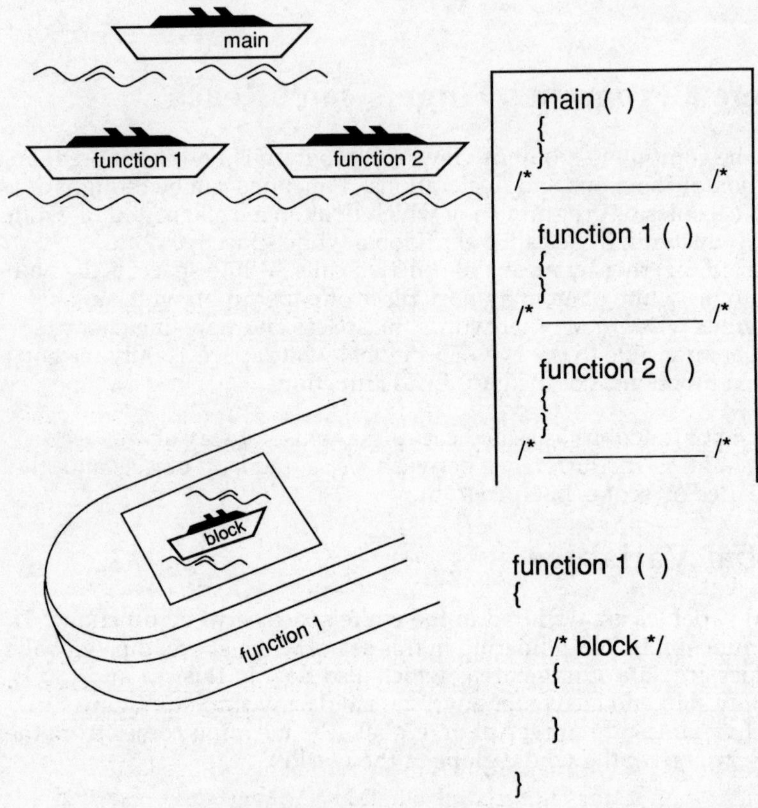

Figure 12.1.Nesting.

of the toys ships), but can't get out of the large ship into the wide beyond. The swimming pool is just like a smaller sea, but one which is restricted to being inside a particular function. Every function has its own swimming pool! The idea can be taken further too. What about even smaller swimming pools onboard the toy ship (ie, functions or blocks inside the functions!)?

```
/* Global white space "sea" */

function ()

{

/* On board ship */

     {

     /* On board a toy ship */

     }
}
```

The same rules apply for the toy ships. Variables can go anywhere inside them but they cannot get out. They just can't escape their block braces { }.

Whenever a pair of block braces is written into a program, it is possible to make variable declarations inside the opening brace as follows:

```
{    int locali;
     char localch;

/* statements */

}
```

These variables do not work outside the braces. They are only created when the opening brace is encountered and they are destroyed when the closing brace is executed, or when control jumps out of the block. Because they only work in this local area of a program, they are called local variables. It is a matter of style and efficiency to use local variables when it does not matter whether variables are preserved outside of a particular block, because the system automatically allocates and disposes of them. The programmer doesn't have to think about this at all.

Where a variable is and is not defined is called the scope of that variable. It tells a programmer what a variable's horizons are!

Intership Communication : Parameters

If functions were sealed capsules and no local variables could ever communicate with other parts of the program, then functions would not be very useful. This is why parameters are allowed. Parameters are a way of communicating local variables to other functions without letting them out! Value parameters (see last chapter) make copies of local variables without actually using them. The copied parameter is then a local variable in another function.

Notice that in this example, if there are two variables of the same name, which are both defined in the same place ('c' in the example below) then the more local one wins. That is, the last variable to be defined takes priority.

Listing 12.1. Scope: the Cllled capsules.

```
/*****************************************************/
/*                                                   */
/* SCOPE : THE CLLLED CAPSULES                       */
/*                                                   */
/*****************************************************/

   #include <stdio.h>

/*****************************************************/

   main ()

   { int a = 1, b = 2, c = 3;

   if (a == 1)
      { int c;
      c = a + b;
      printf ("%d",c);
      }

   handdown (a,b);
   printf ("%d",c);
   }

/*****************************************************/
     handdown (a,b)                /* Some function */
     int a,b;
     {
     }
```

Style Note

Some people complain about the use of global variables in a program. What are they for if not to be used? The main complaint is that it is difficult to see what information is being used by a function unless all that information is passed as parameters. A way to make this clear, is to write global variables in capital letters only, while writing the rest of the variables in mainly small letters.

```
int GLOBALINTEGER;
....

{    int local integer;
}
```

This allows global variables to be easily spotted. Another reason for avoiding global variables is it is easier to debug a program if only local variables are used. The reason is that when a function capsule is tested and sealed, it can be guaranteed to work in all cases, provided it is not affected by any other functions from outside. Global variables punch holes in the sealed function capsules because they allow bugs from other functions to creep into tried and tested ones. An alert and careful programmer can usually control this without difficulty.

The following guidelines may help the reader to decide whether to use local or global data:

1) Always think of using a local variable first. Is it impractical? Yes, if it means passing dozens of parameters to functions, or reproducing a lot of variables. Global variables will sometimes tidy up a program.

2) Global variables generally make the final code longer, as they are stored in a program object file. If this is important, consider global variables. A program should never use entirely global variables, however!

3) Local variables are marginally more efficient than global variables and often make the flow of data in a program clearer.

4) The preference in this book is to use local variables for all work, except where a program centres around a single data structure. Significant data structures are always defined globally.

Advanced Scope and Style

All the programs in this book longer than a couple of lines, are written in an unusual way – with a 'levelled structure' (see Appendix A). There are several good reasons for this. One is that the sealed capsules are shown to be sealed, by using a comment bar between each function.

```
/***************************************/
```

Another good reason is that any function hands parameters down by only one level at a time, and that any return() statement hands values up a single level. The global variables are kept to a single place at the head of each program so that they can be seen to reach into everything.

Questions

1) What is a global variable?

2) What is a local variable?

3) What is meant by calling a block (enclosed by curly braces { }) a 'sealed capsule'?

4) Do parameters make functions leaky? For example, do they spoil them by letting the variables leak out into other functions?

5) Write a program which declares four variables. Two integer types called i,j which are global and two float types called x,y which are local inside the function main(). Then add another function called "another()" and pass x,y to this function. How many different storage spaces are used when this program runs? (Hint: are x,y and their copies the same?)

13 : The Pre-processor

Making Programming Versatile

C is unusual in that it has a 'pre-processor'. As the name suggests, the pre-processor is a phase which occurs prior to compilation of a program. The pre-processor has two main uses. First, it allows external files (such as standard libraries) to be included and second, it allows 'macros' to be defined. Pre-processor commands are given *outside* functions in the global white space area and are distinguished by the hash symbol #. One example of this has already been encountered for the standard library file stdio.h:

```
#include <stdio.h>
```

is a command which tells the pre-processor to treat the file stdio.h as if it were actually part of the program text. In other words, to include it as part of the program to be compiled.

Macros are words which can be defined to stand in place of something complicated, they are a way of reducing the amount of typing in a program and a way of putting long, ungainly pieces of code into short words. For example, the simplest use of macros is to give constant values meaningful names:

```
#define telephnum 720663
```

This allows the programmer to use the word 'telephnum' in the program to mean the number 720663. In this particular case, the word is clearly not any shorter than the number it will replace, but it is more meaningful and would make a program 'read more naturally', than if the raw number were used. For instance, a program which deals with several different fixed numbers like a telephone number, a postcode and a street number, could write:

```
currentnumber = telephnum;
currentnumber = postcode;
currentnumber = streetnum;
```

instead of :

```
currentnumber = 720663;
currentnumber = 345;
currentnumber = 14
```

Using the macros makes the actions much clearer and allows the programmer to forget about what the numbers actually are. It also means that a program is easy to alter because to change a telephone number, or whatever, it is only necessary to change the definition, not to re-type the number in every single instance.

Users of Pascal might easily gain the wrong impression of a macro from this example, because they may compare it to Pascal's constants. The important feature of macros is that they are not merely numerical constants which are referenced at compile time, but are strings which are physically replaced before compilation by the pre-processor! This means that almost anything can be defined:

```
#define sum  1 + 2 + 3 + 4
```

would allow 'sum' to be used instead of 1+2+3+4. Or:

```
#define string "Mary had a little lamb..."
```

would allow a commonly used string to be called by the identifier 'string' instead of typing it out afresh each time. The idea of a define statement then is:

```
#define macroname  definition on rest of line
```

Macros can't define more than a single line to be substituted into a program but they can be used anywhere, except inside strings. Anything enclosed in string quotes is assumed to be complete by the compiler.

Some macros are defined already in the file stdio.h such as:

EOF - the end of file character (= -1 for instance)
NULL - the null character (zero) = 0

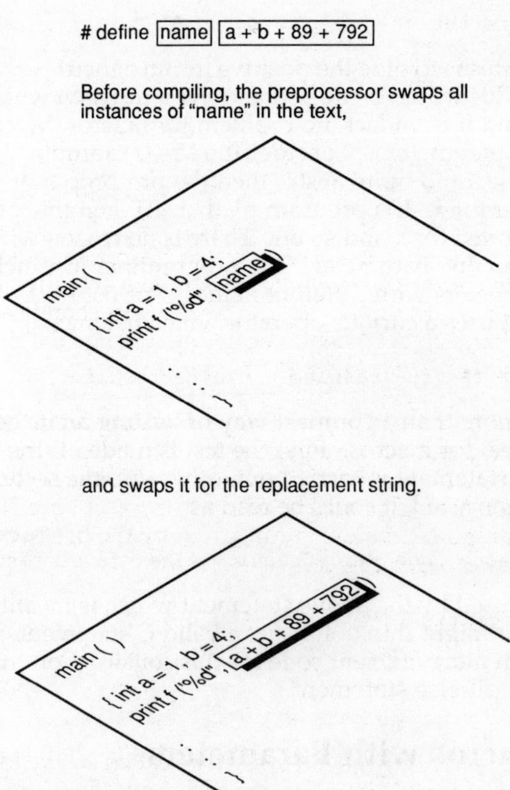

define name a + b + 89 + 792
Before compiling, the preprocessor swaps all instances of "name" in the text,
main ( )
{ int a = 1, b = 4;
print f ("%d", name)
}
and swaps it for the replacement string.
main ( )
{ int a = 1, b = 4;
print f ("%d", a + b + 89 + 792)
}

Figure 13.1.The pre-processor.

Macro Functions

A more advanced use of macros is also permitted by the pre-processor. This involves macros which accept parameters and hand back values. This works by defining a macro with some dummy parameter, say 'x'. For example, a macro which is usually defined in one of the standard libraries is abs() which means the absolute or unsigned value of a number. For example:

```
#define abs(x)          ((x) < 0) ? -(x) : (x)
```

The result of this is to give the positive (or unsigned) part of any number or variable. This would be no problem for a function which could accept parameters and it is, in fact, no problem for macros. Macros can also be made to take parameters. Consider the abs () example. If a programmer were to write abs(4) then the pre-processor would substitute four for x. If a program read abs(i) then the pre-processor would substitute i for x and so on. There is no reason why macros can't take more than one parameter. The programmer just includes two dummy parameters with different names. See listing 13.1. Notice that this definition uses a curious operator which belongs to C:

```
<test> ? <true result> : <false result>
```

This is little more than a compact way of writing an if-then-else statement, ideal for macros. First the test is made. If the test is true then the first statement is carried out, otherwise the second is carried out. As a memory aid, it could be read as:

```
if <test> then <true result> else <false result>
```

Don't be confused by the above statement which is meant to show what a programmer might think. It is *not* a valid C statement. C can usually produce much more efficient code for this construction than for a corresponding if-else statement.

Using Macros with Parameters

It is tempting to forget about the distinction between macros and functions, thinking that it can be ignored. To some extent this is true for absolute beginners, but it is not a good idea as you become more experienced with C. It should always be remembered that macros are substituted whole at every place where they are used in a program. This is potentially a very large amount of repetition of code. The advantage of a macro, however, is speed. No time is taken up in passing control over to a new function, because control never leaves the home function when a macro is used. It simply makes the function a bit longer. There is a limitation with macros though, function calls can't be used as their parameters, such as:

```
abs (function())
```

This will not work. Only variables or number constants will be substituted. Macros are also severely restricted in complexity by the limitations of the pre-processor. It is simply not viable to copy complicated sequences of code all over programs.

Choosing between functions and macros is a matter of personal judgement. No simple rules can be given. In the end (as with all programming choices) it is experience which counts towards the final program.

Listing 13.1. Macro demonstration.

```
/***********************************************************/
/*                                                         */
/* MACRO DEMONSTRATION                                     */
/*                                                         */
/***********************************************************/

   #include "stdio.h"

   #define string1          "A macro definition\n"
   #define string2          "must be all on one line!!\n"
   #define expression       1 + 2 + 3 + 4
   #define expr2            expression + 10
   #define abs(x)           ((x) < 0) ? -(x) : (x)
   #define max(a,b)         (a < b) ? (b) : (a)
   #define biggest(a,b,c)  (max(a,b) < c) ? (c) : (max(a,b))

/***********************************************************/

   main ()                 /* No #definitions inside functions! */

   {
   printf (string1);
   printf (string2);
   printf ("%d\n",expression);
   printf ("%d\n",expr2);
   printf ("%d\n",abs(-5));
   printf ("Biggest of 1 2 and 3 is %d",biggest(1,2,3));
   }
```

Note About #include

When an include statement is written into a program, it is a sign that a compiler should merge another file of C programming with the current one. However, the #include statement is itself valid, so this means that a file which is included may contain #includes itself. The includes are then said to be 'nested'. This often makes includes simpler.

Other Pre-processor Commands

There are a handful more pre-processor commands which largely can be ignored by the beginner. They are commonly used in 'include' files to make sure that things are not defined twice. Note : 'True' has any non zero value in C. 'False' is zero.

#undef This undefines a macro, leaving the name free.

#if This is followed by some expression on the same line. It allows conditional compilation, or compilation only if some condition is true.

#ifdef This is followed by a macro name. If that macro is defined then this is true.

#ifndef This is followed by a macro name. If that name is not defined then this is true.

#else This is part of an #if, #ifdef, #ifndef pre-processor statement.

#endif This marks the end of a pre-processor statement.

#line Has the form:

```
#line constant "filename"
```

This is for debugging mainly. This statement causes the compiler to believe that the next line is line number (constant) and is part of the file (filename).

#error This is a part of the proposed ANSI standard. It is intended for debugging. It forces the compiler to abort compilation.

Listing 13.2. To compile or not.

```
/***********************************************************/
/* To compile or not to compile                            */
/***********************************************************/

      #define somedefinition 6546
      #define choice  1   /* Choose this before compiling */

/***********************************************************/

      #if (choice == 1)
          #define optionstring "The programmer selected this"
          #define ditto        "instead of ....            "
      #else
          #define optionstring "The alternative"
          #define ditto        "i.e. This! "

      #endif

/***********************************************************/

      #ifdef somedefinition
          #define whatever "Something was defined!"
      #else
          #define whatever "Nothing was defined"
      #endif

/************************************************************/

      main ()

      {
      printf (optionstring);
      printf (ditto);
      }
```

Questions:

1) Define a macro called 'birthday' describing the day of the month upon which your birthday falls.

2) Write an instruction to the pre-processor to include to maths library 'math.h'.

3) A macro is always a number. True or false?

4) A macro is always a constant. True or false?

14 : Pointers

Making Maps of Data

Suppose a bold variable-hunter were given a map of a computer's memory with all the storage locations of its variables marked upon it. If there were one single piece of information that he needed in order to be able to point to the place where a variable was stored, what would it be? The answer is the memory address or location of that variable. In other words, a pointer to it.

Pointers, in C, are a special type of variable which holds the addresses or locations of other variables. They do, in a sense, point to their locations by keeping a record of the spot at which they were stored.

Pointers to variables are easily found, or made in programs, by recording the address at which a variable is stored. This is often a useful thing to do in a program (see the section on uses). To make a pointer to a variable, the variable address must be known. It is always possible to find the address of a piece of storage in C using the special '&' operator. For instance: if 'location' were a float type variable, it would be easy to find a pointer to it called 'location_ptr'.

```
float location;
float *location_ptr,*address;

location_ptr = &(location);

/*  or : */

address = &(location);
```

The declarations of pointers look a little strange at first. The star symbol (*) which stands in front of the variable name is C's way of declaring that variable to be a pointer. The four lines above make two identical pointers to a floating point variable called 'location', one of them is called location_ptr and the other is called address. The point is that a pointer is just a place to keep a record of the address of a variable, so they are really the same thing.

For anyone who believes in high-level languages, it is probably a source of wonder why on earth anyone should ever want to know the address of these variables. Having gone to the trouble to design a high-level language, like C, in which variables can be given elegant and meaningful names: it seems like a step in a backward's direction to want to be able to find out the exact number of the memory location. The whole point of variables, after all, is that it is not necessary to know exactly where information is really stored.

This complaint is not quite fair though. It is certainly rare to want to know the actual number of the memory location at which something is stored. That would really make the idea of a high-level language a bit pointless. The idea behind pointers is that a high-level programmer can now find out the exact location of a variable without ever having to know the actual number involved. Remember:

> A pointer is a *variable* which holds the address of the storage location for another given variable.

C provides two operators & and * which allow pointers to be used in many versatile ways.

& and *

The & and * operators have already been used once in chapter 11 to hand back values to variable parameters. They can be read in a program to have the following meanings:

 &   the address of...
 *   the contents of the address held in...

Another way of saying the second of these is:

 *   the contents of the location pointed to by...

This reinforces the idea that pointers reach out an imaginary hand and point to some location in the memory and it is more usual to speak of pointers in this way. The two operators * and & are always written in front of a variable, clinging on, so that they refer without doubt to that one variable. For instance:

&x The address at which the variable x is stored.

*ptr The contents of the variable which is pointed to by ptr.

The following short example might help to clarify the way in which they are used:

```
int somevar;                          /* 1 */
int *ptr_to_somevar;                  /* 2 */
somevar = 42;                         /* 3 */
ptr_to_somevar = &(somevar);          /* 4 */
printf ("%d",*ptr_to_somevar);        /* 5 */
*ptr_to_somevar = 56;                 /* 6 */
```

The key to these statements is as follows:

1) Declare an int type variable called somevar.

2) Declare a *pointer* to an int type called ptr_to_somevar. The * which stands in front of ptr_to_somevar is the way C declares ptr_to_somevar as a pointer to an integer, rather than an integer.

3) Let somevar take the value 42.

4) This gives a value to ptr_to_somevar. The value is the address of the variable somevar. Notice that only at this stage does is become a pointer to the particular variable somevar. Before this, its fate is quite open. The declaration (2) merely makes it a pointer which can point to any integer variable which is around.

5) Print out 'the contents of the location pointed to by ptr_to_somevar' in other words, somevar itself. So this will be just 42.

6) Let the contents of the location pointed to by ptr_to_somevar be 56. This is the same as the more direct statement:

```
somevar = 56;
```

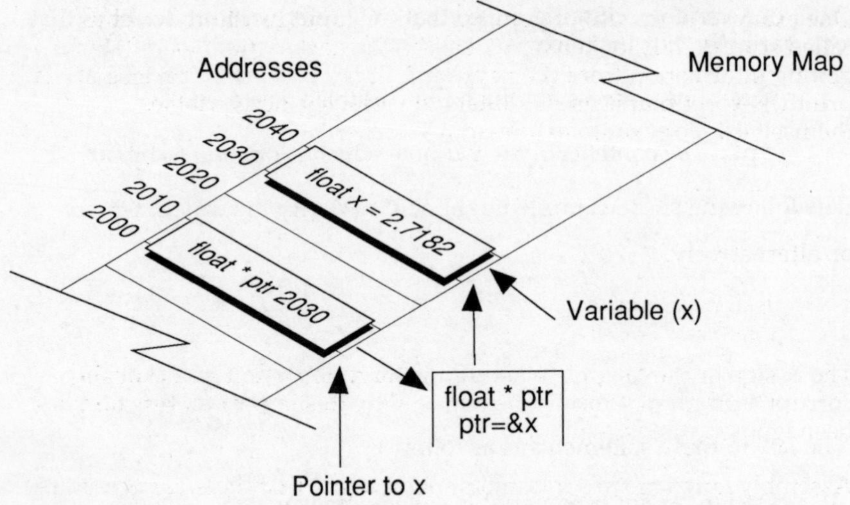

Figure 14.1. Pointers and variables.

Uses for Pointers

It is possible to have pointers which point to any type of data whatsoever. They are always declared with the * symbol. Some examples are given next.

```
int i,*ip;

char ch,*chp;

short s,*sp;

float x,*xp;

double y,*yp;
```

Pointers are extremely important objects in C. They are far more important in C than in Pascal or BASIC (PEEK and POKE are like pointers). In particular they are vital when using strings or arrays or 'linked lists' – in fact these uses are important so they have chapters of their own.

One example of the use of pointers is the C input function, which is called scanf(). It is looked at in detail in the next section. scanf() is for getting information from the keyboard. It is a bit like the reverse of printf(), except that it uses pointers to variables, not variables themselves. For example: to read an integer:

```
int i;
scanf ("%d",&i);
```

or alternatively:

```
int *i;
scanf ("%d",i);
```

The & sign or the * sign is vital. If it is forgotten, scanf will probably corrupt a program. This is one reason why this important function has been ignored up to now.

Assembly language programmers might argue that there are occasions when it would be nice to know the actual *address* of a variable as a number. One reason why you might want to know this, would be for debugging. It is not often a useful thing to do, but it is not inconceivable that in developing some program a programmer would want to know the actual address. The & operator is flexible enough to allow this to be found. It could be printed out as an integer:

```
<type> *ptr:
printf ("Address = %d",(int) ptr);
```

Pointers and Initialisation

Something to be wary of with pointer variables, is the way that they are initialised. It is incorrect, logically, to initialise pointers in a declaration. A compiler will probably not prevent this, however, because there is nothing incorrect about it as far as syntax is concerned.

Think about what happens when the following statement is written. This statement is really talking about two different storage places in the memory:

```
int *a = 2;
```

First of all, what is declared is a pointer. Space for a 'pointer to int' is allocated by the program, and to start off with that space will contain garbage (random numbers) because no statement like :

```
a = &someint;
```

has yet been encountered which would give it a value. It will then attempt to fill the contents of some variable, pointed to by a, with the value two. This is doomed to failure, a only contains garbage so the two could be stored anywhere. There may not even be a variable at the place in the memory which a points to. Nothing has been said about that yet. This kind of initialisation cannot hope to work and will most likely crash the machine or corrupt some other data.

Listing 14.1. Swapping pointers.

```
/*********************************************/
/*                                           */
/* Swapping Pointers                         */
/*                                           */
/*********************************************/
   /* Program swaps the variables which a,b */
   /* point to. Not pointless really !      */

      #include <stdio.h>

      main ()

      {    int *a,*b,*c;           /* Declr ptrs */
      int  A,B;                /* Declare storage */

      A = 12;               /* Initialise storage */
      B = 9;

      a = &A;                  /* Initialise pointers */
      b = &B;

      printf ("%d %d\n",*a,*b);

      c = a;                         /* swap pointers */
      a = b;
      b = c;

      printf ("%d %d\n",*a,*b);
      }
```

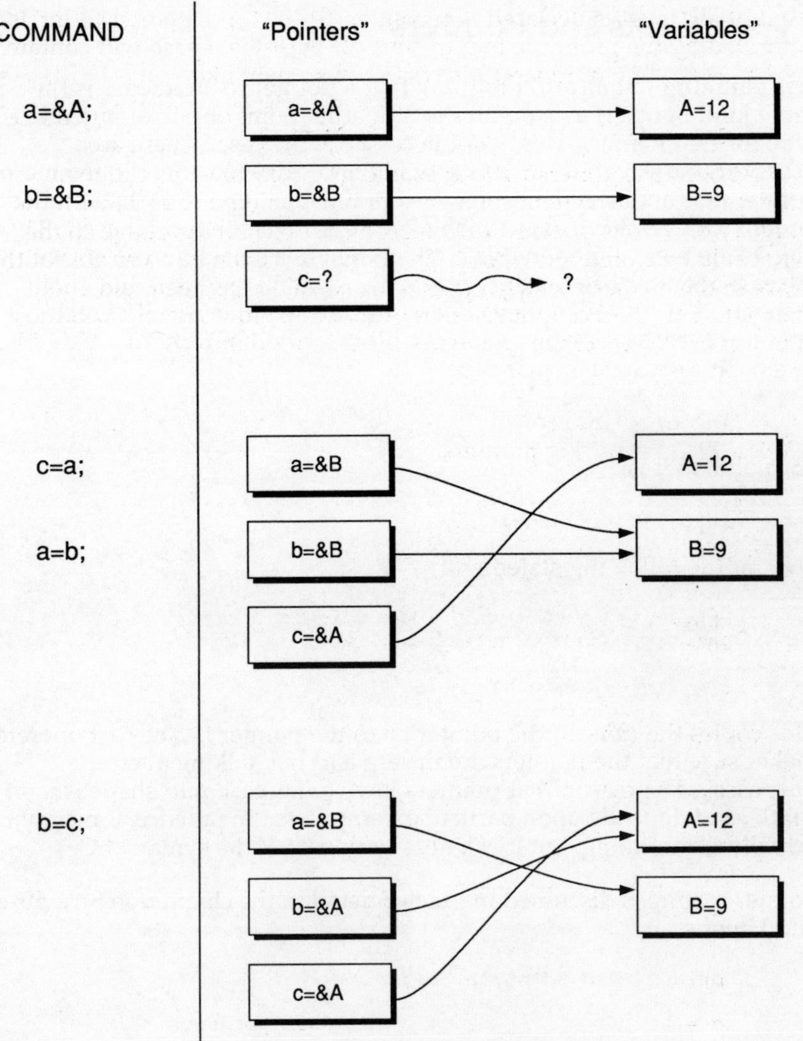

Figure 14.2.Pointers example.

Types, Casts and Pointers

It is tempting but *incorrect* to think that a pointer to an integer is the same kind of object as a pointer to a floating point object, or any other type for that matter. This is not necessarily the case. There are occasions, however, when it is actually necessary to convert one kind of pointer into another. This might happen with a type of variable called 'unions' or even functions which allocate storage for special uses. These objects are met later on in this book. When this situation comes about, the cast operator has to be used to make sure that pointers have compatible types when they are assigned to one another. The cast operator for variables (see Chapter 10) is written in front of a variable, to force it to be a particular type:

```
(type) <variable>
```

For pointers it is:

```
(type *) <pointer>
```

Look at the following statement:

```
char *ch;
int  *i;

i = (int *) ch;
```

This copies the *value* of the pointer ch to the pointer i. The cast operator makes sure that the pointers are in step and not 'talking at cross purposes'. The reason that pointers have to be 'cast' into shape is a bit subtle, and depends upon particular computers. In practice, it may not actually do anything, but it is a necessary part of the syntax of C.

Pointer casting is discussed in greater detail in the chapter on Structures and Unions.

Questions:

1) What is a pointer?

2) How is a variable declared to be a pointer?

3) What data types can pointers 'point to'?

4) Write a statement which converts a pointer to a character into a pointer to a 'double' type. (This is not as pointless as it seems. It is useful in dealing with unions and memory allocation functions).

5) Why is it incorrect to declare: float *number = 2.65; ?

15 : Standard I/O

Talking to the User

Getting information in and out of a computer is the most important thing that a program can do. Without input and output, computers would be quite useless.

C treats all its output as though it were reading or writing to different files. Normally, you would think of a file as a thing on a disc which has to be opened and closed. A file is really just a place where information comes from or can be sent to. Some files can only be read, some can only be written to, others can be both read from and written to. In other situations files are called 'I/O streams'.

C has three 'unusual' files which are always open and ready for use. They are called *stdin*, *stdout* and *stderr*, meaning standard input, standard output and standard error file. Stdin is the input which usually arrives from the keyboard of a computer. Stdout is usually the screen. Stderr is the route by which all error messages pass: usually the screen. This is only 'usually' because the situation can be altered. In fact, what happens is that these files are just handed over to the local operating system to deal with, and it chooses what to do with them. Usually this means the keyboard and the screen, but occasionally this might be redirected to a printer, to a disc file or to a modem and so on. It depends upon how the user runs the program.

The keyboard and screen are referred to as the standard input/output files because this is what most people use, most of the time. Also the programmer never has to open or close these, because C does it automatically. The library stdio.h provides some functions for working with stdin and stdout, which are simplified versions of the functions that can be used on any kind of file. In order of importance, they are:

printf
scanf

getchar
putchar
gets
puts

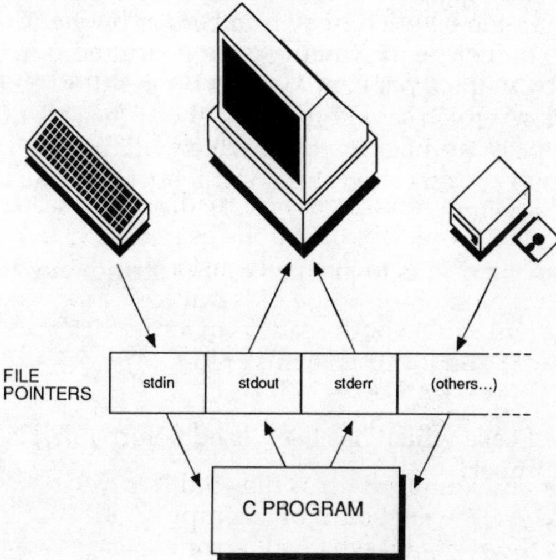

Figure 15.1. Routes to and from a C program.

The printf Function

The printf function has been used widely up to now for output because it provides a neat and easy way of printing text and numbers to stdout (the screen). Its name is meant to signify 'print-formatted' because it gives the user control over how text and numerical data are to be set out on the screen.

Making text look good on screen is important in programming. C makes this easy by allowing the programmer to decide how the text will be printed in the available space. The printf function has general form:

```
printf ("string...",<variables>,<numbers>)
```

It contains a string with some blank 'fields', which is not optional and it contains any number of parameters to follow: one for each blank 'field' in the string.

The blank 'fields' are gaps which the programmer can introduce into the string, which will then be filled in by numbers or by the contents of variables and so on before the final version is printed out. These fields are introduced by using a per cent (%) character, followed by some coded information, which says something about the size of the blank space and the type of number or string which will be filled into that space. The string is often called the 'control string' because it contains these control characters.

The simplest use of printf is to just print out a string with no blank fields to be filled:

```
printf ("A pretty ordinary string..");
printf ("Testing 1,2,3...");
```

The next simplest case which has been used before now, is to print out a single integer number:

```
int number = 42;
printf ("%d",number);
```

The two can be combined as follows:

```
int number = 42;
printf ("Some number = %d",number);
```

The result of this last example is to print out the following on the screen:

```
Some number = 42
```

The text cursor is left pointing to the character just after the two. Notice the way that %d is swapped for the number 42. The %d defines a 'field' which is filled in with the value of the variable.

There are other kinds of data apart from integers! Any kind of variable can be printed out with printf. %d is called a *conversion character* for integers because it tells the compiler to treat the variable to be filled in as an integer. So make sure it is an integer or things will go wrong!

Other characters are used for other kinds of data. Here is a list of the different letters for printf:

d	Signed denary integer
u	Unsigned denary integer
x	Hexadecimal integer
o	Octal integer
s	String
c	Single character
f	Fixed decimal floating point
e	Scientific notation floating point
g	Use f or e, whichever is shorter

The best way to learn these is to experiment with different conversion characters. The example program below and its output below give some impression of how they work:

Listing 15.1. Conversion characters and types of printf.

```
/**************************************************/
/*                                                */
/* printf Conversion Characters and Types         */
/*                                                */
/**************************************************/

        #include "stdio.h"

        main ()

        {    int i = -10;
             unsigned int ui = 10;
             float x = 3.56;
             double y = 3.52;
             char ch = 'z';
             char *string_ptr = "any old string";

        printf ("signed integer %d\n", i);
        printf ("unsigned integer %u\n",ui);

        printf ("This is wrong! %u",i);
        printf ("See what happens when you get the ");
        printf ("character wrong!");

        printf ("Hexadecimal %x %x\n",i,ui);
        printf ("Octal %o %o\n",i,ui);
```

```
printf ("Float and double %f %f\n",x,y);
printf ("       ditto       %e %e\n",x,y);
printf ("       ditto       %g %g\n",x,y);

printf ("single character %c\n",ch);
printf ("whole string -> %s",string_ptr);
}
```

Output

```
signed integer -10
unsigned integer 10
This is wrong! 10 See what happens when you get the
character wrong!
Hexadecimal FFFFFFF6 A Octal 37777777766 12 Float and
double
3.560000 3.520000
          ditto       3.560000E+00 3.520000E+00
          ditto       3.560000 3.520000
single character z
whole string -> any old string
```

Formatting with printf

This example program doesn't produce a very neat layout on the screen. The conversion specifiers in the printf string can be extended to give more information. The % and the character type act like brackets around the extra information. For example:

```
%-10.3f
```

is an extended version of %f, which carries some more information. That extra information takes the form:

```
% [-] [fw] [.p] X
```

where the each bracket is optional and the symbols inside them stand for the following:

[fw] This is a number which specifies the field width of this 'blank field'. In other words, how wide a space will be made in the string for the object concerned. In fact it is the minimum field width because if data needs more room than is written here it will spill out of the box of fixed size. If the size is bigger than the object to be printed, the rest of the field will be filled out with spaces.

[-] If this is included, the output will be left justified. This means it will be aligned with the left-hand margin of the field created with [fw]. Normally all numbers are right justified, or aligned with the right-hand margin of the field 'box'.

[.p] This has different meanings depending on the object which is to be printed. For a floating point type (float or double) p specifies the number of decimal places after the point which are to be printed. For a string it specifies how many characters are to be printed.

Some valid format specifiers are listed below:

```
%10d   %2.2f   %25.21s  %2.6f
```

The table below helps to show the effect of changing these format controls. The width of a field is draw in by using the | bars.

<table>
<tr><th>Object to be printed</th><th>Control Spec.</th><th>Actual Output</th></tr>
<tr><td>42</td><td>%6d</td><td>| 42|</td></tr>
<tr><td>42</td><td>%-6d</td><td>|42 |</td></tr>
<tr><td>324</td><td>%10d</td><td>| 324|</td></tr>
<tr><td>-1</td><td>%-10d</td><td>|-1 |</td></tr>
<tr><td>-1</td><td>%1d</td><td>|-1| (overspill)</td></tr>
<tr><td>'z'</td><td>%3c</td><td>| z|</td></tr>
<tr><td>'z'</td><td>%-3c</td><td>|z |</td></tr>
<tr><td>2.71828</td><td>%10f</td><td>| 2.71828|</td></tr>
<tr><td>2.71828</td><td>%10.2f</td><td>| 2.71|</td></tr>
<tr><td>2.71828</td><td>%-10.2f</td><td>|2.71 |</td></tr>
<tr><td>2.71828</td><td>%2.4f</td><td>|2.7182| (overspill)</td></tr>
<tr><td>2.718</td><td>%.4f</td><td>|2.7180|</td></tr>
<tr><td>2.718</td><td>%10.5f</td><td>| 2.71800|</td></tr>
</table>

Object to be printed	Control Spec.	Actual Output
2.71828	%10e	|2.71828e+00|
2.71828	%10.2e	| 2.17e+00|
2.71828	%10.2g	| 2.71|
"printf"	%s	|printf|
"printf"	%10s	| printf|
"printf"	%2s	|printf| (overspill)
"printf"	%5.3s	| pri|
"printf"	%-5.3s	|pri |
"printf"	%.3s	|pri|

Listing 15.2. Multiplication table.

```
/*********************************************/
/*                                           */
/* Multiplication Table                      */
/*                                           */
/*********************************************/

      #include <stdio.h>

      main ()            /* Printing in columns */

      {    int i,j;

      for (i = 1; i <= 10; i++)
           {
           for (j = 1; j <= 10; j++)
                {
                printf ("%5d",i * j);
                }
           printf ("\n");
           }
      }
```

Output

```
 1   2   3   4   5   6   7   8   9  10
 2   4   6   8  10  12  14  16  18  20
 3   6   9  12  15  18  21  24  27  30
 4   8  12  16  20  24  28  32  36  40
 5  10  15  20  25  30  35  40  45  50
 6  12  18  24  30  36  42  48  54  60
 7  14  21  28  35  42  49  56  63  70
 8  16  24  32  40  48  56  64  72  80
 9  18  27  36  45  54  63  72  81  90
10  20  30  40  50  60  70  80  90 100
```

Special Control Characters

Control characters are invisible on the screen. They have special purposes usually to do with cursor movement. They are written into an ordinary string by typing a backslash character (\) followed by some other character. These characters are listed next:

\b	backspace BS
\f	form feed FF (also clear screen)
\n	new line NL (like pressing RETURN)
\r	carriage return CR (cursor to start of line)
\t	horizontal tab HT
\v	vertical tab
\"	double quote
\'	single quote character '
\\	backslash character \
\ddd	character ddd where ddd is an ASCII code given in octal or base 8. (See Appendix C).

Questions:

1) Write a program which simply prints out 6.23e+00.

2) Investigate what happens when you type the wrong conversion specifier in a program. For example, try printing an integer with %f or a floating point number with %c. This is bound to go wrong – but how will it go wrong?

3) What is wrong with the following statements?
a) printf (x);

b) printf ("%d");
c) printf ();
d) printf ("Number = %d");

Hint: if you don't know, try them in a program!!

The scanf Function

scanf is the input function which gets 'formatted input' from the file stdin (the keyboard). This is a very versatile function, but it is also very easy to go wrong with it. In fact, it is probably the most difficult to understand of all the C standard library functions!

Remember that C treats its keyboard input as a file. This makes quite a difference to the way that scanf works. The actual mechanics of scanf are very similar to those of printf in reverse:

```
scanf ("string...",pointers);
```

with one important exception – namely that it is not variables which are listed after the control string, but pointers to variables. Here are some valid uses of scanf:

```
int i;
char ch;
float x;
scanf ("%d %c %f", &i, &ch, &x);
```

Notice the & characters which make the argument pointers. Also notice the conversion specifiers which tell scanf what types of data it is going to read. The other possibility is that a program might already have pointers to a particular set of variables, in that case the & is not needed. For instance:

```
function (i,ch,x)

int *i;
char *ch;
float *x;
{
scanf ("%d %c %f", i, ch, x);
}
```

In this particular case it would actually be wrong to write the ampersand (&) symbol.

Conversion Characters

The conversion characters for scanf are not identical to those for printf, and it is much more important to be precise and totally correct with these, than it is with printf.

d	Denary integer (int or long int)
ld	Long decimal integer
x	Hexadecimal integer
o	Octal integer
h	Short integer
f	Float type
lf	Long float or double
e	Float type
le	Double
c	Single character
s	Character string

The difference between short integer and long integer can make or break a program. If it is found that a program's input seems to be behaving strangely, check these carefully. See the section on Errors and Debugging for more about this.

How Does scanf 'See' the Input?

When scanf is called in a program it, checks to see what is in the input file, that is, it checks to see what the user has typed in at the keyboard. Keyboard input is usually buffered. This means that the characters are held in a 'waiting bay' in the memory until they are read. The buffer can be thought of as a part of the input file stdin, holding some characters which can be scanned through. If the buffer has some characters in it, scanf will start to look through these; if not, it will wait for some characters to be put into the buffer.

It is important to remember that although scanf will start scanning through characters as soon as they are in the buffer, the operating system often sees to it that scanf doesn't get to know about any of the characters until the user has pressed the RETURN key on the computer or terminal. If the buffer is empty scanf will wait for some characters to be put into it.

To understand how scanf works, it is useful to think of the input as coming in 'lines'. A line is a group of characters ending in a new line character '\n'. This can be represented by a box as follows:

```
--------------------------------------
| some...chars.738/.           |'\n'|
--------------------------------------
```

As far as scanf is concerned, the input is entirely made out of characters. If the programmer says that an integer is to be expected by using the '%d' conversion specifier, then scanf will try to make sense of the characters as an integer. In other words, it will look for some characters which make up a valid integer, such as a group of numbers all between zero and nine. If the user says that floating point type is expected, then it will look for a number which may or may not have a decimal point in it. If the user just wants a character, then any character will do!

First Account of scanf

Consider the example which was given above.

```
int i;
char ch;
float x;

scanf ("%d %c %f", &i, &ch, &x);
```

Here is a simplified, ideal view of what happens.

scanf looks at the control string and finds that the first conversion specifier is '%d' which means an integer. It then tries to find some characters which fit the description of an integer in the input file. It skips over any white space characters (spaces, new lines) which do not constitute a valid integer until it matches one. When it has matched the integer and placed its value in the variable 'i', it carries on and looks at the next conversion specifier '%c', which means a character. It takes the next character and places it in 'ch'. Finally, it looks at the last conversion specifier '%f', which means a floating point number, and finds some characters which fit the description of a floating point number. It passes the value on to the variable 'x' and then quits.

This brief account of scanf does not tell the whole story by a long way! It assumes that all the characters were successfully found and that everything went smoothly: something which very seldom happens in practice!

The Dangerous Function

What happens if scanf doesn't find an integer or a floating point number? The answer is that it will quit at the first item it fails to match, leaving that character and the rest of the input line still to be read in the file. At the first character it meets which does not fit in with the conversion string's interpretation, scanf aborts and control passes to the next C statement. This is why scanf is a 'dangerous' function – because it can quit in the middle of a task and leave a lot of surplus data around in the input file. These surplus data simply wait in the input file until the next scanf is brought into operation, where they can also cause it to quit. It is not safe, therefore, to use scanf by itself – without some check that it is working successfully.

scanf is also dangerous for the opposite reason. What happens if scanf doesn't use up all the characters in the input line before it satisfies its needs? Again the answer is that it quits and leaves the extra characters in the input file stdin for the next scanf to read, exactly where it left off. So if the program was meant to read data from the input and couldn't, it leaves a mess for something else to trip over.

scanf can get out of step with its input, if the user types something even slightly out of line. It should be used with caution.

Keeping scanf Under Control

scanf may be dangerous in sloppy programs which do not check their input carefully, but it is easily tamed by using it as just a part of a more sophisticated input routine, and sometimes even more simply with the aid of a very short function which can be incorporated into almost any program as follows:

```
skipgarb()    /* skip garbage corrupting scanf */

          {
          while (getchar() != '\n')
                {
                }
          }
```

The action of this function simply is to skip to the end of the input line so that there are no characters left in the input. It can't stop scanf from getting out of step before the end of a line, because no function can stop the user from typing in nonsense!

So to get a single integer, for instance, a program could try:

```
int i;

scanf("%d",&i);
skipgarb();
```

The programmer must police user-garbage personally by using a loop to the effect of:

```
while (inputisnonsense)

          {
          printf ("Get your act together out there!!\n");
          scanf (..)
          skipgarb();
          }
```

It is usually as well to use skipgarb every time. Some safe input routines are given in Chapter 29.

Examples

Here are some example programs with example runs to show how scanf either works or fails (Note figures 15.2 and 15.3).

Listing 15.3

```
/***************************************/
/* Example 1                           */
/***************************************/

#include <stdio.h>
```

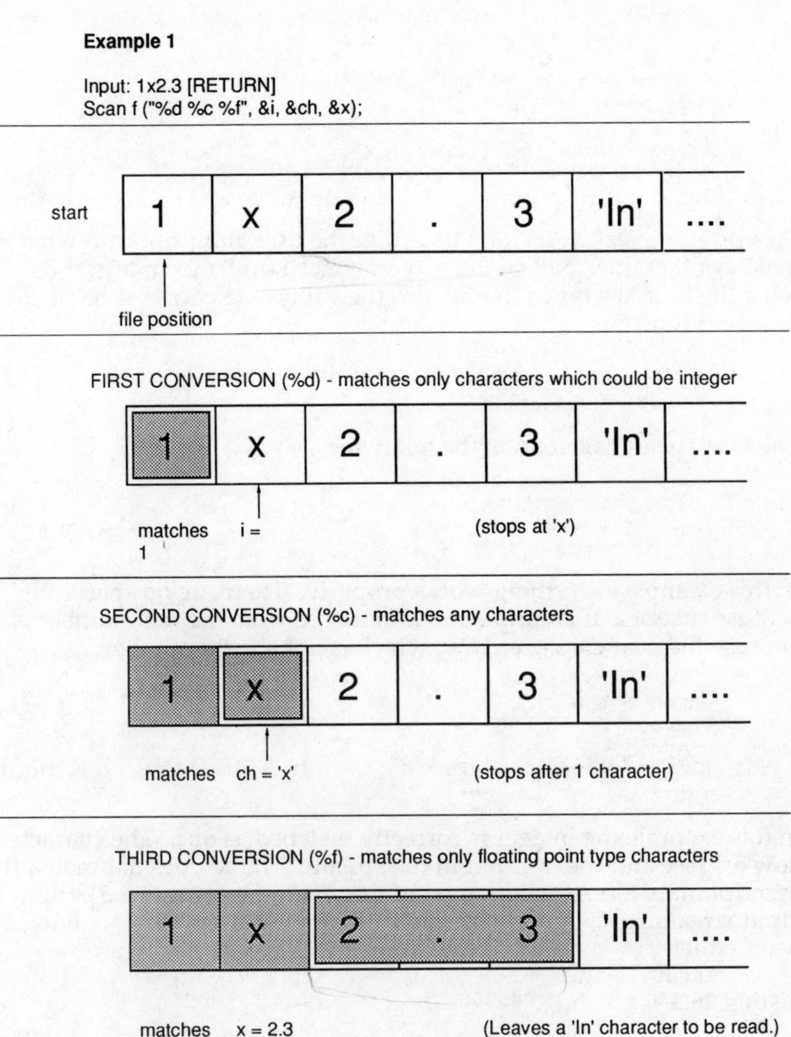

Figure 15.2 - scanf Example 1

```
main ()

{     int i = 0;
      char ch = '*';
      float x = 0;

scanf ("%d %c %f",&i,&ch,&x);
printf ("%d %c %f\n",i,ch,x);
}
```

This program just waits for a line from the user and prints out what it makes of that line. Notice the way in which scanf 'misunderstands' what the user has typed in and also the values the variables had before the scanf function.

```
Input : 1x2.3
Output: 1 x 2.300000
```

The input gets broken up in the following way:

```
 ------------------
| 1 |'x'| 2.3 |'\n'|
 ------------------
```

In this example everything works properly. There are no spaces to confuse matters. It is simple for scanf to see what the first number is because the next character is 'x', which is not a valid number.

```
Input : 1 x 2.3
Output: 1   0.000000
------          ------
|1|' '| <break> |x 2.3|
------          ------
```

In this example the integer is correctly matched as one. The character is now a space and the 'x' is left in the stream. The 'x' does not match the description of a float value so scanf terminates, leaving 'x 2.3' still in the input stream.

```
Input : .
Output: 0 * 0.000000

                       ---
                      |'.'| <break>
                       ---
```

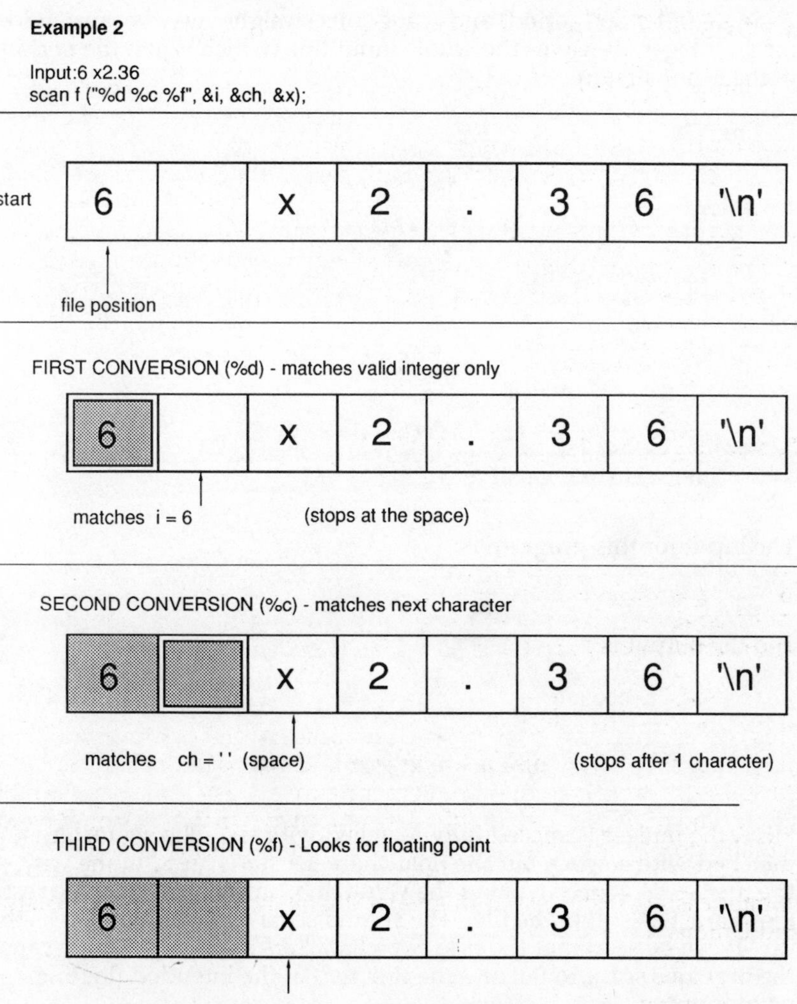
Example 2
Input:6 x2.36
scan f ("%d %c %f", &i, &ch, &x);
start
6
x
2
.
3
6
'\n'
file position
FIRST CONVERSION (%d) - matches valid integer only
matches i = 6
(stops at the space)
SECOND CONVERSION (%c) - matches next character
matches ch = ' ' (space)
(stops after 1 character)
THIRD CONVERSION (%f) - Looks for floating point
No characters matched. x is not valid floating point type. This attempt leaves all the unshaded characters in the input file.

Figure 15.3 - scanf Example 2

A single full-stop (period) and scanf quits straight away because it looks for an integer. It leaves the whole input line (which is just the period '.') in the input stream.

Listing 15.4

```
/****************************************/
/* Example 2                            */
/****************************************/

        #include <stdio.h>
        main ()

        {    int i = 0;
             char ch = '*',ch2,ch3;
             float x = 0;

        scanf ("%d %c %f", &i,&ch,&x);
        scanf ("%c %c", &ch2,&ch3);
        printf ("%d %c %f\n %c %c");
        }
```

The input for this program is:

```
        6 x 2.36
```

and the output is:

```
        6   0.000000
        x 2
         ---------               -------------
        | 6 | ' ' | <break> |'x'|'2'| .36 |
         ---------               -------------
```

Here, the integer is successfully matched with six. The character is matched with a space but the float character finds an 'x' in the way, so the first scanf aborts, leaving the value of 'x' unchanged and the rest of the characters still in the file. The second scanf function then picks these up. It can be seen that the first two characters are the 'x', which caused the previous scanf to fail and the first two of the intended floating point number.

Listing 15.5

```
/**************************************/
/* Example 3                          */
/**************************************/

        #include <stdio.h>

        main()

        {    char ch1,ch2,ch3;
        scanf ("%c %c %c",&ch1,&ch2,&ch3);
        printf ("%c %c %c",ch1,ch2,ch3);
        }
```

Trials:

input : **abc**
output: a b c

input : **a [return] b [return] c [return]**
output: a b c

input : **2.3**
output: 2 . 3

Matching Without Assigning

scanf allows input types to be matched but then discarded without being assigned to any variable. It also allows whole sequences of characters to be matched and skipped. For example:

```
scanf ("%*c");
```

would skip a single character. The '*' character means: do not make an assignment. Note that the following is wrong:

```
scanf ("%*c", &ch);
```

A pointer should not be given for a dummy conversion character. In this simple case above, it probably does not matter but in a string with several items to be matched, it would put the conversion characters out of step with the variables, as scanf does not return a value from a dummy conversion character.

It might seem as though there would be no sense in writing:

```
scanf ("%*s %f %c",&x,&ch);
```

because the whole input file is one long string after all, but this is not true. As far as scanf() is concerned, a string is terminated by any white space character, so the float type 'x' and the character 'ch' would receive values – provided there were a space or new line character after any string.

If any non-conversion characters are typed into the string, scanf will match and skip over them in the input. For example:

```
scanf (" Number = %d",&i);
```

If the input were: 'Number = 256', scanf would simply skip over the 'Number = '. As usual, if the string can't be matched, scanf will abort, leaving the remaining characters in the input stream.

Listing 15.6

```
/****************************************/
/* Example 4                            */
/****************************************/

      #include <stdio.h>

      main()

      {     float x = 0;
            int i = 0;
            char ch = '*';

      scanf("Skipthis! %*f %d %*c",&i);
      printf("%f %d %c",x,i,ch);
      }
```

Input : **Skipthis! 23**
Output: 0.000000 23 *

Input : **26**
Output: 0.000000 0 *

In this last case scanf aborted before matching anything.

Formal Definition of scanf

The general form of the scanf function is as follows:

```
n = scanf ("string...", pointers);
```

The value 'n' returned, is the number of items matched. It will be the end of file character EOF or NULL if the first item did not match. This value is often discarded.

The control string contains a number of conversion specifiers with the following general form:

```
%[*][n]X
```

[*] The optional assignment suppression character.

[n] This is a number giving the maximum field width to be accepted by scanf for a particular item. That is, the maximum number of characters which are to be thought of as being part of one the current variable value.

X Is one of the conversion characters listed above.

Any white space characters in the scanf string are ignored. Any other characters are matched. The pointers must be to correct variables and they must match the conversion specifiers in the exact order in which they are written.

There are two variations on the conversion specifiers for strings, though it is unlikely many compilers will support this. Both of the following imply strings:

%[set of characters] A string made up of the given characters only.

%[^set of characters] A string which is delimited by the set of characters given.

Points to Remember About scanf

1) Scanf works across input lines as though it were dealing with a file. Usually, the user types in a line and hits the RETURN key. The whole line is then thought of as being part of the input file, stdin.

2) If scanf finds the end of a line early, it will try to read past it until all its needs are satisfied.

3) If scanf fails at any stage to match the correct type of string at the correct time, it will quit leaving the remaining input still in the file.

4) If an element is not matched, no value will be assigned to the corresponding variable.

5) White space characters are ignored for all conversion characters except %c. Only a %c type can contain a white space character.

Questions:

1) What is a white space character?

2) Write a program which fetches two integers from the user and multiplies them together. Print out the answer. Try to make the input as safe as possible.

3) Write a program which just echoes all the input to the output.

4) Write a program which strips spaces out of the input and replaces them with a single newline character.

5) scanf always takes pointer arguments. True or false?

Low Level Input/Output

getchar and putchar

scanf and printf are relatively high-level functions. This means they are versatile and do a great deal of hidden work for the user. C also provides some 'functions' for dealing with input and output at a lower level, character by character. These 'functions' are called getchar and putchar but, in fact, they might not be functions: they could be macros instead, as described in Chapter 13 - The Pre-processor.

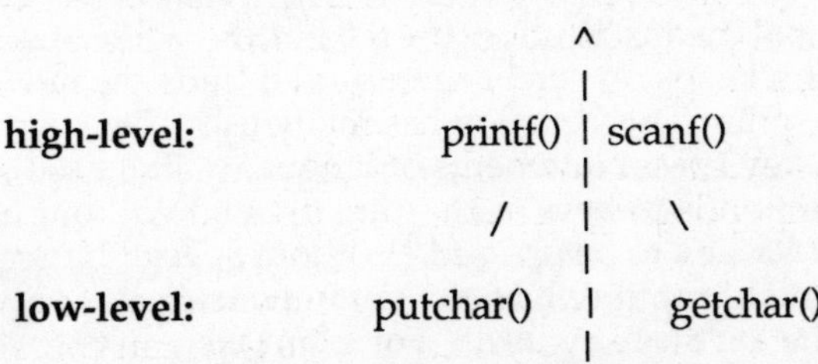

getchar gets a single character from the input file stdin, and putchar writes a single character to the output file, stdout. getchar returns a character type – the next character on the input file. For example:

```
char ch;
ch = getchar();
```

This places the next character, whatever it might be, into the variable 'ch'. Notice that no conversion to different data types can be performed by getchar as it deals with single characters only. It is a low-level function and does not 'know' anything about data types other than about characters.

getchar was used in the function skipgarb to tame the scanf function. This function was written in a very compact way.

Another way of writing it would be as follows:

```
skipgarb ()    /* skip garbage corrupting scanf */

{     char ch;

ch = getchar();
while (ch != '\n')
      {
      ch = getchar();
      }
}
```

The != symbol means 'is not equal to' and the while statement is a loop. This function keeps on getchar-ing until it finds the new line character and then it quits. This function has many uses. One of these is to copy immediate key press statements of languages like BASIC, where a program responds to keys as they are pressed without having to wait for the RETURN key to be pressed. Without special library functions to give this kind of input (which are not universal), it is only possible to do this with the RETURN key itself. For example:

```
printf("Press RETURN to continue\n");
skipgarb();
```

skipgarb does not receive any input until the user presses Return, and then it simply skips over it in one go! The effect is that it waits for RETURN to be pressed.

putchar writes a character type and also returns a character type. For example:

```
char ch = '*';
putchar (ch);
ch = putchar (ch);
```

These two alternatives have the same effect. The value returned by putchar is the character which was written to the output. In other words, it just hands the same value back again. This can simply be discarded, as in the first line. putchar is not much use without loops to repeat it over and over again.

An important point to remember is that putchar and getchar could well be implemented as macros, rather than functions. This means that it might not be possible to use functions as parameters inside them:

```
putchar( function() );
```

This depends entirely upon the compiler, but it is something to watch out for.

gets and puts

Two 'functions' which are similar to putchar and getchar are puts and gets which mean 'putstring' and 'getstring', respectively. Their purpose is either to read a whole string from the input file stdin, or write a whole string to the output stdout. Strings are groups or arrays of characters. For instance:

```
char *string[length];
string = gets(string);
puts(string);
```

More information about these is contained in Chapter 20 - Strings.

Questions:

1) Is the following statement possible? (It could depend upon your compiler: try it!)

```
putchar(getchar());
```

What might this do? (Hint: re-read the chapter about the pre-processor.)

2) Re-write the statement in question one, assuming that putchar and getchar are macros.

16 : Assignments

Thinking in C
Working Things Out
Paving the Way...

'Operator' is a word used a lot in connection with C. Generally, an operator takes one or more values and does something useful with those values. It *operates* on them. The terminology which is found in most books dealing with operators is as following:

Operator Something which operates on some 'things'

Operand Each thing which is operated upon by the operator is called an operand

Operation The action which was carried out upon the operands by the operator!

There are lots of operators in C. Some of them may already be familiar:

+ - * / = & ==

Most operators can be thought of as belonging to one of three groups, divided up arbitrarily according to what they do with their operands. These rough groupings are thought of as follows:

1) Operators which produce new values from old ones. They make a result from their operands. For example: the addition operator (+) takes two numbers, or two variables or a number and a variable, and adds them together to give a new number.

2) Operators which make comparisons. For example, less than, equal to, greater than.

3) Operators which produce new variable types: like the cast operator.

The majority of operators fall into the first group. C has no less than 39 different operators. This is more than, say, Pascal and BASIC put together! The operators serve a variety of purposes and they can be used very freely. The object of this chapter is to explain the functions of operators in C. The more intricate operators are looked at separately in another chapter.

Expressions and Values

The most common operators in any language are simple arithmetic operators. In C these are the following:

+	plus (unary)
-	minus (force value to be negative)
+	addition
-	subtraction
*	multiplication
/	floating point division
/	integer division 'div'
%	integer remainder 'mod'

These operators would not be useful without a partner operator which could attach the values they produce to variables. Perhaps the most important operator then is the assignment operator:

= assignment operator

This has been used extensively up to now. For example:

```
double x,y;

x = 2.356;
y = x;
x = x + 2 + 3/5;
```

The assignment operator takes the value of whatever is on the right-hand side of the '=' symbol and puts it into the variable on the left-hand side. As usual there is some standard jargon for this, which is useful to know because compilers tend to use this when handing out error messages. The assignment operator can be summarised succinctly in the following way:

```
lvalue = expression;
```

This statement says no more than what has been said about assignments already: namely that it takes something on the right-hand side and attaches it to whatever is on the left-hand side of the '=' symbol. An 'expression' is simply the name for any string of operators, variables and numbers. All of the following could be called expressions:

```
1 + 2 + 3
a + somefunction()
32 * x/3
i % 4
x
1
(22 + 4*(function() + 2))
function ()   /* provided it returns a sensible value */
```

On the other hand, 'lvalues' are simply names for memory locations: in other words variable names, or identifiers. The name comes from 'left values' meaning anything which can legally be written on the left-hand side of an assignment. The definition is circular!

Listing 16.1. Arithmetic and sign operators.

```
/**************************************/
/*                                    */
/* Operators Demo # 1                 */
/*                                    */
/**************************************/

      #include <stdio.h>

/**************************************/

      main ()

      {     int i;

      printf ("Arithmetic Operators\n\n");
      i = 6;
      printf ("i = 6, -i is : %d\n", -i);
```

```
printf ("int 1 + 2 = %d\n", 1 + 2);
printf ("int 5 - 1 = %d\n", 5 - 1);
printf ("int 5 * 2 = %d\n", 5 * 2);

printf ("\n9 div 4 = 2 remainder 1:\n");
printf ("int 9 / 4 = %d\n", 9 / 4);
printf ("int 9 % 4 = %d\n", 9 % 4);

printf ("double 9 / 4 = %f\n", 9.0 / 4.0);
}
```

Output

```
Arithmetic operators:

i = 6, -i is : -6
int 1 + 2 = 3
int 5 - 1 = 4
int 5 * 2 = 10
9 div 4 = 2 remainder 1:
int 9 / 4 = 2
int 9  4 = 1
double 9 / 4 = 2.250000
```

Brackets and Priority

Brackets are classed as operators by the compiler, although their position is a bit unclear. They have a value in the sense that they assume the value of whatever is inside them. Brackets are used for forcing a priority over operators. If an expression is written out in an ambiguous way, such as:

a + b / 4 * 2

It is not clear what is meant by this. It could be interpreted in several different ways:

((a + b) / 4) * 2

or:

(a + b)/ (4 * 2)

or:

a + (b/4) * 2

By using brackets, any doubt about what the expression means is removed. Brackets are said to have a higher priority than +, * or /

because they are evaluated as 'sealed capsules' before other operators can act on them. Putting brackets in may remove the ambiguity of expressions, but it does not alter the fact that:

```
a + b / 4 * 2
```

is ambiguous. What will happen in this case? The answer is that the C compiler has a convention about the way in which expressions are evaluated: it is called *operator precedence*. The convention is that some operators are stronger than others and that the stronger ones will always be evaluated first. Otherwise, expressions like the one above, are evaluated from left to right: so an expression will be dealt with from left to right unless a strong operator overrides this rule. Use brackets to be on the safe side.

A table of all operators and their priorities is given in the reference section.

Unary Operator Precedence

Unary operators are operators which have only a single operand – that is, they operate on only one object. For instance:

```
++
--
+
-
&
```

The precedence of unary operators is from right to left, so an expression something like:

```
*ptr++;
```

would do ++ before *.

Special Assignment Operators, ++ and --

C has some special operators which cut down on the amount of typing involved in a program. To get the most out of these operators it is essential to think in C. The simplest of these perhaps are the increment and decrement operators:

++ increment: add one to
-- decrement: subtract one from

These attach to any variable, or integer, or floating point type (character types too, with care). They are used simply to add or subtract one from a variable. Normally, in other languages, this is accomplished by writing the following:

```
variable = variable + 1;
```

In C this would also be quite valid, but there is a much better way of doing this:

```
variable++;
```

or alternatively:

```
++variable;
```

would do the same thing more neatly. Similarly:

```
variable = variable - 1;
```

is equivalent to:

```
variable--;
```

or the following:

```
--variable;
```

Notice particularly that these two operators can be placed in front or after the name of the variable. In some cases the two are identical, but in the more advanced uses of C operators, which appear later in this book, there is a subtle difference between the two.

More Special Assignments

Here are some of the nicest operators in C. Like ++ and -- these are short ways of writing longer expressions. Consider the statement:

```
variable = variable + 23;
```

In C this would be a long-winded way of adding 23 to 'variable'. It could be done more simply using the general increment += operator.
For example:

```
variable += 23;
```

This performs exactly the same operation. Similarly you could write:

```
variable1 = variable1 + variable2;
```

as the following:

```
variable1 += variable2;
```

and so on. There is a handful of these 'operation=' operators, one for each of the major operations which can be performed. There is, naturally, one for subtraction too:

```
variable = variable - 42;
```

which can be written:

```
variable -= 42;
```

More surprisingly, perhaps, the multiplicative assignment:

```
variable = variable * 2;
```

can may be written as:

```
variable *= 2;
```

and so on. The main arithmetic operators all follow this pattern:

+=	Add assign
-=	Subtract assign
*=	Multiply assign

/= Divide (double) and (int) types
%= Remainder (int) type only

There are more exotic kinds too which are used for bit operations or machine-level operations, which will be ignored at this stage:

>>=
<<=
^=
|=
&=

Listing 16.2. Operators demo #2.

```
/***********************************/
/*                                 */
/* Operators Demo # 2              */
/*                                 */
/***********************************/

      #include <stdio.h>

/***********************************/

      main ()

      {   int i;
      printf ("Assignment Operators\n\n");

      i = 10;               /* Assignment */
      printf("i = 10 : %d\n",i);

      i++;                  /* i = i + 1 */
      printf ("i++ : %d\n",i);

      i += 5;               /* i = i + 5 */
      printf ("i += 5 : %d\n",i);

      i--;                  /* i = i = 1 */
      printf ("i-- : %d\n",i);

      i -= 2;               /* i = i - 2 */
      printf ("i -= 2 : %d\n",i);

      i *= 5;               /* i = i * 5 */
      printf ("i *= 5 :%d\n",i);
```

```
    i /= 2;                    /* i = i / 2 */
    printf ("i /= 2 : %d\n",i);

    i %= 3;                    /* i = i % 3 */
    printf ("i %%= 3 : %d\n",i);

    }
```

Output

```
Assignment operators:

i = 10 : 10
i++ : 11
i += 5 : 16
i-- : 15
i -= 2 : 13
i *= 5 :65
i /= 2 : 32
i %= 3 : 2
```

The Cast Operator

The cast operator is an operator which forces a particular type-mould or type-cast onto a value, hence the name. For instance, a character type variable could be forced to fit into an integer type box by using the following statement:

```
char ch;
int i;

i = (int) ch;
```

This operator was introduced in Chapter 10 : Variables, Types and Declarations. It will always produce some value, whatever the conversion, however improbable it might seem. For instance, it is quite possible to convert a character into a floating point number – the result will be a floating point representation of its ASCII code!

Expressions and Types

There is a rule in C that all arithmetic and mathematical operations must be carried out with 'long' variables. That is, the following types:

double
long float

int
long int

If the programmer tries to use other types, like short or float, in a mathematical expression, they will be cast into long types automatically by the compiler. This can cause confusion because the compiler will spot an error in the following statement:

```
short i, j = 2;
i = j * 2 + 1;
```

A compiler will claim that there is a type mismatch between 'i' and the expression on the right-hand side of the assignment. The compiler is perfectly correct of course, even though it appears to be wrong. The subtlety is that arithmetic cannot be done in short type variables, so that the expression is automatically converted into 'long' type or int type. So the right-hand side is 'int' type and the left-hand side is 'short' type: hence there is indeed a type mismatch. The programmer can get around this by using the cast operator to write:

```
short i, j = 2;
i = (short) j * 2 + 1;
```

A similar thing would happen with float:

```
float x, y = 2.3;
x = y * 2.5;
```

It is incorrect for the reasons as just mentioned.

Comparisons and Logic

Six operators in C are for making logical comparisons. The relevance of these operators will quickly become clear in the next chapter, which is about decisions and comparisons. The six operators which compare values are:

==	Is equal to
!=	Is not equal to
>	Is greater than
<	Is less than
>=	Is greater than or equal to
<=	Is less than or equal to

These operators belong to the second group according to the scheme above, but they do actually result in values so that they could be thought of as being a part of the first group of operators too. The values which they produce are called true and false. As words, 'true' and 'false' are not defined normally in C, but it is easy to define them as macros and they may well be defined in a library file. For example:

```
#define true  1
#define false 0
```

It is assumed 'false' as it has the value zero, and 'true' is assumed to be anything which is non-zero. These comparison operators are used for making decisions, but they are themselves operators and thus expressions can be built up with them.

1 == 1 has the value 'true' (which could be anything except zero)

The statement:

```
int i;
i = (1 == 2);
```

would be false, so i would be false. In other words, i would be zero.

Comparisons are often made in pairs or even in groups and linked together with words like OR and AND. For instance, you might want to find out whether:

```
(A is greater than B) AND (A is greater than C)
```

C does not have words for these operations but gives symbols instead. The 'logical operators', as they are called, are as follows:

&&	Logical AND
||	Logical OR inclusive
!	Logical NOT

The statement which was written in words above could be translated as:

```
(A > B) && (A > C)
```

The statement:

```
(A is greater than B) AND (A is not greater than C)
```

translates to:

```
(A > B) && !(A > C)
```

Shakespeare might have been disappointed to learn that, whatever the value of a variable 'tobe' the result of:

```
thequestion = tobe || !tobe
```

must always be true. The NOT operator always creates the logical opposite: !true is false and !false is true! One or the other of these must be true. 'thequestion' is therefore always true. Fortunately, this is not a matter of life or death!

Summary of Operators and Precedence

The highest priority operators are listed first.

Operator	Operation	Evaluated
( )	parentheses	left to right
[ ]	square brackets	left to right
++	increment	right to left
--	decrement	right to left
(type)	cast operator	right to left
*	the contents of	right to left
&	the address of	right to left
-	unary minus	right to left
~	one's complement	right to left
!	logical NOT	right to left

<table>
<tr><th>Operator</th><th>Operation</th><th>Evaluated</th></tr>
<tr><td>*</td><td>multiply</td><td>left to right</td></tr>
<tr><td>/</td><td>divide</td><td>left to right</td></tr>
<tr><td>%</td><td>remainder (MOD)</td><td>left to right</td></tr>
<tr><td>+</td><td>add</td><td>left to right</td></tr>
<tr><td>-</td><td>subtract</td><td>left to right</td></tr>
<tr><td>>></td><td>shift right</td><td>left to right</td></tr>
<tr><td><<</td><td>shift left</td><td>left to right</td></tr>
<tr><td>></td><td>is greater than</td><td>left to right</td></tr>
<tr><td>>=</td><td>greater or equal to</td><td>left to right</td></tr>
<tr><td><=</td><td>less or equal to</td><td>left to right</td></tr>
<tr><td><</td><td>less than</td><td>left to right</td></tr>
<tr><td>==</td><td>is equal to</td><td>left to right</td></tr>
<tr><td>!=</td><td>is not equal to</td><td>left to right</td></tr>
<tr><td>&</td><td>bitwise AND</td><td>left to right</td></tr>
<tr><td>^</td><td>bitwise exclusive OR</td><td>left to right</td></tr>
<tr><td>|</td><td>bitwise inclusive OR</td><td>left to right</td></tr>
<tr><td>&&</td><td>logical AND</td><td>left to right</td></tr>
<tr><td>||</td><td>logical OR</td><td>left to right</td></tr>
<tr><td>=</td><td>assign</td><td>right to left</td></tr>
<tr><td>+=</td><td>add assign</td><td>right to left</td></tr>
<tr><td>-=</td><td>subtract assign</td><td>right to left</td></tr>
<tr><td>*=</td><td>multiply assign</td><td>right to left</td></tr>
<tr><td>/=</td><td>divide assign</td><td>right to left</td></tr>
<tr><td>%=</td><td>remainder assign</td><td>right to left</td></tr>
<tr><td>>>=</td><td>right shift assign</td><td>right to left</td></tr>
<tr><td><<=</td><td>left shift assign</td><td>right to left</td></tr>
<tr><td>&=</td><td>AND assign</td><td>right to left</td></tr>
<tr><td>^=</td><td>exclusive OR assign</td><td>right to left</td></tr>
<tr><td>|=</td><td>inclusive OR assign</td><td>right to left</td></tr>
</table>

Questions

1) What is an operand?

2) Write a statement which prints out the remainder of five divided by two.

3) Write a short statement which assigns the remainder of five divided by two to a variable called 'rem'.

4) Write a statement which subtracts -5 from 10.

5) Write in C: If one is not equal to 23, print out 'Thank goodness for mathematics!'

17 : Decisions

Testing and Branching
Making Conditions

Suppose that a fictional traveller, some character in a book like this one, came to the end of a straight, unfinished road and waited there for his author to decide where the road would lead. The author might decide a number of things about this road and its traveller:

1) The road will carry on in a straight line. If the traveller is thirsty he will stop for a drink.

2) The road will fork and the traveller will have to decide whether to take the left branch or the right branch.

3) The road might have a crossroads or a meeting point where many roads come together. Again the traveller has to decide which way to go.

Programs and programmers are often faced with just this dilemma: a situation in which decisions have to be made. Up to now, the simple example programs in this book have not had any choice about the way in which they progressed. They have all followed narrow paths without any choice about which way they were going. This is a very limited way of expressing ideas. The ability to make decisions and to choose different options is very useful in programming. For instance, you might want to implement the following ideas in different programs:

1) If the user hits the jackpot, write some message to say so: 'You've won the game!'

2) If a bank balance is positive then print C for credit, otherwise print D for debit.

3) If the user has typed in one of five things, then do something special for each special case, otherwise do something else.

These choices are actually just the same choices that the traveller had to make on his undecided road, thinly disguised. In the first case there is a simple choice: a do or don't choice. The second case gives two choices: do thing one or thing two. The final choice has several possibilities.

C offers four ways of making decisions like the ones above. They are listed here. The method which is numbered 2b was encountered in connection with the C pre-processor; its purpose is very similar to 2a.

1)

```
if (something_is_true)
     {
     /* do something */
     }
```

2a)

```
if (something_is_true)
     {
     /* do one thing */
     }
else
     {
     /* do something else */
     }
```

2b)

```
? (something_is_true)
/* do one thing */
:
/* do something else */
```

3)

```
switch (choice)
     {
     case first_possibility : /* do something */
     case second_possibility : /* do something */
      ....
     }
```

if

The first form of the 'if' statement is an all or nothing choice. 'if' some condition is satisfied, do what is in the braces, otherwise just skip what is in the braces. Formally, this is written:

```
if (condition) statement;
```

or:

```
if (condition)
    {
    compound statement
    }
```

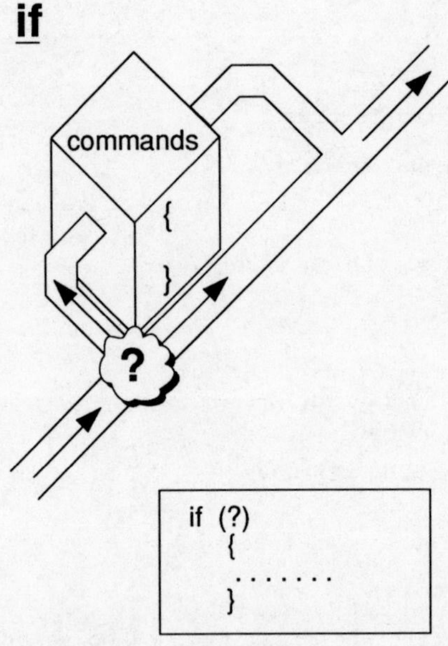

Figure 17.1. If some condition is satisfied, do the contents of this box then rejoin the main path.

Notice that, as well as a single statement, a whole statement block can be written under the 'if' statement. In fact, there is an unwritten rule in C that wherever a single statement will do, a 'compound statement' will do instead. A compound statement is a block of single statements enclosed by curly braces.

A condition is usually some kind of comparison, like the ones discussed in the previous chapter. It must have a value which is either true or false (one or zero) and it must be enclosed by the brackets (and). If the condition has the value 'true' then the statement or compound statement following the condition will be carried out, otherwise it will be ignored. Some of the following examples help to show this:

```
int i;

printf ("Type in an integer");
scanf ("%ld",&i);

if (i == 0)
     {
     printf ("The number was zero");
     }

if (i > 0)
     {
     printf ("The number was positive");
     }

if (i < 0)
     {
     printf ("The number was negative");
     }
```

The same code could be written more briefly, but perhaps less consistently in the following way:

```
int i;

printf ("Type in an integer");
scanf ("%ld",&i);

if (i == 0) printf ('The number was zero');
if (i > 0) printf ('The number was positive');
if (i < 0) printf ('The number was negative');
```

The preference in this book usually is to include the block braces, even when they are not strictly required. This does no harm. It is no more or less efficient, but the programmer will often find that some extra statements have to go into those braces, so it is wise to include them from the start. It also has the appeal that it makes 'if' statements look the same as all other block statements. It also makes them clearly stand out in the program text. This rule of thumb is only dropped in very simple examples like:

```
        if (i == 0) i++;
```

The 'if' statement alone allows only a very limited kind of decision: it makes do or don't decisions; it could not decide whether our traveller should take the left-hand fork or the right-hand fork of this road, for instance – it could only tell the traveller whether to get up and go at all. To do more it needs to be extended. This is the purpose of the 'else' statement, described after some example listings.

Example Listings

Listing 17.1. If demo #1.

```
/******************************************/
/*                                        */
/* If... #1                               */
/*                                        */
/******************************************/

       #include <stdio.h>
       #define true     1
       #define false    0

/*******************************************/

       main ()
       {    int i;

       if (true)
            {
            printf ("This is always printed");
            }
       if (false)
            {
            printf ("This is never printed");
            }
       }
```

Listing 17.2. If demo #2.

```
/****************************************/
/*                                      */
/* If demo #2                           */
/*                                      */
/****************************************/

  /* On board car computer. Works out the */
  /* number of kilometers to the litre    */
  /* that the car is doing at present     */

       #include <stdio.h>

/****************************************/
/* Level 0                              */
/****************************************/

       main ()

       {    double fuel,distance;

       FindValues (&fuel,&distance);
       Report (fuel,distance);
       }

/*****************************************/
/* Level 1                               */
/*****************************************/

       FindValues (fuel,distance)/* from car */

     /* These values would be changing in */
     /* a real car, independently of the  */
     /* program.                          */

       double *fuel,*distance;

       {

/* how much fuel used since last check on values */

       printf ("Enter fuel used");
       scanf ("%lf",fuel);

/* distance travelled since last check on values */

       printf ("Enter distance travelled");
       scanf ("%lf",distance);
       }
```

```
/*******************************************/

      Report (fuel,distance) /* on dashboard */

      double fuel,distance;

      {    double kpl;

      kpl = distance/fuel;

      printf ("fuel consumption: %2.1lf",kpl);
      printf (" kilometers per litre\n");

      if (kpl <= 1)
         {
         printf ("Predict fuel leak or car");
         printf (" needs a service\n");
         }

      if (distance > 500)
         {
         printf ("Remember to check tyres\n");
         }

      if (fuel > 30)          /* Tank holds 40 l */
         {
         printf ("Fuel getting low\n");
         }
      }
```

if...else

The 'if...else' statement has the following form:

```
if (condition) statement1; else statement2;
```

This is most often written in the compound statement form:

```
if (condition)
   {
   /* statements */
   }

else
```

```
{
/* statements */
}
```

The if...else statement is a two-way branch, it means do one thing or do the other. When it is executed, the condition is evaluated and if it has the value 'true' (ie, not zero) then *statement1* is executed. If the condition is 'false' (or zero) then *statement2* is executed.

if...else

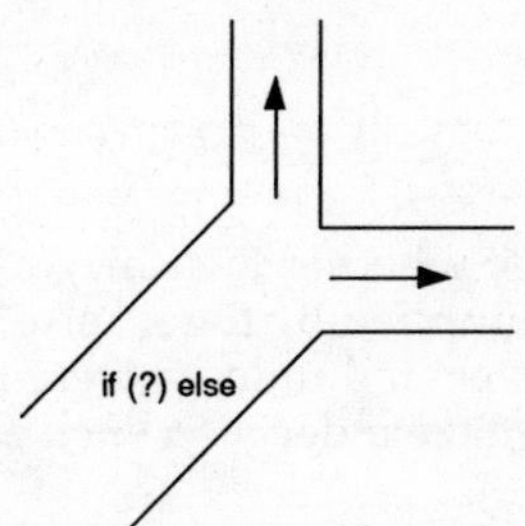
if (?) else

Nested if...else

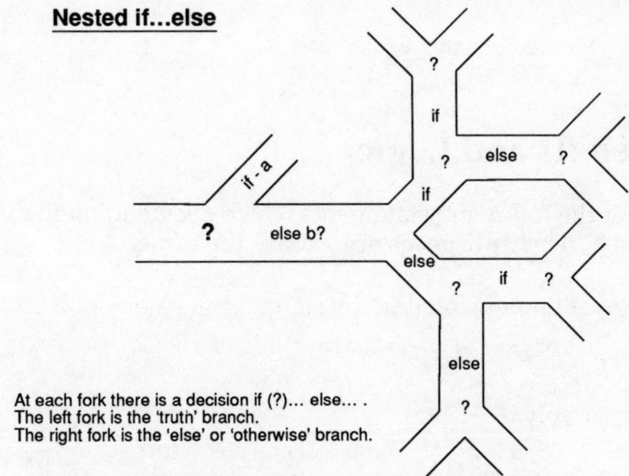
?
if
?
else
?
if
if - a
?
else b?
else
?
if
?
else
?
At each fork there is a decision if (?)... else... .
The left fork is the 'truth' branch.
The right fork is the 'else' or 'otherwise' branch.

Figure 17.2. Which route – if...else selects.

The if...else construction often saves an unnecessary test from having to be made. For instance:

```
int i;

scanf ("%ld",i);

if (i > 0)
     {
     printf ("That number was positive!");
     }

else
     {
     printf ("That number was negative or zero!");
     }
```

It is not necessary to test whether i was negative in the second block, because it was already implied by the if...else structure. That is, the block would not have been executed unless i were not greater than zero. Our weary traveller might make a decision such as:

```
if (rightleg > leftleg)
     {
     take_left_branch();
     }
else
     {
     take_right_branch();
     }
```

Nested ifs and Logic

Consider the following statements which decide upon the value of variable 'i'. Their purposes are exactly the same.

```
if ((i > 2) && (i < 4))
     {
     printf ("i is three");
     }
```

or alternatively:

```
if (i > 2)
     {
     if (i < 4)
          {
          printf ("i is three");
          }
     }
```

Both of these test i for the same information, but they do it in different ways. The first method might have been born out of the following sequence of thought:

> If i is greater than two and i is less than four, both at the same time, then i has to be three.

The second method is more complicated. Think carefully. It says:

> If i is greater than two, do what is in the curly braces. Inside these curly braces i is always greater than two, because otherwise the program would never have arrived inside them. Now, if i is also less than four, then do what is inside the new curly braces. Inside these curly braces i is always less than four. But wait! The whole of the second test is held inside the 'i is greater than two' braces, which is a sealed capsule: nothing else can get in, so, if the program gets into the 'i is less than four' braces as well, then both facts must be true at the same time. There is only one integer which is bigger than two and less than four at the same time: it is three. So i is three.

The aim of this demonstration is to show that there are two ways of making multiple decisions in C. Using the logical comparison operators &&, || (AND,OR) and so on, several multiple tests can be made. In many cases though, it is too difficult to think in terms of these operators and the sealed capsule idea begins to look attractive. This is another advantage of using the curly braces: it helps the programmer to see that if statements and if...else statements are made up of sealed capsule parts. When inside a sealed capsule:

```
if (i > 2)
     {
     /* i is greater than 2 in here! */
     }

else
```

```
        {
        /* i is not greater than 2 here! */
        }
```

The programmer can rest assured that nothing illegal can get in. The block braces are like regions of grace, they can't be penetrated by anything which does not satisfy the right conditions. This is an enourmous weight off the mind! The programmer can sit back and think: I have accepted that i is greater than two inside these braces, so I can stop worrying about that now. This is how programmers learn to think in a structured way. They learn to be satisfied that certain things have already been proven and thus save themselves from the onset of madness as the ideas become too complex to think of all in one go.

Listing 17.3. If demo #3.

```
/***********************************************/
/*                                             */
/* If demo #3                                  */
/*                                             */
/***********************************************/

       #include <stdio.h>

/***********************************************/

       main ()

       {     int persnum,usernum,balance;

       persnum = 7462;
       balance = -12;

       printf ("The Plastic Bank Corporation\n");
       printf ("Please enter your personal number :");

       usernum = getnumber();

       if (usernum == 7462)
            {
            printf ("\nThe current state of your account\n");
            printf ("is %d\n",balance);

            if (balance < 0)
                 {
                 printf ("The account is overdrawn!\n");
                 }

            }
```

```
      else
           {
           printf ("This is not your account\n");
           }

      printf ("Have a splendid day! Thank you.\n");
      }

/***************************************************/

      getnumber () /* get a number from the user */

      { int num = 0;

      scanf ("%d",&num);

      if ((num > 9999) || (num <= 0))
           {
           printf ("That is not a valid number\n");
           }

      return (num);

      }
```

Stringing Together if...else

What is the difference between the following programs (listings 17.4 and 17.5)? They both interpret some imaginary exam result in the same way. They both look identical when compiled and run. Why, then, are they different?

Listing 17.4

```
/***************************************************/
/* Program 1                                       */
/***************************************************/

      #include <stdio.h>

      main ()

      {    int result;
```

```
        printf("Type in exam result");

        scanf ("%d",&result);

        if (result < 10)
            {
            printf ("That is poor");
            }

        if (result > 20)
            {
            printf ("You have passed.");
            }

        if (result > 70)
            {
            printf ("You got an A!");
            }

        }
            /* end */
```

Listing 17.5

```
/***********************************************/
/* Program 2                                   */
/***********************************************/

        #include <stdio.h>

        main ()

        {   int result;

        printf("Type in exam result");

        scanf ("%d",&result);

        if (result < 10)
            {
            printf ("That is poor");
            }

        else

            {
            if (result > 20)
                {
                printf ("You have passed.");
                }
```

```
        else

            {
            if (result > 70)

                {
                printf ("You got an A!");
                }
            }
        }
    }
```

The answer is that the second of these programs can be more efficient, insofar as the number of times it has to work something out is concerned. This because it uses the 'else' form of the 'if' statement. Program one makes every single test, because the program meets every if statement, one after the other. The second program does not necessarily do this however. The nested 'if' statements make sure that the second two tests are only made if the first one fails. Similarly, the third test is only performed if the first two failed. So the second program could end up doing a third of the work of the first program, in the best possible case. Nesting decisions like this can be an efficient way of controlling long lists of decisions. Nested loops make a program branch into lots of possible paths, but choosing one path would preclude any others.

switch: Integers and Characters

The 'switch' construction is another way of making a program path branch into lots of different limbs. It can be used as a different way of writing a string of if...else statements, but it is more versatile in that it only works for integers and character type values. It works like a multi-way switch (see figure 17.1). The switch statement has the following form:

```
switch (int or char expression)

    {
    case constant : statement;
         break;       /* optional line*/
    ...
    }
```

It has an expression which is evaluated and a number of constant 'cases' which are to be chosen from, each of which is followed by a statement or compound statement. An extra statement called 'break' can also be incorporated into the block at any point. Break is a reserved word in C.

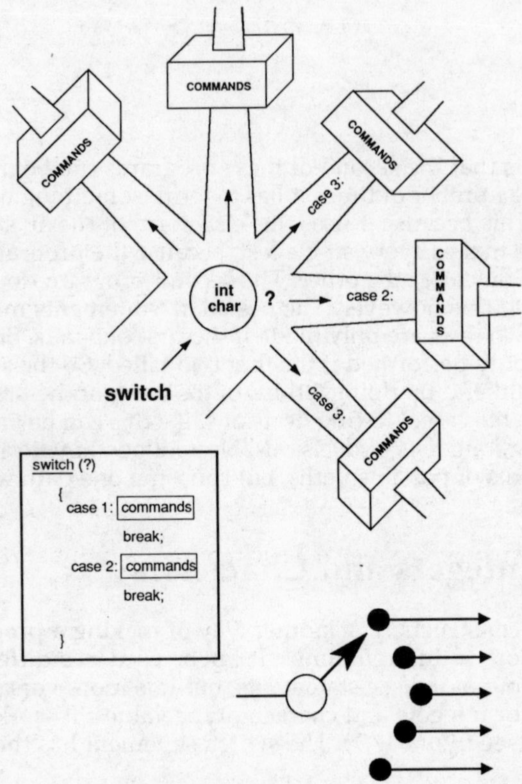

Figure 17.3. switch.

The switch statement can be written more specifically for integers, as the follows shows:

```
switch (integer value)

    {

    case 1:  statement1;
        break;              /* optional line */

    case 2:  statement2;
        break;              /* optional line */

    ....

    default: default statement
        break;              /* optional line */

    }
```

When a switch statement is encountered, the expression in the brackets is evaluated. The program then checks to see whether the result of that expression matches any of the constants labelled with 'case'. If a match is made (for instance, if the expression is evaluated to 23 and there is a statement beginning 'case 23 : ...'), execution will start just after that case statement and will carry on until either the closing brace is encountered or a break statement is found. 'Break' is a handy way of jumping straight out of the switch block. One of the cases is called 'default'. Statements which follow the 'default' case are executed for all cases which are not specifically listed.

Switch is a way of choosing some action from a number of known instances. See listing 17.6 below.

Listing 17.6. switch example.

```
/**********************************************/
/*                                            */
/* switch  .. case                            */
/*                                            */
/**********************************************/
   /* Morse code program. Enter a number and */
   /* find out what it is in Morse code      */

      #include <stdio.h>

      #define code 0

/***********************************************/

      main ()
```

```
    { short digit;

    printf ("Enter any digit in the range 0..9");
    scanf ("%h",&digit);

    if ((digit < 0) || (digit > 9))
        {
        printf ("Number was not in range 0..9");
        return (code);
        }

    printf ("The Morse code of that digit is ");
    Morse (digit);
    }

/*********************************************/

    Morse (digit)     /* print out Morse code */
    short digit;

    {
    switch (digit)
        {

        case 0 : printf ("-----");
                 break;
        case 1 : printf (".----");
                 break;
        case 2 : printf ("..---");
                 break;
        case 3 : printf ("...--");
                 break;
        case 4 : printf ("....-");
                 break;
        case 5 : printf (".....");
                 break;
        case 6 : printf ("-....");
                 break;
        case 7 : printf ("--...");
                 break;
        case 8 : printf ("---..");
                 break;
        case 9 : printf ("----.");
        }
    }
```

The program selects one of the printf statements using a switch construction. At every 'case' in the switch, a 'break' statement is used. This causes control to jump straight out of the switch statement to its closing brace. If break wasn't included, it would go right on executing the statements to the end, testing the cases in turn. Break gives a way of jumping out of a switch quickly .

There might be cases where it is not necessary, or not desirable, to jump out of the switch immediately. Think of a function yes() which gets a character from the user, and tests whether it was 'y' or 'Y'.

```
yes ()          /* A sloppy but simple function */

{

switch (getchar())
      {
      case 'y' :
      case 'Y' : return (true);
      default  : return (false);
      }
}
```

If the character is either 'y' or 'Y', then the function meets the statement 'return(true)'. If there had been a break statement after case 'y', then control would not have been able to reach case 'Y' as well. However, the return statement does more than break out of switch, it breaks out of the whole function, so break was not required in this case. The default option ensures that whatever else the character is, the function returns false.

Things to try

1) Write a program to get a lot of numbers from the user and print out the maximum and minimum of those numbers.

2) Try to make a counter which is reset to zero when it reaches the number 9999.

3) Write a program incorporating the statement if (yes()) {...}.

18 : Loops

Controlling Repetitive Processes
Nesting Loops

Decisions can also be used to make up loops. Loops free a program from the constriction of doing things only once. They allow the programmer to build up a sequence of instructions which can be executed again and again, with some condition deciding when they will stop.

There are three kinds of loop in C. They are called:

while
do ... while
for

These three loops offer a great amount of flexibility to programmers and can be used in some surprising ways!

while

The simplest of the three loops is the 'while' loop. In common language 'while' has a fairly obvious meaning – the while loop has a condition:

```
while (condition)
        {
        statements;
        }
```

and the statements in the curly braces are executed *while* the condition has the value 'true' (1). There are dialects in the English language, however, in which 'while' does not have its commonplace meaning, so it is worthwhile explaining the steps which take place in a while loop.

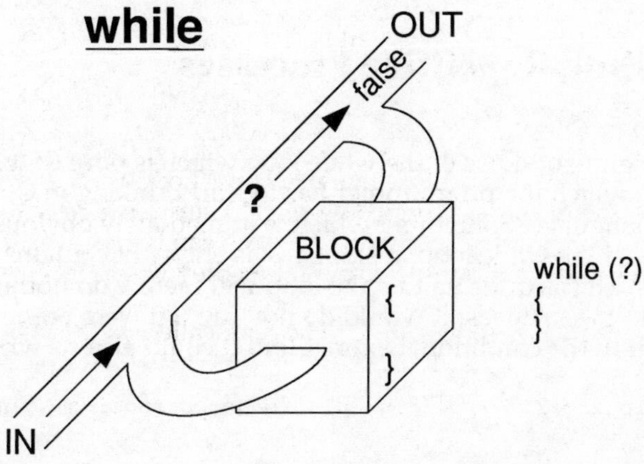

Figure 18.1. The structure of the while command.

The first important thing about this loop is that it has a conditional expression (something like a > b and so on) which is evaluated every time the loop is executed by the computer. If the value of the expression is true, then it will carry on with the instructions in the curly braces. If the expression evaluates to 'false' (or zero) then the instructions in the braces are ignored and the entire 'while' loop ends. The computer then moves on to the next statement in the program.

The second thing to notice about this loop, is that the conditional expression comes at the start of the loop. This means that the condition is tested at the start of every 'pass', not at the end. This is important because if the condition has the value false before the loop has been executed even once, the statements inside the braces will not get executed at all – not even once.

The best way to illustrate a loop is to give an example of its use. One example was sneaked into Chapter 15 before its time, in order to write the 'skipgarb' function which complemented scanf. That was:

```
skipgarb ()      /* skip garbage corrupting scanf */

{
while (getchar() != '\n')
      {
      }
}
```

This is a slightly odd use of the while loop which is pure C. It is one instance in which the programmer has to start thinking in C, and not any other language. Something which is immediately obvious from the listing, is that the while loop in skipgarb is empty, it contains no statements. This is quite valid – the loop will merely do nothing a number of times. At least it would do nothing if it were not for the assignment in the conditional expression! It could also be written:

```
skipgarb ()      /* skip garbage corrupting scanf */

{
while (getchar() != '\n');
}
```

The assignment inside the conditional expression makes this loop special. When the loop is encountered, the computer attempts to evaluate the expression inside the brackets. There, inside the brackets, it finds a function call to 'getchar()', so it calls 'getchar()', which fetches the next character from the input. Getchar() then takes on the value of the character which it fetched from the input file. Next, the computer finds the '!=' (is not equal to) symbol and the new line character '\n'. This means that there is a comparison to be made. The computer compares the character fetched by getchar with the new line character. If they are 'not equal', the expression is true. If they are equal, the expression is false. Now, if the expression is true, the while statement will loop and start again – and it will evaluate the expression on every pass of the loop, to check whether or not it is true. When the expression eventually becomes false, the loop will quit. The net result of this is that skipgarb skips all the input characters up to and including the next new line ('\n') character and that usually means the rest of the input.

Another use of while is to write a better function called yes. The idea of this function was introduced in the previous section. It uses a while loop which is always true to repeat the process of getting a response from the user. When the response is either 'yes' or 'no', it quits using the return function to jump right out of the loop.

Listing 18.1. Give me your answer.

```
/*********************************************/
/*                                           */
/* Give me your answer!                      */
/*                                           */
/*********************************************/

      #include <stdio.h>

      #define true     1
      #define false    0

/***********************************************/
/* Level 0                                     */
/***********************************************/

      main ()

      {
      printf ("Yes or no? (Y/N)\n");

      if (yes())
         {
         printf ("YES!");
         }

      else
         {
         printf ("NO!");
         }
      }

/***********************************************/
/* Level 1                                     */
/***********************************************/

      yes ()           /* get response Y/N query */

      {   char getkey();

      while (true)
         {
```

```
            switch (getkey())
                {
                case 'y' : case 'Y' : return (true);
                case 'n' : case 'N' : return (false);
                }
            }
        }

/*************************************************/
/* Toolkit                                       */
/*************************************************/

        char getkey();  /* get a character+RETURN */

        {    char ch;

        ch = getchar();
        skipgarb();

        }

/**************************************************/

        skipgarb ()

        {
        while (getchar() != '\n');
        }

            /* end */
```

Listing 18.2. while loop.

This example listing prompts the user to type in a line of text and it counts all the spaces in that line. It quits when there is no more input left and prints out the number of spaces.

```
/**********************************************/
/* while loop                                 */
/**********************************************/
 /* count all the spaces in an line of input */

        #include <stdio.h>
        main ()

        {    char ch;
             short count = 0;
```

```
printf ("Type in a line of text\n");

while ((ch = getchar()) != '\n')
     {
     if (ch == ' ')
          {
          count++;
          }
     }

printf ("Number of space = %d\n",count);
}
```

do...while

The do...while loop resembles most closely the repeat...until loops of Pascal and BBC BASIC, except that it is the 'logical opposite'. The do loop has the form:

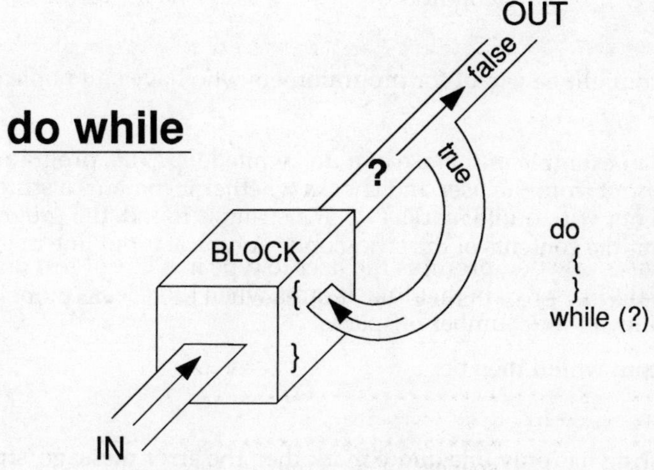

Figure 18.2. The do...while command structure.

```
do

      {
      statements;
      }

while (condition)
```

Notice that the condition is at the end of this loop. This means that a do...while loop will always be executed at least once, before the test is made to determine whether it should continue. This is the only difference between while and do...while.

A do...while loop is like the, 'repeat...until', of other languages in the following sense – if the condition is NOTed using the (!) operator, then the two are identical.

```
repeat                          do
                ==
until(condition)                while (!condition)
```

This fact might be useful for programmers who have still not learnt to think in C!

Here is an example of the use of a do...while loop. This program gets a line of input from the user and checks whether it contains a string marked out with quote marks (" "). If a string is found, the program prints out the contents of the string only. A typical input line might be:

Once upon a time "Here we go round the..."what a terrible..

The output would then be:

```
Here we go round the...
```

If the string has only one quote mark then the error message 'string was not closed before end of line' will be printed.

Listing 18.3. do...while demo.

```
/*******************************************/
/*                                         */
/* do...while demo                         */
/*                                         */
/*******************************************/
   /* print a string enclosed by quotes " " */
   /* gets input from stdin i.e. keyboard   */
   /* skips anything outside the quotes     */

    #include <stdio.h>

/**********************************************/
/* Level 0                                    */
/**********************************************/

    main ()

    {    char ch,skipstring();

    do

         {
         if ((ch = getchar()) == '"')
              {
              printf ("The string was:\n");
              ch = skipstring();
              }
         }

    while (ch != '\n');
    }

/**********************************************/
/* Level 1                                    */
/**********************************************/

    char skipstring () /* skip a string "..." */

    {    char ch;

    do
         {
         ch = getchar();
         putchar(ch);

         if (ch == '\n')
              {
              printf ("\nString was not closed ");
              printf ("before end of line\n");
```

```
            break;
            }
        }

    while (ch != '"');

    return (ch);
    }
```

for

The most interesting and also the most difficult of all the loops, is the 'for' loop. The name 'for' is a hangover from earlier days and other languages. It is not altogether appropriate for C's version of 'for'. The name comes from the typical description of a classic 'for' loop:

> 'for all values of <variable> from <some value> to <some value> in steps of <some value>, repeat the following sequence of commands....'

In BASIC this looks like:

```
FOR <variable> = <value> TO <value> STEP <value>
:
NEXT <variable>
```

The C 'for' loop is much more versatile than its BASIC counterpart. It is actually based on the 'while' construction. A 'for' loop normally has the characteristic feature of controlling one particular variable, called the *control variable*. That variable is somehow associated with the loop. For example it might be a variable which is used to count 'for values from zero to 10' or whatever.

The form of the for loop is as follows:

```
for (statement1; condition; statement2)
    {
    }
```

For normal usage, these expressions have the following significance.

statement1 This is some kind of expression which initialises the control variable. This statement is only carried out once before the start of the loop. For example: i = 0;

condition This is a condition which behaves like the while loop. The condition is evaluated at the beginning of every loop and the loop is only carried out while this expression is true. For example: i < 20;

statement2 This is some kind of expression for altering the value of the control variable. In languages such as Pascal this always means adding or subtracting one from the variable. In C it can be absolutely anything. Eg: i++ or i *= 20 or i /= 2.3 ...

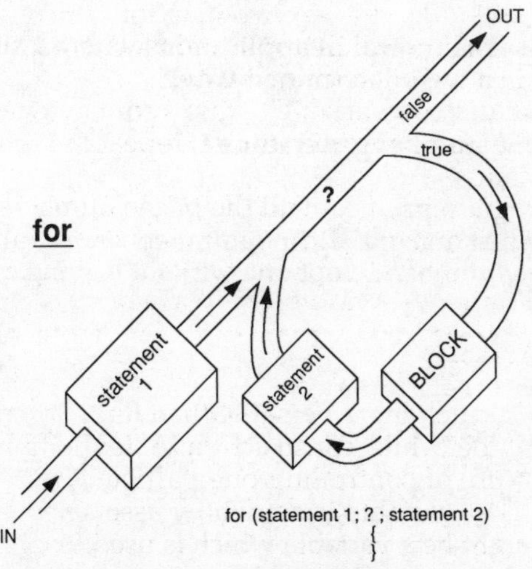

Figure 18.3. The structure of a for loop.

Compare a C 'for' loop to the BASIC 'for' loop. Here is an example in which the loop counts from zero to 10 in steps of 0.5:

```
FOR X = 0 TO 10 STEP 0.5
NEXT X

for (x = 0; x <= 10; x += 0.5)
    {
    }
```

The C translation looks peculiar in comparison, because it works on a different principle. It does not contain information about when it will stop, as the BASIC version does, instead it contains information about when it should be looping. The result is that a C 'for' loop often has the '<=' symbol in it.

The 'for' loop has plenty of uses. It could be used to find the sum of the first n natural numbers very simply:

```
sum = 0;

for (i = 0; i <= n; i++)
      {
      sum += i;
      }
```

It generally finds itself useful in applications where a single variable has to be controlled in a well-determined way.

Listing 18.4. Prime number generator #1.

This example program prints out all the prime numbers between one and the macro value 'maxint'. Prime numbers are numbers which can't be divided by any number except one without leaving a remainder.

```
/**********************************************/
/*                                            */
/* Prime Number Generator #1                  */
/*                                            */
/**********************************************/
   /* Check for prime number by raw number */
   /* crunching. Try dividing all numbers  */
   /* up to half the size of a given i, if */
   /* remainder == 0 then not prime!       */

      #include <stdio.h>

      #define maxint  500
      #define true      1
      #define false     0

/**********************************************/
/* Level 0                                    */
/**********************************************/

      main ()
```

```
{ int i;
for (i = 2; i <= maxint; i++)
     {

     if (prime(i))
          {
          printf ("%5d",i);
          }
     }
}

/**********************************************/
/* Level 1                                    */
/**********************************************/

prime (i)      /* check for a prime number */
int i;

{ int j;

for (j = 2; j <= i/2; j++)
     {

     if (i % j == 0)
          {
          return (false);
          }

     }
     return (true);

}
```

The Flexible 'for' Loop

The word 'statement' was chosen carefully to describe what goes into a 'for' loop. Look at the loop again:

```
for (statement1; condition; statement2)
     {
     }
```

Statement really means what it says. C will accept any statement in the place of those above, including the empty statement. The while loop could be written as a 'for' loop!

```
for (; condition; )      /* while ?? */
    {
    }
```

Here there are two empty statements, which are just wasted. This flexibility can be put to better uses though. Consider the following loop:

```
for (x = 2; x <= 1000; x = x * x)
    {
    ....
    }
```

This loop begins at two and each time the statements in the braces are executed, x squares itself! Another 'odd' looking loop is the following one below:

```
for (ch = '*'; ch != '\n'; ch = getchar())
    {
    }
```

This could be used to make yet another different kind of skipgarb function. The loop starts off by initialising ch with a star character. It checks that ch != '\n' (which it isn't, first time around) and proceeds with the loop. On each new pass, ch is reassigned by calling the function getchar.

Statement2 can be any statement at all which the programmer would like to be executed on every pass of the loop. The reader might ask: 'Why not put that statement in the curly braces?' In most cases that would be the best thing to do, but in special instances it might keep a program tidier or more readable to put it in a 'for' loop instead. There is no hard and fast rule for when to do this, you will be able to decide which is best when you become more aquainted with C.

It is not only the statements which are flexible. An unnerving feature of the 'for' construction (according to some programmers!) is that even the conditional expression in the 'for' loop can be altered by the program from within the loop itself if it is written as a variable.

```
int i, number = 20;

for (i = 0; i <= number; i++)
    {

    if (i == 9)
        {
```

```
            number = 30;
            }
        }
```

This is so nerve-shattering that many languages totally forbid it! It is not often a very good idea to use this facility, but in the right hands, it is a powerful one to have around.

Quitting Loops and Hurrying Them Up!

It is an infuriating waste of time to find, during the course of a loop, that a program has to wait for the rest of a loop to finish when it does not really need to. C provides a simple way of jumping out of any of the three loops above whether it has finished or not. The statement which performs this action is the same statement which was used to jump out of 'switch' statements in last section.

```
break;
```

If this statement is encountered, a loop will quit where it stands. For instance, an expensive way of assigning i to be 12 would be:

```
for (i = 1; i <= 20; i++)

        {
        if (i == 12)
            {
            break;
            }
        }
```

Still another way of making skipgarb, would be to perform the following loop:

```
while (true)
        {
        ch = getchar();

        if (ch == '\n')
            {
            break;
            {
        }
```

Of course, another way to do this would be to use the return function, which jumps right out of a whole function. 'Break' only jumps out of the loop, so it is less drastic.

As well as wanting to quit a loop, a programmer might want to hurry a loop on to the next pass – perhaps to avoid executing a lot of irrelevant statements. C gives a statement for this too, called:

```
continue;
```

When a continue statement is encountered, a loop will stop whatever it is doing and will go straight to the start of the next loop pass. This might be useful to avoid dividing by zero in a program:

```
for (i = -10; i <= 10; i++)

        {
        if (i == 0)
                {
                continue;
                }

        printf ("%d", 20/i);
        }
```

Nested Loops

Like decisions, loops will also nest – that is, loops can be placed inside other loops. Although this feature will work with any loop at all, it is most commonly used with the 'for' loop, because this is easiest to control. The idea of nested loops is important for *multi-dimensional arrays* which will be examined in the next chapter. A 'for' loop controls the number of times that a particular set of statements will be carried out. Another 'greater' loop could be used to control the number of times that a whole loop is carried out. To see the benefit of nesting loops, the following example shows how a square could be printed out using two printf statements and two loops.

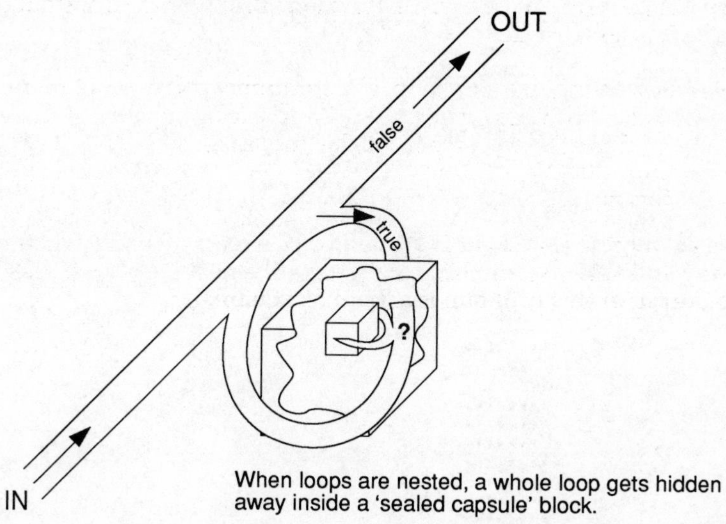
OUT
false
true
?
IN
When loops are nested, a whole loop gets hidden away inside a 'sealed capsule' block.

Figure 18.4. Nested loops.

Listing 18.5. The square.

```
/****************************************/
/*                                      */
/* A "Square"                           */
/*                                      */
/****************************************/

     #include <stdio.h>

     #define size  10

/****************************************/

     main ()

     { int i,j;
```

```
for (i = 1; i <= size; i++)
     {
     for (j = 1; j <= size; j++)
          {
          printf("*");
          }

     printf ("\n");
     }
}
```

The output of this program is a 'kind of' square:

Questions:

1) How many kinds of loop does C offer, and what are they?

2) When is the condition tested in each of the loops?

3) Which of the loops is always executed once?

4) Write a program which copies all input to output line by line.

5) Write a program to get 10 numbers from the user and add them together.

19 : Arrays

Rows and Grids of Storage
Initialisation

Arrays are a convenient way of grouping a lot of variables under a *single variable name*. Arrays are like pigeon-holes or chessboards, with each compartment or square acting as a storage place – they can be one-dimensional, two-dimensional or more-dimensional!

An array is defined using square brackets []. For example: an array of three integers called 'triplet' would be declared like this:

```
int triplet[3];
```

Notice that there is no space between the square bracket [and the name of the array. This statement would cause space for three integers type variables to be created in memory next to each other as in the diagram below.

```
                  ------------------------------------
int triplet:      |           |           |           |
                  ------------------------------------
```

The number in the square brackets of the declaration is referred to as the 'index' (*plural: indices*) or 'subscript' of the array and it must be an integer number between zero and (in this case) two. The three integers are called elements of the array and they are referred to in a program by writing the following:

```
triplet[0]
triplet[1]
triplet[2]
```

Note that the indices start at zero and run up to one less than the number which is placed in the declaration (which is called the *dimension* of the array.) The reason for this will become clear later. Also notice that every element in an array is of the same *type* as every other. It is not possible (at this stage) to have arrays which contain many different data-types. When arrays are declared inside a function, storage is allocated for them, but that storage space is not initialised – that is, the memory space contains garbage (random values). It is usually necessary, therefore, to initialise the array before the program truly begins, to prepare it for use. This normally means that all the elements in the array will be set to zero.

Why Use Arrays?

Arrays are most useful when they have a large number of elements – that is, in cases where it would be completely impractical to have a different name for every storage space in the memory. It is then highly beneficial to move over to arrays for storing information for two particular reasons:

1) The storage spaces in arrays have indices. These numbers can often be related to variables in a problem and so there is a logical connection to be made between an array an a program.

2) In C, arrays can be initialised very easily indeed. It is far easier to initialise an array than it is to initialise 20 or so variables.

The first reason is probably the most important as far as C is concerned, since information can be stored in other ways with equally simple initialisation facilities in C.

One example of the use of an array might be in taking a census of the types of car passing on a road. By defining macros for the names of the different cars, they could easily be linked to the elements in an array.

Type	**Array Element**
car	0
auto	1
bil	2

The array could then be used to store the number of cars of a given type which had driven past. For example, look at listing 19.1.

Listing 19.1. Car census.

```
/**********************************************/
/*                                            */
/* Census                                     */
/*                                            */
/**********************************************/

       #include "stdio.h"

       #define notfinished 1
       #define car         0
       #define auto        1
       #define bil         2

/***********************************************/

       main ()

       {    int type[3];
            int index;

       for (index = 0; index < 3; index++)
            {
            type[index] = 0;
            }

       while (notfinished)
            {
            printf ("Enter type number 0,1, or 2");
            scanf ("%d", &index);
            skipgarb();

            type[index] += 1;     /* See text below */
            }
       }
```

This program, first of all, initialises the elements of the array to be zero. It then enters a loop which repeatedly fetches a number from the user and increases the value stored in the array element, labelled by that number, by one. The effect is to count the cars as they go past. This example program is actually not a very good one for two reasons in particular:

1) First, it does not check that the number which the user typed is actually one of the elements of the array. See the section below about this.

2) The loop goes on for ever and the program never gives up the information which is stores. In short: it is not very useful!

Another example, which comes readily to mind, would be the use of a two-dimensional array for storing the positions of chess pieces in a chess game. Two-dimensional arrays have a chessboard-like structure already and they require two numbers (two indicies) to pinpoint a particular storage 'cell'. This is just like the numbers on a chess board, so there is an immediate and logical connection between an array and the problem of keeping track of the pieces on a chess board.

Arrays play an important role in the handling of string variables. Strings are important enough to have a section of their own. See Chapter 20 - Strings, for more information.

Limits and the Dimension of an Array

C does not do much hand holding for programmers. It is invariably up to the programmer to make sure that programs are free from errors. This is true with arrays too. C does not complain if a program tries to write to elements of an array which do not exist! For example:

```
char array[5];
```

is an array with five elements. If the user then writes:

```
array[7] = '*';
```

C would happily try to write the character * at the location which would have corresponded to the seventh element, had it been declared that way. Unfortunately, this would probably be memory taken up by some other variable, or perhaps even by the operating system. The result would be either:

The value in the incorrect memory location would be corrupted and no harm would be done.

or:

> The value would totally corrupt the memory and crash the system completely!

This is a common source of error. Remember that array limits run from zero to the size of the array *minus one*.

Arrays and 'for' Loops

Arrays have a natural partner in programs – the 'for' loop. The 'for' loop provides a simple way of counting through the numbers of an index in a controlled way.

Consider a one-dimensional array called 'array'. A 'for' loop can be used to initialise the array, so that all its elements contain zero:

```
#define size  10;

main ()

{   int i, array[size];

for (i = 0; i < size; i++)
    {
    array[i] = 0;
    }
}
```

It could equally well be used to fill the array with different values. Consider the following:

```
#define size  10;

main ()

{   int i, array[size];

for (i = 0; i < size; i++)
    {
    array[i] = i;
    }
}
```

This fills each successive space with the number of its index:

```
index       0   1   2   3   4   5   6   7   8   9
          -----------------------------------------
element   | 0 | 1 | 2 | 3 | 4 | 5 | 6 | 7 | 8 | 9 |
contents  -----------------------------------------
```

The 'for' loop can be used to work on an array sequentially at any time during a program, not only when it is being initialised. The example listing, 19.2, shows an example of how this might work for a one-dimensional array, called an *Eratosthenes sieve*. This sieve is an array which is used for weeding out prime numbers – that is: numbers which cannot be divided by any number except one without leaving a remainder or a fraction. It works by filling an array with numbers from zero to some maximum value in the same way that was shown previously and then by going through the numbers in turn and deleting (setting equal to zero) every multiple of every number from the array. This eliminates all the numbers which could be divided by something exactly and leaves only the prime numbers at the end. Try to follow through the listing below.

Listing 19.2. Eratosthenes sieve.

```
/*******************************************************/
/*                                                     */
/* Prime Number sieve                                  */
/*                                                     */
/*******************************************************/

      #include <stdio.h>

      #define size     5000
      #define deleted     0

/********************************************************/
/* Level 0                                              */
/********************************************************/

      main ()

      {    short sieve[size];

      printf ("Eratosthenes sieve \n\n");

      FillSieve(sieve);
      SortPrimes(sieve);
```

```
      PrintPrimes(sieve);
      }

/**********************************************************/
/* Level 1                                                */
/**********************************************************/

      FillSieve (sieve)              /* Fill with integers */

      short sieve[size];
      {    short i;

      for (i = 2; i < size; i++)
           {
           sieve[i] = i;
           }
      }

/**********************************************************/

      SortPrimes (sieve)               /* Delete non primes */

      short sieve[size];

      {    short i;

      for (i = 2; i < size; i++)
           {

           if (sieve[i] == deleted)
                {
                continue;
                }

           DeleteMultiplesOf(i,sieve);
           }
      }

/**********************************************************/

      PrintPrimes (sieve)                 /* Print out array */

      short sieve[size];

      {    short i;

      for (i = 2; i < size; i++)
           {

           if (sieve[i] == deleted)
                {
```

```
              continue;
               }

         else
              {
              printf ("%5d",sieve[i]);
               }
          }

     }

/***********************************************************/
/* Level 2                                                 */
/***********************************************************/

     DeleteMultiplesOf (i,sieve) /* Delete.. of an integer */

     short i,sieve[size];
     {    short j, mult = 2;

     for (j = i*2; j < size; j = i * (mult++))
          {
          sieve[j] = deleted;
           }
      }
```

Arrays of More than One Dimension

There is no limit, in principle, to the number of indicies which an array can have. (Though there is a limit to the amount of memory available for their storage.) A two-dimensional array could be declared in the following way:

```
     float numbers[size][size];
```

Size is some macro constant. The sizes of the two 'dimensions' do not have to be the same. This is called a two-dimensional array because it has two indicies, or two labels in square brackets. It has (size * size) or size-squared elements in it, which form an imaginary grid, like a chess board, in which every square is a variable or storage area as follows:

```
------------------------------------
| 0 | 1 | 2 | 3 | 4 | 5 | 6 | 7 | 8 | ... (up to size)
------------------------------------
| 1 |   |   |   |   |   |   |   |   |
------------------------------------
| 2 |   |   |   |   |   |   |   |   |
------------------------------------
| 3 |   |   |   |   |   |   |   |   |
------------------------------------
| 4 |   |   |   |   |   |   |   |   |
------------------------------------
| 5 |   |   |   |   |   |   |   |   |
------------------------------------
| 6 |   |   |   |   |   |   |   |   |
------------------------------------
| 7 |   |   |   |   |   |   |   |   |
-------------------------------------
(up to size)
```

Every element in this grid needs two indices to pin-point it. The elements are accessed by giving the co-ordinates of the element in the grid. For instance to set the element two – three to the value 12, you would write:

```
array[2][3] = 12;
```

The usual terminology for the two indices is that the first gives the row number in the grid and that the second gives the column number in the grid. Rows go along, columns hold up the ceiling.

An array can't be stored in the memory as a grid, as computer memory is a one-dimensional thing. Arrays are therefore stored in rows. The following array:

```
-------------
| 1 | 2 | 3 |
-------------
| 4 | 5 | 6 |
-------------
| 7 | 8 | 9 |
-------------
```

would be stored as:

```
-------------------------------------
| 1 | 2 | 3 | 4 | 5 | 6 | 7 | 8 | 9 |
-------------------------------------
*  ROW # 1  *  ROW # 2  *  ROW #3   *
```

Another way of saying that arrays are stored row-wise, is to say that the second index varies fastest because a two-dimensional array is always thought of as:

```
array[row][column]
```

So for every row stored, there will be lots of columns inside that row. That means the column index goes from zero to size inside every row, so it is changing faster as the line of storage is followed.

A three-dimensional array, like a cube or a cuboid, could also be defined in the same kind of way:

```
double cube[size][size][size];
```

or with different limits on each dimension:

```
short  notcubic[2][6][8];
```

Three-dimensional arrays are stored according to the same pattern as two-dimensional arrays. They are kept in computer memory as a linear sequence of variable stores and the last index is always the one which varies fastest.

Arrays and Nested Loops

Arrays of more than one dimension are usually handled by nested for loops. A two-dimensional array might be initialised in the manner shown below:

```
main ()

{ int i,j;
  float array[size1][size2];

for (i = 0; i < size1; i++)

    {
    for (j = 0; j < size2; j++)
        {
```

```
            array[i][j] = 0;
            }
        }
    }
```

In three dimensions, three nested loops would be needed:

```
main ()

{ int i,j,k;
  float array[size1][size2][size3];

for (i = 0; i < size1; i++)
    {

    for (j = 0; j < size2; j++)
        {

          for (k = 0; k < size3; k++)
              {
              array[i][j][k] = 0;
              }
          }
    }
}
```

An example program helps to show how this happens in practice. The aim is to mimic something like cell reproduction by applying some rigid rules to a pattern of dots (.) and stars (*). A dot is a place where there is no life (as we know it!) and a star is a place in which there is a living thing. The rules will be clear from the listing. Things to notice are the way the program traverses the arrays and the way in which it checks that it is not over-stepping the boundaries of the arrays.

Listing 19.3. The Game of Life.

```
/*******************************************************/
/*                                                     */
/* Game of Life                                        */
/*                                                     */
/*******************************************************/
   /* Based upon an article from Scientific American */
   /* in 1970. Simulates the reproduction of cells   */
   /* which depend on one another. The rules are     */
   /* that cells will only survive if they have a    */
   /* certain number of neighbours to support them   */
   /* but not too many, or there won't be enough     */
   /* food!                                          */

    #include <stdio.h>
```

```
      #define size            20
      #define maxnum          15
      #define inbounds        (a>=0)&&(a<size)&&(b>=0)&&(b<size)
      #define noresponse      1

/**********************************************************/
/* Level 0                                                */
/**********************************************************/

      main ()

      {   int count[size][size];
          char array[size][size];
          int generation = 0;

      printf ("Game of Life\n\n\n");
      InitializeArray(array);
      while (noresponse)
          {
          CountNeighbours(array,count);
          BuildNextGeneration(array,count);
          UpdateDisplay(array,++generation);

          printf ("\n\nQ for quit. RETURN to continue.\n");
          if(quit()) break;
           }
      }
/**********************************************************/
/* Level 1                                                */
/**********************************************************/

      InitializeArray (array) /* Get starting conditions */

      char array[size][size];

      {   int i,j;
          char ch;

      printf ("\nEnter starting setup. Type '.' for empty");
      printf ("\nand any other character for occupied.\n");
      printf ("RETURN after each line.\n\n");
      printf ("Array size guide:\n\n");

      for (i=0; i++ < size; printf("%c",'^'));
      printf ("\n\n");

      for (i = 0; i < size; i++)
          {
          for (j = 0; j < size; j++)
              {
```

```
            scanf ("%c",&ch);
            if (ch == '.')
                 {
                 array[i][j] = '.';
                 }
            else
                 {
                 array[i][j] = '*';
                 }
            }
       skipgarb();
       }

  printf ("\n\nInput is complete. Press RETURN.");
  skipgarb();
  }

/*****************************************************/

  CountNeighbours (array,count) /* count all neighbours */

  char array[size][size];
  int count[size][size];

  {    int i,j;

  for (i = 0; i < size; i++)
       {
       for (j = 0; j < size; j++)
            {
             count[i][j] = numalive(array,i,j);
             }
         }
  }

/*****************************************************/

  BuildNextGeneration (array,count)

 /* A cell will survive if it has two or three  */
 /* neighbours. New life will be born to a dead */
 /* cell if there are exactly three neighbours  */

  char array[size][size];
  int count[size][size];

  {    int i,j;

  for (i = 0; i < size; i++)
       {
       for (j = 0; j < size; j++)
            {
```

```
                if (array[i][j] == '*')
                        {
                        switch (count[i][j])
                                {
                                case 2 :
                                case 3 : continue;

                                default: array[i][j] = '.';
                                         break;
                                }
                        }
          else
                        {
                        switch (count[i][j])
                                {
                                case 3 : array[i][j] = '*';
                                         break;
                                default: continue;
                                }
                        }
                }
        }
    }

/*****************************************************/

    UpdateDisplay (array,g) /* print out life array */

    char array[size][size];
    int g;

    {    int i,j;

    printf ("\n\nGeneration %d\n\n",g);

    for (i = 0; i < size; i++)
         {
         for (j = 0; j < size; j++)
              {
              printf("%c",array[i][j]);
              }
         printf("\n");
         }
    }

/*****************************************************/
/* Level 2                                           */
/*****************************************************/

    numalive (array,i,j)
```

```
    /* Don't count array[i,j] : only its neighbours */
    /* Also check that haven't reached the boundary */
    /* of the array                                 */
      char array[size][size];
      int i,j;

      { int a,b,census;
        census = 0;

      for (a = (i-1); (a <= (i+1)); a++)
           {
           for (b = (j-1); (b <= (j+1)); b++)
                {
                if (inbounds && (array[a][b] == '*'))
                     {
                     census++;
                     }
                }
           }

      if (array[i][j] == '*') census--;
      return (census);
      }

/*******************************************************/
/* Toolkit input                                       */
/*******************************************************/

      quit()

      {    char ch;

      while (noresponse)
           {
           scanf ("%c",&ch);
           if (ch != '\n') skipgarb();
           switch (ch)
                {
                case 'q' : case 'Q' : return (1);
                default  :            return (0);
                }
           }
      }

/*******************************************************/

      skipgarb ()
      {
      while (getchar() != '\n');
      }
```

Example run of the Game of Life

```
Game of Life

Enter starting setup. Type '.' for empty and any other
character for occupied. RETURN after each line.

Array size guide:
^^^^^^^^^^^^^^^^^^^^
(user types in:
....................
....................
.....................
.....................
.....................
..........***........
...........*.........
......................
.....................
.....................
.....................
*********************
.....................
......................
....................
.....................
......................
......................
......................
...................... )
```

It doesn't matter if the input spills over the size guide, because 'skipgarb()' discards it.

```
Input is complete. Press RETURN.

Generation 1
....................
....................
....................
....................
...........*........
..........***.......
..........***.......
....................
....................
....................
.******************.
.******************.
.******************.
....................
....................
....................
....................
....................
....................
....................
```

```
Q for quit. RETURN to continue.

Generation 2
....................
....................
....................
....................
..........***.......
....................
..........*.*.......
...........*........
....................
..****************..
.*................*.
*..................*
.*................*.
..****************..
....................
....................
....................
....................
....................
....................

Q for quit. RETURN to continue.

Generation 3
....................
....................
....................
...........*........
...........*........
..........*.*.......
...........*........
...........*........
...*******...****...
..****************..
.******************.
**................**
.******************.
..****************..
...**************...
....................
....................
....................
....................
....................

Q for quit. RETURN to continue.
```

```
Generation 4
....................
....................
....................
....................
..........***.......
..........*.*.......
..........***.......
....*****.*.*.**....
..*..............*..
.*................*.
*..................*
*..................*
*..................*
.*................*.
..*..............*..
....************....
....................
....................
....................
....................

Q for quit. RETURN to continue.
```

Try experimenting with different starting patterns.

Initialising Arrays

Arrays can be initialised in two ways. The first way is by assigning every element to some value with a statement as follows:

```
array[2] = 42;
array[3] = 12;
```

or perhaps with the aid of one or more for loops. Because it is tedious and uneconomical to initialise the values of each element as different values, C provides another method, which employs a single assignment operator ('=') and curly braces, { }. This method only works for *static variables* and *external variables.*

Recall that arrays are stored 'row-wise' or with the last index varying fastest. A three by three array could be initialised in the following way:

```
static int array[3][3] =

{
{10,23,42},
{1,654,0},
{40652,22,0}
};
```

The internal braces are unnecessary, but help to distinguish the rows from the columns. The same thing could be written as follows:

```
int array[3][3] =

{
10,23,42,
1,654,0
40652,22,0
};
```

Take care to include the semicolon at the end of the curly brace which closes the assignment.

Note that, if there are not enough elements in the curly braces to account for every single element in an array, the remaining elements will be filled out with zeros. Static variables are always guaranteed to be initialised to zero anyway, whereas auto or local variables are guaranteed to be garbage. This is because static storage is created by the compiler in the body of a program, whereas auto or local storage is created at run-time.

Arrays and Pointers

The information about how arrays are stored was not included just for interest. There is another way of looking at arrays which follows the BCPL idea of an array as simply a block of memory. An array can be accessed with pointers as well as with square brackets ([]):

> The name of an array variable, standing alone, is actually a pointer to the first element in the array.

For example, if an array is declared:

```
float numbers[34];
```

then 'numbers' is a pointer to the first floating point number in the array – 'numbers' is a pointer in its own right. In this case it is type 'pointer to float'. So the first element of the array could be accessed by writing:

```
numbers[0] = 22.3;
```

or by writing:

```
*numbers = 22.3;
```

For character arrays, which are dealt with in some depth in Chapter 20, this gives an alternative way of getting at the elements in the array.

```
char arrayname[5];
char *ptr;

for (ptr = arrayname; ptr <= arrayname+4; ptr++)
    {
    *ptr = 0;
    }
```

The code above sets the array ('arrayname') to zero. I do not recommend this method of getting at array data, except in very simple computer environments. If a program is running on a normal micro, then there should be few problems with this alternative method of handling arrays. On the other hand, if the micro is multi-tasking, or the program is running on a larger system which has a limited manager, then memory ceases to be something which can be thought of as a sequence of boxes standing next to one another. A multi-tasking system shares memory with other programs and it takes what it can find, where it can find it. It is therefore not possible to guarantee that arrays will be stored in one simple string of memory locations, it might be scattered around in different places. So:

```
ptr = arrayname + 5;
```

might not be a pointer to the fifth character in a character array. This could be found instead using the & operator. A pointer to the fifth element can be reliably found with:

```
ptr = &(arrayname[5]);
```

Be warned!

Arrays as Parameters

What happens if the programmer wants to pass an array as a parameter? Does the program copy the entire array into local storage? The answer is 'no', because it would be an enormous waste of time and memory. Arrays can be passed as parameters, but only as variable ones.

This is a simple matter, because the name of the array is a pointer to the array. The Game of Life program does this. Notice from that program how the declarations for the parameters are made.

```
main ()

{ char array[23];

function (array);
.....
}

function (arrayformal)
char arrayformal[23];

{
}
```

Any function which writes to the array, passed as a parameter, will affect the original copy. Array parameters are always *variable parameters*.

Questions:

1) Given any array, how would you find a pointer to the start of it?

2) How do you pass an array as a parameter? When the parameter is received by a function does C allocate space for a local variable and copy the whole array to the new location?

3) Write a statement which declares an array of type double which measures four by five. What numbers can be written in the indicies of the array?

20 : Strings

Communication with Strings and Arrays

Strings are pieces of text which can be treated as 'values' for variables. In C a string is represented as some characters enclosed by double quotes as follows.

```
"This is a string"
```

A string may contain any character, including special control characters, such as '\n', '\r', '\7' and so on:

```
"Beep! \7 Newline \n..."
```

Conventions and Declarations

There is an important distinction between a string and a single character in C. The convention is that single characters are enclosed by single quotes, eg: '*' and have the type *char*. Strings, on the hand, are enclosed by double quotes eg: "string..." and have the type "*pointer to char*" (char *) or array of *char*. Here are some declarations for strings which are given without immediate explanations.

Listing 20.1. String declaration.

```
/**********************************************************/
/*                                                        */
/* String Declaration                                     */
/*                                                        */
/**********************************************************/

      #define size    10

      char *global_string1;
      char  global_string2[size];
      main ()
```

```
{     char *auto_string;
      char  arraystr[size];
      static char *stat_strng;
      static char statarraystr[size];
 }
```

Strings, Arrays and Pointers

A string is really an array of characters. It is stored in memory and is given an end marker which standard library functions can recognize as being the end of the string. The end marker is called the zero (or null) byte because it is just a byte which contains the value zero: '\0'. The programmer rarely gets to 'see' this end marker, as most functions which handle strings use it or add it automatically.

Strings can be declared in two main ways. First, as an array of characters and second, as a pointer to some pre-assigned array.

Perhaps the simplest way of seeing how C stores arrays is to give an extreme example which would probably never be used in practice! Think of how a string called 'string' might be used to store the message 'Tedious!'. The knowledge that a string is an array of characters might lead a programmer to write something like:

```
#define length 9;

main ()

{    char string[length];

string[0] = 'T';
string[1] = 'e';
string[2] = 'd';
string[3] = 'i';
string[4] = 'o';
string[5] = 'u';
string[6] = 's';
string[7] = '!';
string[8] = '\0';
printf ("%s", string);
}
```

This method of handling strings is perfectly acceptable, if there is time to waste, but it is so laborious that C provides a special initialisation service for strings, which bypasses the need to assign every single character with a new assignment! There are six ways of assigning constant strings to arrays. A constant string is one which is actually typed into the program, not one which is typed in by the user. They are written into a short compilable program, listing 20.2. The explanation follows after.

Listing 20.2. String initialisation.

```
/**********************************************************/
/*                                                        */
/* String Initialisation                                  */
/*                                                        */
/**********************************************************/

      char *global_string1 = "A string declared as a pointer";
      char  global_string2[] = "Declared as an array";

      main ()

      { char *auto_string = "initializer...";
        static char *stat_strng = "initializer...";
        static char statarraystr[] = "initializer....";

     /* char arraystr[] = "initializer....";  IS ILLEGAL! */
     /* This is because the array is an "auto" type      */
     /* which cannot be preinitialized, but...           */

        char arraystr[20];
        printf ("%s %s", global_string1, global_string2);
        printf ("%s %s %s", auto_string, stat_strng,
statarraystr);
      }
          /* end */
```

The details of what goes on with strings can be difficult to grasp for a newcomer to C. It is worth being totally familiar with pointers and arrays before reading the explanations that follow. Notice the diagrams too – they are probably more helpful than words.

The first of these assignments is a global, static variable, or more correctly, it is a pointer to a global, static array. Static variables are assigned storage space in the body of a program when the compiler creates the executable code. This means that they are saved on disc along with the program code, so they can be initialised at compile time. That is the reason for the rule which says, only static arrays can be initialised with a constant expression in a declaration. The first statement allocates space for a pointer to an array. Notice that, because the string which is to be assigned to it is typed into the program, the compiler can also allocate space for that in the executable file too. In fact, the compiler stores the string, adds a zero byte to the end of it and assigns a pointer to its first character to the variable called global_string1.

The second statement works almost identically, with the exception that, this time the compiler sees the declaration of a static array, which is to be initialised. Notice that there is no size declaration in the square brackets. This is quite legal – the compiler counts the number of characters in the initialisation string and allocates just the right amount of space, filling the string into that space, along with its end marker as it goes. Remember also that the name of the array is a pointer to the first character, so, in fact, the two methods are identical.

The third expression is the same kind of thing, only this time the declaration is inside the function main(), so the type is not *static* but *auto*. The difference between this and the other two declarations is that this pointer variable is created every time the function main() is called. It is new each time – the same thing holds for any other function which it might have been defined in. When the function is called, the pointer is created and when it ends, it is destroyed. The string which initialises it is stored in the executable file of the program (because it is typed into the text). The compiler returns a value which is a pointer to the string's first character and uses that as a value to initialise the pointer. This is a slightly round about way of defining the string constant. The normal thing to do would be to declare the string pointer as being static, but this is just a matter of style. In fact this is exactly what is done in the fourth example.

The fifth example is again identical, in practice to other static types, but is written as an 'open' array with an unspecified size.

The sixth example is forbidden! The reason for this might seem rather trivial, but it is made in the interests of efficiency. The array declared is of type *auto* – the whole array is created when the function is called and destroyed afterwards. Auto-arrays can't be initialised with a string (see Chapter 19) because they would have to be re-initialised every time the array were created – that is, each time the function were called. The final example could be used to overcome this, if the programmer were inclined to do so. Here an auto-array of characters is declared (with a size this time, because there is nothing for the compiler to count the size of). There is no single assignment which will fill this array with a string though - the programmer would have to do it character by character so that the inefficiency is made as plain as possible!

Arrays of Strings

In Chapter 19, programs progressed from one-dimensional arrays to two-dimensional arrays, or arrays of arrays! The same thing works well for strings which are declared static. Programs can take advantage of C's easy assignment facilities to let the compiler count the size of the string arrays and define arrays of messages. For example listing 20.3 prints out a menu for an application program:

Listing 20.3. Print a menu.

```
/*********************************************************/
/*                                                       */
/* MENU : program which prints out a menu                */
/*                                                       */
/*********************************************************/

      main ()

      {   int str_number;

      for (str_number = 0; str_number < 13; str_number++)
          {
          printf ("%s",menutext(str_number));
          }
      }

/*********************************************************/

      char *menutext(n)        /* return n-th string ptr */

      int n;
```

```
{
static char *t[] =

{
"  --------------------------------------  \n",
"  |              ++ MENU ++             |\n",
"  |             ~~~~~~~~~~~~            |\n",
"  |     (1) Edit Defaults               |\n",
"  |     (2) Print Charge Sheet          |\n",
"  |     (3) Print Log Sheet             |\n",
"  |     (4) Bill Calculator             |\n",
"  |     (q) Quit                        |\n",
"  |                                     |\n",
"  |                                     |\n",
"  |     Please Enter Choice             |\n",
"  |                                     |\n",
"  --------------------------------------  \n"
};

return (t[n]);
}
```

Notice the way the static declaration works. It is initialised once at compile time, so there is effectively only one statement in this function and that is the return() function. This function retains the pointer information from call to call.

The morse coder program from Chapter 17 could be rewritten more economically using static strings.

Listing 20.4. Static string array.

```
/***********************************************/
/*                                             */
/* static string array                         */
/*                                             */
/***********************************************/
   /* Morse code program. Enter a number and */
   /* find out what it is in Morse code      */

      #include <stdio.h>

      #define code 0

/*************************************************/

      main ()
```

```
{    short digit;

printf ("Enter any digit in the range 0..9");
scanf ("%h",&digit);

if ((digit < 0) || (digit > 9))
     {
     printf ("Number was not in range 0..9");
     return (code);
     }

printf ("The Morse code of that digit is ");
Morse (digit);

}

/*********************************************/

     Morse (digit)     /* print out Morse code */
     short digit;

     {
     static char *code[] =

          {
          "dummy",            /* index starts at 0 */
          "-----",
          ".----",
          "..---",
          "...--",
          "....-",
          ".....",
          "-....",
          "--...",
          "---..",
          "----.",
          };

     printf ("%s\n",code[digit]);
     }
```

Strings from the User

All the strings mentioned so far have been typed into a program by the programmer and stored in a program file, so it has not been necessary to worry about where they were stored. However, it is just as often necessary to fetch a string from the user and store it somewhere in the memory for later use. It might even be necessary to get a whole bunch of strings and store them all. But how will the program know in advance how much array space to allocate to these strings? The answer is that it won't and it doesn't matter at all!

One way of getting a simple, *single* string from the user is to define an array and to read the characters one by one. An example of this was the Game of Life program in Chapter 19:

1) Define the array to be a certain size.

2) Check that the user does not type in too many characters.

3) Use the string in that array.

Another way is to define a static string with an initialiser as in the following example. The function filename asks the user to type in a filename, for loading or saving by and return it to a calling function:

```
char *filename()

{    static char *filenm = "........................";

do
     {
     printf ("Enter filename :");
     scanf ("%24s",filenm);
     skipgarb();
     }
while (strlen(filenm) == 0);

return (filenm);
}
```

The string is made static and given an initialising expression and this forces the compiler to make some space for the string. It makes exactly 24 characters plus a zero byte in the program file, which can be used by an application. Notice that the conversion string in scanf prevents the characters from spilling over the bounds of the string. The function strlen is a standard library function – it returns the length of a string. 'skipgarb' is the function which was introduced in Chapter 15.

Neither of thsee methods is very useful if a program is going to be fetching a lot of strings from a user. It isn't practical to define lots of static strings and expect the user to type into the right size boxes! The next step in string handling is, therefore, to allocate memory for strings personally. In other words to be able to say how much storage is needed for a string while a program is running. C has special memory allocation functions which can do this, not only for strings but for any kind of object.

Suppose then that a program is going to get 10 strings from the user. Here is one way in which it could be done:

1) Define one large, static string (or array) for getting one string at a time. Call this a string buffer, or waiting place.

2) Define an array of 10 pointers to characters, so that the strings can be recalled easily.

3) Find out how long the string in the string buffer is.

4) Allocate memory for the string.

5) Copy the string from the buffer to the new storage and place a pointer to it in the array of pointers for reference.

6) Release the memory when it is finished with.

The function which allocates memory in C is probably called 'malloc' (check individual compiler manuals for this) and it works like this:

1) malloc should be declared as returning the type pointer to character, with the statement:

```
char *malloc();
```

2) malloc takes one argument which should be an unsigned integer value telling the function how many bytes of storage to allocate. It returns a pointer to the first memory location in that storage position:

```
char *ptr;
unsigned int size;
ptr = malloc(size);
```

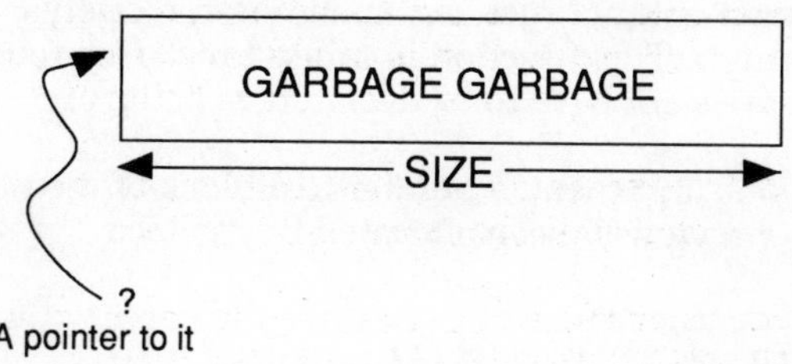
(1) malloc ( ) creates some storage and returns
GARBAGE GARBAGE
SIZE
?
A pointer to it

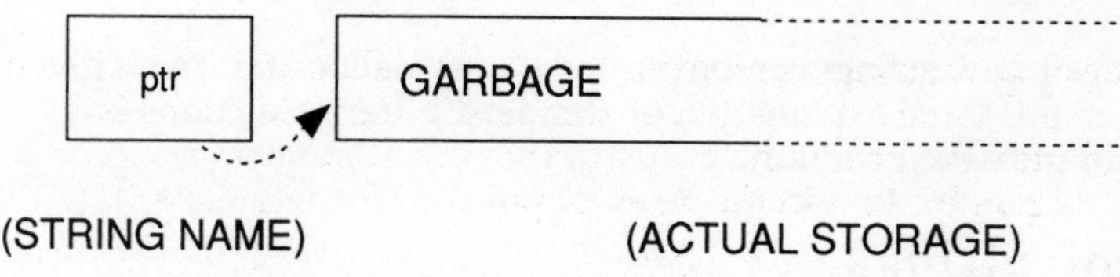
(2) This pointer is assigned to a pointer variable.
ptr = malloc (size)
ptr
GARBAGE
(STRING NAME)
(ACTUAL STORAGE)

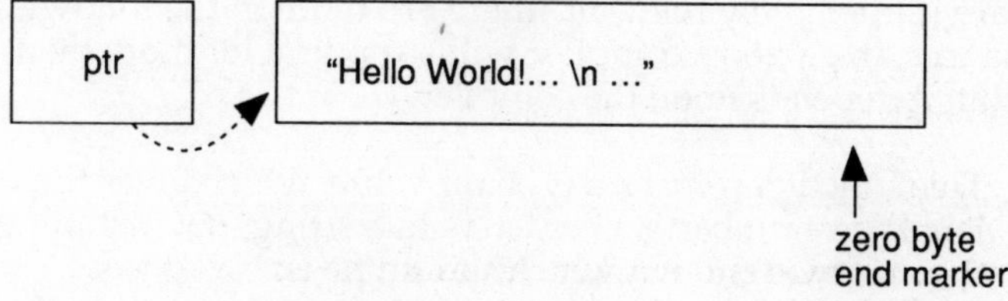
3) Finally the storage is filled with meaningful characters using strcpy ( );
ptr
"Hello World!... \n ..."
zero byte
end marker

Figure 20.1. Strings from the user.

3) The pointer returned has the value NULL (==0) if there was no memory left to allocate. This should always be checked.

The fact that malloc always returns a pointer to a character doesn't stop it from being used for other types of data too. The cast operator can force malloc to give a pointer to any data type. This method is used for building data structures in C with 'struct' types.

malloc has a complementary function which does precisely the opposite – de-allocates memory. This function is called 'free'. free returns an integer code, so it does not have to be declared as being any special type:

1) free takes one argument: a pointer to a block of memory which has previously been allocated by malloc:

```
int returncode;
returncode = free (ptr);
```

2) The pointer should be declared:

```
char *ptr;
```

3) The return code is zero if the release was successful.

An example of how strings can be created using malloc and free is given next. First of all, some explanation of standard library functions is useful to simplify the program.

Handling Strings

The C standard library commonly provides a number of very useful functions which handle strings. Here is a short list of some common ones which are immediately relevant (there are more in the following chapter). Chances are, a good compiler will support a lot more than those listed, but it depends upon the compiler.

strlen() This function returns a type int value, which gives the length or number of characters in a string, not including the null byte end marker. An example is:

```
int len;
char *string;
len = strlen (string);
```

strcpy() This function copies a string from one place to another. Use this function in preference to custom routines: it is set up to handle any peculiarities in the way data are stored. An example is:

```
char *to,*from;
to = strcpy (to,from);
```

Where 'to' is a pointer to the place to which the string is to be copied and 'from' is the place where the string is to be copied from.

strcmp() This function compares two strings and returns a value which indicates how they compared. An example:

```
int value;
char *s1,*s2;

value = strcmp(s1,s2);
```

The value returned is zero if the two strings were identical. If the strings were not the same, this function indicates the (ASCII) alphabetical order of the two. S1 > s2, alphabetically, then the value is >0. If s1 < s2 then the value is <0. Note numbers come before letters in the ASCII code sequence and upper case is before lower case.

More string functions are described in the next chapter along with a host of standard library functions.

The program in listing 20.5 aims to get 10 strings from the user. The strings may not contain any spaces or white space characters. It works as follows:

The user is prompted for a string which he/she types into a buffer. The length of the string is tested with strlen, and a block of memory is allocated for it using malloc. Notice that this block of memory is one byte longer than the value returned by strlen, because strlen() does not count the end of string marker '\0'. Malloc returns a pointer to the space allocated, which is then stored in the array called 'array'. Finally, the string is copied from the buffer to the new storage with the library function strcpy. This process is repeated for each of the 10 strings. Notice that the program exits through a low-level function called QuitSafely. The reason for doing this is to exit from the program neatly, while at the same time remembering to perform all of a programmer's duties, such as de-allocating the memory which is no longer needed. QuitSafely uses the function exit which should be provided as a standard library function. exit can end a program at any point.

Listing 20.5. String storage allocation.

```
/****************************************************/
/*                                                  */
/* String storage allocation                        */
/*                                                  */
/****************************************************/

     #include <stdio.h>
    /* #include another file for malloc() and    */
    /* strlen() ???. Check the compiler manual! */

     #define noofstr    10
     #define bufsize    255
     #define code       0

/****************************************************/
/* Level 0                                          */
/****************************************************/

     main ()

     {    char *array[noofstr], *malloc();
          char buffer[bufsize];
          int i;

     for (i = 0; i < noofstr; i++)
          {
          printf (“Enter string %d :”,i);
          scanf  (“%255s”,buffer);

          array[i] = malloc(strlen(buffer)+1);

          if (array[i] == NULL)
               {
               printf (“Can’t allocate memory\n”);
               QuitSafely (array);
               }
          strcpy (array[i],buffer);
          }

          for (i = 0; i < noofstr; i++)
               {
               printf (“%s\n”,array[i]);
               }
```

```
        QuitSafely(array);
        }

/*************************************************************/
/* Snakes & Ladders!                                         */
/*************************************************************/

    QuitSafely (array)    /* Quit & de-alloc memory */

    char *array[noofstr];

    {    int i, len;

        for (i = 0; i < noofstr; i++)
        {
        len = strlen(array[i]) + 1;
        if (free (array[i]) != 0)
            {
            printf ("Debug: free failed\n");
            }
         }

    exit (code);
    }
                        /* end */
```

String Input/Output

Because strings are recognised to be special in C, some special library functions for reading and writing are provided for them. These make it easier to deal with strings, without the need for special user routines. There are four of these functions:

```
    gets()
    puts()
    sprintf()
    sscanf()
```

gets()

This function fetches a string from the standard input file stdin and places it into some buffer which the programmer must provide:

```
#define size    255
char *sptr, buffer[size];
strptr = gets(buffer);
```

If the routine is successful in getting a string, it returns the value 'buffer' to the string pointer 'strptr'. Otherwise it returns null (==0). The advantage of gets over scanf("%s"..) is that gets will read spaces in strings, whereas scanf will not. gets quits reading when it finds a new line character: that is, when the user presses RETURN.

puts()

puts sends a string to the output file stdout, until it finds a null end of string marker. The null byte is not written to stdout, instead a new line character is written:

```
char *string;
int returncode;
returncode = puts(string);
```

Puts returns an integer value, whose value is only guaranteed if there is an error. Returncode == EOF if an end of file was encountered or there was an error.

sprintf()

This is an interesting function which works in almost the same way as printf(), the exception being that it prints *to a string*. In other words, it treats a string as though it were an output file. This is useful for creating formatted strings in the computer's memory. It works in the following way:

```
int n;
char *ds;
n = sprintf (ds, "control string", parameters, values);
```

n is an integer which is the number of characters printed; ds is a pointer to the 'destination string' or the string which is to be written to.

Note carefully, that this function does not perform any check on the output string to make sure that it is long enough to contain the formatted output. If the string is not large enough, then a crash could be in store!

sscanf()

This function is the complement of sprintf. It reads its input from a string, as though it were an input file:

```
int n;
char *ss;

n = sscanf (ss,"control string", pointers...);
```

ss is a pointer to the string which is to be read from. The string must be null terminated (it must have a zero byte end marker '\0').sscanf returns an integer value which holds the number of items successfully matched, or EOF, if an end of file marker was read or an error occurred. The conversion specifiers are identical to those for scanf.

Listing 20.6. Formatted strings.

```
/************************************************/
/*                                              */
/* Formatted strings                            */
/*                                              */
/************************************************/
   /* program rewrites s1 in reverse into s2 */

      #include <stdio.h>

      #define size   20
      #define code    0

/************************************************/

      main ()

      {    static char *s1 = "string 2.3 55x";
           static char *s2 = "....................";
           char ch, *string[size];

      int i,n;
      float x;

      sscanf (s1,"%s %f %d %c", string, &x, &i, &ch);
      n = sprintf (s2,"%c %d %f %s", ch, i, x, string);

      if (n > size)
           {
           printf ("Error: string overflowed!\n");
```

```
        exit (code);
        }

    puts (s2);
    }
```

Questions:

1) What are the two main ways of declaring strings in a program?

2) How would you declare a static array of strings?

3) Write a program which gets a number between zero and nine and prints out a different message for each number. Use a pre-initialised array to store the strings.

21 : Functions & Macros

Checking Character Types
Handling Strings
Doing Maths

C provides a repertoire of standard library functions and macros for specialised purposes, and for the advanced user. These may be divided into three categories:

1) Character identification: (ctype.h)

2) String manipulation: (string.h)

3) Mathematical functions: (math.h)

A program has to include header files in order to use special functions. The names of the appropriate files can be found in compiler manuals. They commonly take the names given in brackets, ie, ctype.h, string.h and math.h.

Character Identification

Some or all of the following functions/macros will be available for identifying and classifying single characters. The programmer ought to be aware that it is natural for many of these facilities to exist as macros rather than functions, so the usual remarks about macro parameters apply (see Chapter 13 on the pre-processor for more information).

Assume that 'true' has any non-zero, integer value and that 'false' has the integer value zero. The 'ch' in brackets stands for some character, or char type variable.

Function/Macro	Description
isalpha(ch)	This returns true if ch is alphabetic and false otherwise. Alphabetic means a to z, or A to Z
isupper(ch)	Returns true if the character is upper case. If ch is not an alphabetic character, this returns false
islower(ch)	Returns true if the character is lower case. If ch is not an alphabetic character, this returns false.
isdigit(ch)	Returns true if the character is a digit in the range zero to nine
isxdigit(ch)	Returns true if the character is a valid hexadecimal digit, that is, a number from zero to nine or a letter a to f or A to F
isspace(ch)	Returns true if the character was a white space character, ie, a space, tab character or a new line
ispunct(ch)	Returns true if ch is a punctuation character
isalnum(ch)	Returns true if a character is alphanumeric, that is, alphabetic or digit
isprint(ch)	Returns true if the character is printable, that is, the character is not a control character
isgraph(ch)	Returns true if the character is graphic, ie, if the character is printable (excluding the space)
iscntrl(ch)	Returns true if the character is a control character, ie, ASCII values zero to 31 and 127
isascii(ch)	Returns true if the character is a valid ASCII character, that is, it has a code in the range 0 to 127
iscsym(ch)	Returns true if the character is a character which could be used in a C identifier

Function/Macro	Description
toupper(ch)	This converts the character ch into its upper case counterpart. This does not affect characters which are already upper case, or characters which do not have a particular case, such as digits
tolower(ch)	This converts a character into its lower case counterpart. It does not affect characters which are already lower case
toascii(ch)	This strips off bit 7 of a character so that it is in the range zero to 127, that is, a valid ASCII character

Listing 21.1. Character utility functions.

```
/*******************************************************/
/*                                                     */
/* Demonstration of character utility functions       */
/*                                                     */
/*******************************************************/
   /* prints out all the ASCII characters which give */
   /* the value "true" for the listed character fns  */

     #include <stdio.h>
     #include <ctype.h> /* contains character utilities */
     #define  allchars    ch = 0; isascii(ch); ch++

/*******************************************************/

     main ()        /* A criminally long main program! */

     {   char ch;

     printf ("VALID CHARACTERS FROM isalpha()\n\n");

     for (allchars)
         {
         if (isalpha(ch))
             {
             printf ("%c ",ch);
             }
         }

     printf ("\n\nVALID CHARACTERS FROM isupper()\n\n");

     for (allchars)
         {
```

```
        if (isupper(ch))
            {
            printf ("%c ",ch);
            }
        }

    printf ("\n\nVALID CHARACTERS FROM islower()\n\n");

    for (allchars)
        {
        if (islower(ch))
            {
            printf ("%c ",ch);
            }
        }

    printf ("\n\nVALID CHARACTERS FROM isdigit()\n\n");

    for (allchars)
        {
        if (isdigit(ch))
            {
            printf ("%c ",ch);
            }
        }

    printf ("\n\nVALID CHARACTERS FROM isxdigit()\n\n");

    for (allchars)
        {
        if (isxdigit(ch))
            {
            printf ("%c ",ch);
            }
        }
    printf ("\n\nVALID CHARACTERS FROM ispunct()\n\n");
    for (allchars)
        {
        if (ispunct(ch))
            {
            printf ("%c ",ch);
            }
        }

    printf ("\n\nVALID CHARACTERS FROM isalnum()\n\n");

    for (allchars)
        {
        if (isalnum(ch))
            {
            printf ("%c ",ch);
```

```
            }
        }

    printf ("\n\nVALID CHARACTERS FROM iscsym()\n\n");

    for (allchars)
        {
        if (iscsym(ch))
            {
            printf ("%c ",ch);
            }
        }
    }
```

Output

```
VALID CHARACTERS FROM isalpha()
A B C D E F G H I J K L M N O P Q R S T U V W X Y Z a b c
 d e f g h i j k l m n o p q r s t u v w x y z

VALID CHARACTERS FROM isupper()
A B C D E F G H I J K L M N O P Q R S T U V W X Y Z

VALID CHARACTERS FROM islower()
a b c d e f g h i j k l m n o p q r s t u v w x y z

VALID CHARACTERS FROM isdigit()
0 1 2 3 4 5 6 7 8 9

VALID CHARACTERS FROM isxdigit()
0 1 2 3 4 5 6 7 8 9 A B C D E F a b c d e f

VALID CHARACTERS FROM ispunct()
! " # $ % & ' ( ) * + , - . / : ; < = > ? @ [ \ ] ^ _ ` {
 | } ~

VALID CHARACTERS FROM isalnum()
0 1 2 3 4 5 6 7 8 9 A B C D E F G H I J K L M N O P Q R S
 T U V W X Y Z a b c d e f g h i j k l m n o p q r s t u v
 w x y z

VALID CHARACTERS FROM iscsym()
0 1 2 3 4 5 6 7 8 9 A B C D E F G H I J K L M N O P Q R S
 T U V W X Y Z _ a b c d e f g h i j k l m n o p q r s t u
 v w x y z
```

String Manipulation

The following functions perform useful functions for string handling (See Chapter 20 on strings for more information).

Function **Description**

strcat() This function 'concatenates' two strings, that is, it joins them together into one string. The effect of:

```
char *new,*this, onto[255];

new = strcat(onto,this);
```

is to join the string 'this' onto the string 'onto'. 'new' is a pointer to the complete string – it is identical to 'onto'. Memory is assumed to have been allocated for the starting strings. The string which is to be copied to must be large enough to accept the new string tagged onto the end. If it is not, then unpredictable effects will result. (In some programs the user might get away without declaring enough space for the 'onto' string, but in general the results will be garbage, or even a crashed machine.)

To join two static strings together, the following code is required:

```
char *s1 = "string one";
char *s2 = "string two";

main ()

{    char buffer[255];

strcat(buffer,s1);
strcat(buffer,s2);

}
```

buffer would then contain 'string onestring two'.

strlen() This function returns a type int value, which gives the length or number of characters in a string, *not* including the NULL byte end-marker. An example is:

```
int len;

char *string;

len = strlen (string);
```

strcpy() This function copies a string from one place to another. Use this function in preference to custom routines. It is set up to handle any peculiarities in the way data is stored. An example is:

```
char *to,*from;

to = strcpy (to,from);
```

Where 'to' is a pointer to the place to which the string is to be copied and 'from' is the place where the string is to be copied from.

strcmp() This function compares two strings and returns a value which indicates how they compared. An example:

```
int value;
char *s1,*s2;

value = strcmp(s1,s2);
```

The value returned is zero, if the two strings are identical. If the strings are not the same, this function indicates the (ASCII) alphabetical order of the two. If s1 > s2, alphabetically, then the value is >0. If s1 < s2, then the value is <0. Note that numbers come before letters in the ASCII code sequence and also that upper case comes before lower case.

There are also variations on the theme of the aforementioned functions which begin with 'strn' instead of 'str'. These enable the programmer to perform the same actions with the first 'n' characters of a string.

strncat() This function 'concatenates' two strings by copying the first n characters of 'this' to the end of the 'onto' string.

```
char *onto,*new,*this;

new = strncat(onto,this,n);
```

strncpy() This function copies the first n characters of a string from one place to another.

```
char *to,*from;
int n;

to = strncpy (to,from,n);
```

strncmp() This function compares the first n characters of two strings

```
int value;
char *s1,*s2;

value = strcmp(s1,s2,n);
```

The following functions perform conversions between strings and floating point/integer types, without needing to use sscanf. They take a pre-initialised string and work out the value represented by that particular string.

atof() ASCII to floating point conversion:

```
double x;
char *stringptr;

x = atof(stringptr);
```

atoi() ASCII to integer conversion:

```
int i;
char *stringptr;

i = atoi(stringptr);
```

atol() ASCII to long integer conversion:

```
long i;
char *stringptr;

i = atol(stringptr);
```

Listing 21.2. String comparison.

```
/*****************************************************/
/*                                                   */
/* String comparison                                 */
/*                                                   */
/*****************************************************/

     #include <stdio.h>

     #define true   1
     #define maxlen 30

/*****************************************************/

     main ()

     { char string1[maxlen],string2[maxlen];
         int result;

     while (true)

         {
         printf ("Type in string 1:\n\n");
         scanf ("%30s",string1);

         printf ("Type in string 2:\n\n");
         scanf ("%30s",string2);

         result = strcmp (string1,string2);

         if (result == 0)
             {
             printf ("Those strings were the same!\n");
             }

         if (result > 0)
             {
             printf ("string1 > string2\n");
             }

         if (result < 0)
             {
             printf ("string1 < string 2\n");
             }
         }
     }
```

Mathematical Functions

C has a library of standard mathematical functions which can be accessed by including the appropriate header files ('math.h' and so on). Note that all of these functions work with 'double' or 'long float' type variables. All of C's mathematical capabilities are written for long variable types. Here is a list of the functions which can be expected in the standard library file. The variables used are *all* to be declared 'long'

```
int i;                     /* long int */

double x,y,result;         /* long float */
```

The functions themselves must be declared long float or double (which might be done automatically in the mathematics library file, or in a separate file) and any constants must be written in floating point form – for instance, write 7.0 instead of just 7.

Function	Description
abs()	Macro returns the unsigned value of the value in brackets. See fabs() for a function version.
fabs()	Find the absolute or unsigned value of the value in brackets:

```
result = fabs(x);
```

Function	Description
ceil()	Find out what the 'ceiling' integer is, that is, the integer which is just above the value in brackets. This is like rounding up:

```
i = ceil(x);          /* ceil (2.2) is 3 */
```

Function	Description
floor()	Find out what the floor integer is, that is, the integer which is just below the floating point value in brackets:

```
i = floor(x);     /* floor(2.2) is 2 */
```

exp() Find the exponential value:

```
result = exp(x);
result = exp(2.7);
```

log() Find the natural (Naperian) logarithm. The value used in the brackets must be unsigned, that is, it must be greater than zero. It does not have to be declared unsigned:

```
result = log(x);
result = log(2.71828);
```

log10() Find the base 10 logarithm. The value used in the brackets must be unsigned, that is, it must be greater than zero. It does not have to be declared specifically as unsigned:

```
result = log10(x);
result = log10(10000);
```

pow() Raise a number to the power. (As x^y in BASIC):

```
result = pow(x,y); /*raise x to the power y */
result = pow(x,2); /*find x-squared */
result = pow(2.0,3.2); /* find 2 to the power
                           3.2 ...*/
```

sqrt() Find the square root of a number:

```
result = sqrt(x);
result = sqrt(2.0);
```

sin() Find the sine of the angle in radians:

```
result = sin(x);
result = sin(3.14);
```

cos() Find the cosine of the angle in radians:

```
result = cos(x);
result = cos(3.14);
```

tan() Find the tangent of the angle in radians:

```
result = tan(x);
result = tan(3.14);
```

asin() Find the arc-sine or inverse sine of the value which must lie between +1.0 and -1.0:

```
result = asin(x);
result = asin(1.0);
```

acos() Find the arc-cosine or inverse cosine of the value which must lie between +1.0 and -1.0:

```
result = acos(x);
result = acos(1.0);
```

atan() Find the arc-tangent or inverse tangent of the value:

```
result = atan(x);
result = atan(200.0);
```

atan2() This is a special inverse tangent function for calculating the inverse tangent of X divided by Y. This function is set up to find this result more accurately than atan():

```
result = atan2(x,y);
result = atan2(x/3.14);
```

sinh() Find the hyperbolic sine of the value, pronounced 'shine' or 'sinch':

```
result = sinh(x);
result = sinh(5.0);
```

cosh() Find the hyperbolic cosine of the value:

```
result = cosh(x);
result = cosh(5.0);
```

tanh() Find the hyperbolic tangent of the value:

```
result = tanh(x);
result = tanh(5.0);
```

Listing 21.3. Maths function demo #2.

```
/*****************************************************/
/*                                                   */
/* Maths functions demo #1                           */
/*                                                   */
/*****************************************************/
     /* use sin(x) to work out an animated model */

      #include <stdio.h>
      #include <math.h>
      #include <limits.h>

      #define true          1
      #define amplitude     30
      #define inc           0.02

      double pi;            /* this may already be defined */
                            /* in the math file */
/*****************************************************/
/* Level 0                                           */
/*****************************************************/

      main ()          /* The simple pendulum program */

      { pi = asin(1.0)*2;     /* if PI is not defined */

      printf ("\nTHE SIMPLE PENDULUM:\n\n\n");

      Pendulum();

      }

/****************************************************/
/* Level 1                                          */
/****************************************************/

      Pendulum ()

      { double x, twopi = pi * 2;
        int i,position;

      while (true)
          {
          for (x = 0; x < twopi; x += inc)
              {
              position = (int)(amplitude * sin(x));

              for (i = -amplitude; i <= amplitude; i++)
                  {
```

```
                if (i == position)
                    {
                    putchar('*');
                    }
                else
                    {
                    putchar(' ');
                    }
                }
            startofline();
            }
        }
    }

/****************************************************/
/* Toolkit                                          */
/****************************************************/

    startofline()
    {
    putchar('\r');
    }
```

Mathematical Errors

Mathematical functions can be delicate animals. Mathematical functions exist which simply *cannot* produce sensible answers in all possible cases. Mathematical functions are not 'user friendly'! One example of an unfriendly function is the inverse sine function, asin(x), which only works for values of X in the range +1.0 to -1.0. The reason for this is a mathematical one – the sine function (of which asin is the opposite) only has values in this range. The statement:

```
y = asin (25.3);
```

is nonsense, and it cannot possibly produce a value for Y, because none exists. Similarly, there is no simple number which is the square root of a negative value, so an expression such as:

```
x = sqrt(-2.0);
```

would also be nonsense. This doesn't stop the programmer from writing these statements though, and it doesn't stop a faulty program from straying out of bounds. What happens then, when an erroneous statement is executed? Some sort of error condition would certainly have to be the result.

In many languages errors are terminal – they cause a program to stop without any option to recover the damage. In C, as the reader might have come to expect, this is not the case. It is possible (in principle) to recover from any error, while still maintaining in total firm control of a program.

Errors like the ones above are called *domain errors* (the set of values which a function can accept is called the domain of the function). There are other errors which can occur too. For example, *division by zero* is illegal, because dividing by zero is 'mathematical nonsense' – it can be done, but the answer can be all the numbers which exist at the same time! Obviously a program can't work with any idea as vague as this. Finally, in addition to these 'pathological' cases, mathematical operations can fail just because the numbers they deal with get too large or small for the computer to handle.

Error Type	**Comment**
Domain error	Illegal value put into function
Division by zero	Dividing by zero is nonsense.
Overflow	Number became too large
Underflow	Number became too small.
Loss of accuracy	No meaningful answer could be calculated

Errors are investigated by calling the function matherr. The mathematical functions, listed above, call this function automatically when an error is detected. The function responds by returning a value which gives information about the error. The exact details will depend upon a given compiler. Here's a hypothetical example to illustrate this – if the error could be recovered from, matherr returns 0, otherwise it returns -1. matherr uses a 'struct' type variable called an 'exception' to diagnose faults in mathematical functions. (See Chapter 26 : Structures and Unions). This can be examined by programs which trap their errors dutifully. Information about this structure must be found in a given compiler manual.

Although it is not possible to generalise, the following remarks about the behaviour of mathematical functions may help to avoid any surprises about their behaviour in error conditions:

1) A function which fails to produce a sensible answer, for any of the reasons mentioned, might simply return zero or it might return the maximum value of the computer. Be careful to check this. (Division by zero and underflow probably return zero, whereas overflow returns the maximum value which the computer can handle.)

2) Some method of signalling errors must clearly be used. This is the exception 'structure' (a special kind of C variable) which gives information about the last error which occurred. Find out what it is and trap errors!

3) Obviously, wherever possible, the programmer shouldn't let errors occur in the first place.

Here is an example for the mathematically-minded. Program 21.4 below performs numerical integration by the simplest possible method of adding up the area under small strips of a graph of the function f(y) = 2*y. The integral is found between the limits zero and five and the exact answer is 25. (See diagram.) The particular compiler used for this program returns the largest number which can be represented by the computer when numbers overflow, although, in this simple case, it is impossible for the numbers to overflow.

Listing 21.4. Numerical estimation of integral.

```
/*******************************************************/
/*                                                     */
/*  Numerical Estimation of Integral                   */
/*                                                     */
/*******************************************************/

      #include <stdio.h>
      #include <math.h>
      #include <limits.h>

      #define limit 5

      double inc = 0.001;  /* Increment width - arbitrary */
      double twopi;
```

```
/**********************************************************/
/** LEVEL 0                                             */
/**********************************************************/

     main ()

     { double y,integrand();
       double integral = 0;

     twopi = 4 * asin(1.0);
     for ( y = inc/2;  y < limit;  y += inc )

          {
          integral += integrand (y) * inc;
          }

     printf ("Integral value = %.10f \n",integral);
     }

/**********************************************************/
/** LEVEL 1                                            **/
/**********************************************************/

     double integrand (y)
     double y;

     { double value;
     value = 2*y;

     if (value > 1e308)

          {
          printf ("Overflow error\n");
          exit (0);
          }

     return (value);
     }
```

More Examples

More examples of the uses of special library functions can be found in the section on programming examples (Chapter 30).

Questions:

1) What type of data is returned from mathematical functions?

2) All calculations are performed using long variables. True or false?

3) What information is returned by strlen()?

4) What action is performed by strcat()?

5) Name five different kinds of error which can occur in a mathematical function.

22 : Hidden Operators

Tidying Up Programs
Writing Smaller Source Files

Many operators in C are more versatile than they appear to be at first glance. None of these operators concerned are new – they have all been described in Chapter 16, but up to now they have been used cautiously. They are:

= ++ -- += -= (and so on)

the assignment, increment and decrement operators. These innocent looking operators can be used in some surprising ways, which make C source code very neat and compact.

The first thing to notice is that ++ and -- are unary operators, that is, they are applied to a single variable and they affect that variable alone. They therefore produce one unique value each time they are used. The assignment operator, on the other hand, has the unusual position of being both unary, in the sense that it works out only one expression, and also binary or dyadic because it sits between two separate objects – an 'lvalue' on the left-hand side and an expression on the right-hand side. Both kinds of operator have one thing in common however – both form statements which have values in their own right. What does this mean? It means that certain kinds of C statements do not have to be thought of as being complete and sealed off from the rest of a program. To paraphrase John Donne: 'In C, no statement is an island'. A statement can be taken as a whole – as a 'black box' – and can be treated as a single value, which can be assigned and compared to things! The value of a statement is the result of the operation which was carried out in the statement.

Increment/decrement operator statements, taken as a whole, have a value which is one greater or one less than the value of the variable which they act upon. So:

```
c = 5;
c++;
```

The second of these statements ('c++;') has the value six, and similarly:

```
c = 5;
c--;
```

The second of these statements ('c--;') has the value four.

Entire assignment statements have values too. A statement such as:

```
c = 5;
```

has the value which is the value of the assignment. So the example above has the value five. This has some important implications.

Extended and Hidden =

The idea that an assignment statement has a value, can be used to make C programs neat and tidy for one simple reason – it means that whole assignment statements can be used in place of a value! For instance, the value 'c = 0;' could be assigned to a variable b:

```
b = (c = 0);
```

or simply:

```
b = c = 0;
```

These equivalent statements set b and c to the value zero, provided b and c are of the same type! It is equivalent to the more usual:

```
b = 0;
c = 0;
```

Indeed, any number of these assignments can be strung together:

```
a = (b = (c = (d = (e = 5))))
```

or simply:

```
a = b = c = d = e = 5;
```

This very neat syntax compresses five lines of code into one line!

There are other uses for the valued assignment statement, of course. It can be used anywhere where a value can be used. For instance:

1) In other assignments

2) As a parameter for functions

3) Inside a comparison (== > < etc.)

4) As an index for arrays

The uses are many-fold. Consider how an assignment statement might be used as a parameter to a function. The next example gets a character from the input file stdin and passes it to a function called 'ProcessCharacter':

```
ProcessCharacter (ch = getchar());
```

This is a perfectly valid statement in C, because the hidden assignment statement passes on the value which it assigns. The actual order of events is that the assignment is carried out first and then the function is called. It would not make sense the other way around, because, that way around, there would be no value to pass as a parameter. So this is a more compact way of writing:

```
ch = getchar();
ProcessCharacter (ch);
```

The two methods are entirely equivalent. If you've any doubt, examine a little more of this imaginary character processing program:

```
ProcessCharacter(ch = getchar());
if (ch == '*')
     {
     printf ("Starry, Starry Night...");
     }
```

The purpose in adding the second statement is to impress the fact that ch has been assigned quite legitimately and it is still defined in the next statement, and the one after, until it is re-assigned by a new assignment statement. The fact that the assignment was hidden inside another statement does not make it any less valid. All the same remarks apply about the specialised assignment operators += *= /= etc.

Listing 22.1. Hidden assignment #1.

```
/*********************************************/
/*                                           */
/* Hidden Assignment #1                      */
/*                                           */
/*********************************************/
      main ()
      {
      do
          {
          switch (ch = getchar())
              {
              default   : putchar(ch);
                          break;
              case 'Q'  : /* Quit */
              }
          }
      while (ch != 'Q');
      }
                  /* end */
```

Listing 22.2. Hidden Assignment #2.

```
/*********************************************/
/*                                           */
/* Hidden Assignment #2                      */
/*                                           */
/*********************************************/
      main ()

      {   double x = 0;

      while ((x += 0.2) < 20.0)
          {
          printf ("%lf",x);
          }
      }
                     /* end */
```

Hidden ++/--

The increment and decrement operators also form statements which have intrinsic values and, like assignment expressions, they can be hidden away in inconspicuous places. These two operators are slightly more complicated than assignments because they exist in two forms – as a postfix and as a prefix:

Postfix	**Prefix**
var++	++var
var--	--var

and these two forms have slightly different meanings. Look at the following example:

```
int i = 3;
PrintNumber (i++);
```

The increment operator is hidden in the parameter list of the function PrintNumber(). This example is not as clear cut as the assignment statement examples however, because the variable 'i' has both a value before the ++ operator acting upon it, and a different value afterwards. The question is then – which value is passed to the function? Is 'i' incremented before or after the function is called? The answer is that this is where the two forms of the operator come into play.

> **If the operator is used as a prefix, the operation is performed** *before* **the function call. If the operator is used as a postfix, the operation is performed after the function call.**

In the example the value three is passed to the function and when the function returns, the value of 'i' is incremented to four. The alternative is to write:

```
int i = 3;
PrintNumber (++i);
```

in which case the value four is passed to the function PrintNumber. The same remarks apply to the decrement operator.

Arrays, Strings and Hidden Operators

Arrays and strings are one area of programming in which the increment and decrement operators are used a lot. Hiding operators inside array subscripts or hiding assignments inside loops can often make light work of tasks such as array initialisation. Consider the following example of a one-dimensional array of integers:

```
#define size   20

int i, array[size];

for (i = 0; i < size; array[i++] = 0)
     {
     }
```

This is a neat way of initialising an array to zero. Notice that the postfixed form of the increment operator is used. This prevents the element array[0] from assigning zero to memory which is out of the bounds of the array. A lucky programmer might get away with the prefixed form without any noticeable damage to a program, but that would be sloppy work, and programmers should worry about such things as this.

Strings, too, can benefit from hidden operators. If the standard library function strlen (which finds the length of a string), were not available, then it would be a simple matter to write the function for simply connected memory (see remarks on arrays, Chapter 19):

```
strlen (string)     /* count the characters in a string */

char *string;

{    char *ptr;
     int count = 0;

for (ptr = string; *(ptr++) != NULL; count++)
     {
     }
return (count);
}
```

NULL is a macro which has the value zero. This function increments count while the end of string marker is not found.

Listing 22.3. Hidden operators demo #1.

```
/*******************************************************/
/*                                                     */
/* Hidden Operator Demo #1                             */
/*                                                     */
/*******************************************************/
   /* Any assignment or increment operator has a value */
   /* which can be handed straight to printf() ...     */
   /* Also compare the prefix / postfix forms of ++/-- */

     #include <stdio.h>

/*******************************************************/

     main ()

     {    int a,b,c,d,e;

     a = (b = (c = (d = (e = 0))));
     printf ("%d %d %d %d %d\n", a, b++, c--, d = 10, e += 3);

     a = b = c = d = e = 0;
     printf ("%d %d %d %d %d\n", a, ++b, --c, d = 10, e += 3);
     }
                         /* end */
```

Listing 22.4. Hidden operator demo #2.

```
/*****************************************************/
/*                                                   */
/* Hidden Operator demo #2                           */
/*                                                   */
/*****************************************************/

     #include <stdio.h>

/*****************************************************/

     main ()                       /* prints out zero! */

     {
     printf ("%d",Value());
     }

/*****************************************************/

     Value()                       /* Check for zero .... */
```

```
{ int value;
if ((value = GetValue()) == 0)

     {
     printf ("Value was zero\n");
     }

return (value);
}

/****************************************************/

GetValue()          /* Some function to get a value */

{
return (0);
}
                     /* end */
```

Cautions about Style

Hiding operators away inside other statements can certainly make programs look very elegant and compact, but, as with all neat tricks, it can make programs harder to understand. Never forget that programming is about communication to other programmers, so be kind to the potential reader of your program! (It could be you in years to come!) Statements such as:

```
if ((i = (int)ch++) <= --comparison)

     {
     }
```

are not recommended programming style and they are no more efficient than the more long-winded:

```
ch++;
i = (int)ch;

if (i <= comparison)
     {
     }

comparison--;
```

There is always a happy medium in which to settle on a readable version of the code. The statement above might perhaps be written as:

```
        i = (int) ch++;

        if (i <= --comparison)
             {
             }
```

Listing 22.5. Arrays and hidden operators.

```
/**************************************************/
/*                                                */
/* Arrays and Hidden Operators                    */
/*                                                */
/**************************************************/

        #include <stdio.h>

        #define size 10

/**************************************************/
/* Level 0                                        */
/**************************************************/

        main ()   /* Demo prefix & postfix ++ in arrays */

        {    int i, array[size];

        Initialise(array);
        i = 4;
        array[i++] = 8;
        Print (array);

        Initialise(array);
        i = 4;
        array[++i] = 8;
        Print(array);
        }

/**************************************************/
/* Level 1                                        */
/**************************************************/

        Initialise (array)               /* set to zero */
        int array[size];
        {    int i;

        for (i = 0; i < size; array[i++] = 0)
```

```
        {
        }
    }
/*****************************************************/

    Print (array)                          /* to stdout */

    int array[size];
    {   int i = 0;

    while (i < size)

        {
        printf ("%2d",array[i++]);
        }

    putchar ('\n');
    }
                        /* end */
```

Listing 22.6. Hidden operator.

```
/****************************************************/
/*                                                  */
/* Hidden Operator                                  */
/*                                                  */
/****************************************************/

    #include <stdio.h>

    #define maxno  20

/*****************************************************/

    main ()                    /* Print out 5 x table */

    { int i, ctr = 0;

    for (i = 1; ++ctr <= maxno; i = ctr*5)

        {
        printf ("%3d",i);
        }
    }
```

Questions:

1) Which operators can be hidden inside other statements?

2) Give a reason why you would not want to do this in every possible case.

3) Hidden operators can be used in return statements. For example:

```
return (++x);
```

Would there be any point in writing:

```
return (x++);;
```

23 : Advanced Data Types

Special Constants
More Types
User Defined Data Types

This section is about the remaining data types which C has to offer programmers. These extra data types are for more advanced uses of the language. They are called:

FILE	The type which files are classified under
enum	Enumerated type for abstract data
void	The 'empty' type
volatile	New ANSI standard type for memory mapped I/O
const	New ANSI standard type for fixed data
struct	Groups of variables under a single name
union	Multi-purpose storage areas

Special Constant Expressions

Constant expressions are often used without any thought, until a programmer needs to know how to do something special with them. It is worth making a brief remark about some special ways of writing integer constants, for the latter half of this book.

Up to now the distinction between long and short integer types has largely been ignored. Constant values can be declared explicitly as long values, in fact, by placing the letter L after the constant.

```
long int variable = 23L;
variable = 236526598L;
```

Advanced programmers writing systems software often find it convenient to work with hexadecimal or octal numbers as these number bases have a special relationship to binary. A constant in one of these types is declared by placing either '0' (zero) or '0x' in front of the appropriate value. If ddd is a value, then:

Octal number Oddd
Hexadecimal number Oxddd

For example:

```
oct_value = 077;            /* 77 octal */
hex_value = 0xFFEF;         /* FFEF hex */
```

This kind of notation has already been applied to strings and single character constants with the backslash notation, instead of the leading '0' (zero) character:

```
ch = '\ddd';
ch = '\xdd';
```

The values of character constants can't be any greater than 255.

FILE

In previous chapters, the files stdin, stdout and stderr alone have been used in programs. These special files are always handled implicitly by functions like printf() and scanf() – the programmer never gets to know that they are, in fact, files. Programs do not have to use these functions however – standard input/output files can be treated explicitly by general file handling functions just as well. Files are distinguished by filenames and by file pointers. File pointers are variables which pass the location of files to file handling functions; being variables, they have to be declared as being some data type. That type is called FILE and file pointers have to be declared 'pointer to FILE'. For example:

```
FILE *fp;
FILE *fp = stdin;
FILE *fopen();
```

File handling functions which return file pointers must also be declared as pointers to files. Notice that, in contrast to all the other reserved words, FILE is written in upper case. This is because FILE is not a simple data, type such as char or int, but a 'structure' which is only defined by the input/output file 'stdio.h' and so, strictly speaking, it is not a reserved word itself. See chapter 24 for comprehensive information about files.

enum

Abstract data are usually the realm of exclusively high-level languages such as Pascal. 'enum' is a way of incorporating limited 'high-level' data facilities into C.

enum is short for enumerated data. The user defines a type of data which is made up of a fixed set of *words,* instead of numbers or characters. These words are given substitute integer numbers by the compiler which are used to identify and compare 'enum' type data. For example:

```
enum countries

     {
     England,
     Scotland,
     Wales,
     Eire,
     Norge,
     Sverige,
     Danmark,
     Deutschland
     };

main ()

{ enum countries variable;
variable = England;
}
```

Why go to all this trouble? The point about enumerated data is that it they allow the programmer to forget about any numbers which the computer might need in order to deal with a list of words, like the previous example, and simply concentrate on the logic of using them. Enumerated data are called 'abstract' because the low-level number form of the words is removed from the users attention. In fact, enumerated data are made up of integer constants, which the compiler generates itself. For this reason, they have a natural partner in programs – the switch statement. Here is an example, which uses the countries listed in the program to make a kind of airport 'help computer' in age of electronic passports!

Listing 23.1. Enumerated data.

```
/**********************************************************/
/*                                                        */
/* Enumerated Data                                        */
/*                                                        */
/**********************************************************/

        #include <stdio.h>

        enum countries

             {
             England,
             Ireland,
             Scotland,
             Wales,
             Danmark,
             Island,
             Norge,
             Sverige
             };

/**********************************************************/

        main ()          /* Electronic Passport Program */

        {    enum countries birthplace, getinfo();

        printf ("Insert electronic passport\n");
        birthplace = getinfo();

        switch (birthplace)
             {
             case England : printf("Welcome home!\n");
                                break;
             case Danmark :
             case Norge   : printf("Velkommen til England\n");
                                break;
             }
        }

/**********************************************************/

        enum countries getinfo() /* interrogate passport */
```

```
            {
            return (England);
            }
                        /* end */
```

'enum' makes words into constant integer values for a programmer. Data which are declared enum, is not the kind of data which it makes sense to do arithmetic with (even integer arithmetic), so in most cases it should not be necessary to know or even care about what numbers the compiler gives to the words in the list. However, some compilers allow the programmer to force particular values on words. The compiler then tries to give the values successive integer numbers unless the programmer states otherwise. For instance:

```
enum planets

     {
     Mercury,
     Venus,
     Earth = 12,
     Mars,
     Jupiter,
     Saturn,
     Uranus,
     Neptune,
     Pluto
     };
```

This would probably yield values Mercury = 0, Venus = 1, Earth = 12, Mars = 13, Jupiter = 14 ... etc.

If the user tries to force a value which the compiler has already used then the compiler will complain.

The following example program listing shows two points:

1) enum types can be local or global

2) The words can be forced to have certain values

Listing 23.2. Enumerated data.

```
/**********************************************************/
/*                                                        */
/* Enumerated Data                                        */
/*                                                        */
/**********************************************************/
      /* The smallest adventure game in the world */

     #include <stdio.h>
     #define true  1
     #define false 0

     enum treasures                   /* Adventure Treasures */

          {
          rubies,
          sapphires,
          gold,
          silver,
          mask,
          scroll,
          lamp
          };

/**********************************************************/
/* Level 0                                                */
/**********************************************************/

     main ()                          /* Tiny Adventure! */

     {    enum treasures object = gold;

     if (getobject(object))

          {
          printf ("Congratulations you've found the gold!\n");
          }
     else

          {
          printf ("Too bad you just missed your big-chance");
          }
     }

/**********************************************************/
/* Level 1                                                */
/**********************************************************/

     getobject (ob)                             /* yes or no ? */
```

```
enum treasures ob;

{    enum answer
          {
          no = false,
          yes = true
          };

if (ob == gold)
     {
     printf ("Pick up object? Y/N\n");
     switch (getchar())

          {
          case 'y' :
          case 'Y' : return ((int) yes);
          default  : return ((int) no);
          }
     }
else
     {
     printf ("You grapple with the dirt\n");
     return (false);
     }
}
                         /* end */
```

Suggested uses for enum

Here are some suggested uses for enum:

```
enum numbers
     {
     zero,
     one,
     two,
     three
     };

enum animals
     {
     cat,
     dog,
     cow,
     sheep,
     };
```

```
enum plants
     {
     grass,
     roses,
     cabbages,
     oaktree
     };

enum diseases
     {
     heart,
     skin,
     malnutrition,
     circulatory
     };

enum quarks
     {
     up,
     down,
     charmed,
     strange,
     top,
     bottom,
     truth,
     beauty
     }
```

Other uses could include types of car, colours, names of roads or train numbers.

void

Void is a peculiar data type which has some debatable uses. A variable or function can be declared void in the following ways:

```
void function();
void variable;
void *ptr;

(void) returnvalue();
```

The following points can be made about void:

1) A variable which is declared void is useless – it cannot be used in an expression and it cannot be assigned to a value

2) A function which is declared void has no return value and returns simply with:

```
return ();
```

3) A function can be cast (void) in order to explicitly discard a return value (though this is done by the compiler anyway). For instance, scanf() returns the number of items it matches in the control string, but this is usually discarded:

```
scanf ("%c",&ch);
```

or:

```
(void) scanf("%c",&ch);
```

4) A void pointer can point to to any kind of object. This means that any pointer can be assigned to a void pointer, regardless of its type. This is always possible using the cast operator anyway.

volatile

This is a type which has been proposed in the ANSI standard of C. The idea behind this type is to allow memory-mapped input/output to be held in C variables. Variables which are declared volatile will be able to have their values altered in ways which a program does not explicitly define, that is, by external influences such as clocks, external ports, hardware, interrupts and so on. This type will be useful for optimising compilers which copy the values of local variables into register storage and use the copied values for reference. The keyword volatile will force such compilers to read the variable itself, each time its value is required.

const

The reserved word const is used to declare data which can only be assigned once, either because they are in ROM (for example) or because they are data whose values must not be corrupted. Types declared const must be assigned when they are first initialised and they exist as stored values only at compile time:

```
const double pi = 3.14;
const int one = 1;
```

Since a constant array only exists at compile time, it can be initialised by the compiler.

```
const int array[] =
      {
      1,
      2,
      3,
      4
      };
```

Array[0] then has the value one, array[1] has the value two and so on. Any attempt to assign values to const types, will result in various compilation errors.

It is worth comparing the const declaration to enumerated data, as they are connected in a very simple way. The following two sets of statements are the same:

```
enum numbers

      {
      zero,
      one,
      two,
      three,
      four
      };
```

and:

```
const zero = 0;
const one = 1;
const two = 2;
const three = 3;
const four = 4;
```

Constant types and enumerated data are therefore just different aspects of the same thing. Enumerated data provide a convenient way of classifying constants while the compiler keeps track of the values and types. The programmer personally has to keep track of constant values.

struct

Structures are called records in Pascal and many other languages. They are packages of variables which are all wrapped up under a single name. Structures are described in detail in Chapter 26.

union

Unions are often grouped together with structures, but they are quite unlike them in almost all respects. They are like general purpose storage containers, which can hold a variety of different variable types, at different times. The compiler makes a container which is large enough to take any of these. Unions are described in detail in Chapter 26.

typedef

C allows programmers to define their own data types or to re-name existing ones by using a compiler 'directive' called typedef. This statement is used as follows:

```
typedef type newtypename;
```

So, for example, a program could define a type called 'byte', which was exactly one byte in size by redefining the word 'char':

```
typedef char byte;
```

The compiler type checking facilities then treat byte as a new type which can be used to declare variables:

```
byte variable, function();
```

The typedef statement may be written inside functions or in the global white space of a program.

```
/**************************************************/
/* Program                                        */
/**************************************************/

      typedef int newname1;

      main ()

      {
      typedef char newname2;
      }
```

This program will compile and run, but won't do anything useful!

It is not very often that a programmer wishes to re-name existing types. The most important use for typedef is in conjunction with structures and unions. Structures and unions can, by their very definition, be all kinds of shape and size and so their names can become long and tedious to declare. Typedef makes dealing with these simple, because it means that the user can define a structure or union with a simple typename. See Chapter 26 about structures and unions.

Questions:

1) Is FILE a reserved word? If so why is it in upper case?

2) Write a statement which declares a file pointer called fp.

3) Enumerated data are given values by the compiler so that it can do arithmetic with them. True or false?

4) Does 'void' do anything which C cannot already do without this type?

5) What type might a timer device be declared if it were to be called by a variable name?

6) Write a statement which declares a new type 'real' to be like the usual type 'double'.

7) Variables declared 'const' can be of any type. True or false?

24 : Low-level Operations

Bits and Bytes
Flags/Messages
Shifting

This section is advanced. First time readers may wish to omit it until they are more acquainted with C.

Down in the depths of a computer, below even the operating system are 'bits' of memory. Bits (or binary digits) are the lowest level software objects in a computer – there is nothing more primitive. For precisely this reason, it is extremely rare for high-level languages to even acknowledge the existence of bits, let alone manipulate them. Manipulating bit patterns is usually the preserve of assembly language programmers. C, however, is quite different from most other high level-languages in that it allows a programmer full access to bits and even provides high-level operators for manipulating them.

As this book is an introductory text, bit operations will be dealt with superficially. Many of the facilities which are available for bit operations need not concern the majority of programs. This chapter concerns the main uses of bit operations for high-level programs and it assumes a certain amount of knowledge about programming at the low-level. Inexperienced programmers may wish to consult a book on assembly language programming to learn about low-level memory operations, in more detail.

Bit Patterns

All computer data, of any type, are bit patterns. The only difference between a string and a floating point variable is the way in which human beings choose to interpret the patterns of bits in a computer's memory. For the most part, it is quite unnecessary to think of computer data as bit patterns. Systems programmers, on the other hand, frequently find that they need to handle bits directly in order to make efficient use of memory when using 'flags'. A flag is a message which is either one thing or the other. In system terms, the flag is said to be 'on' or 'off' or alternatively 'set' or 'cleared'. The usual place to find flags is in a status register of a CPU (central processing unit) or in a pseudo-register (this is a status register for an imaginary processor, which is held in memory). A status register is a group of bits (a byte perhaps) in which each bit signifies something special. In an ordinary byte of data, bits are grouped together and are interpreted to have a collective meaning, but in a status register they are thought of as being independent. Programmers are interested to know about the contents of bits in these registers, perhaps to find out what happened in a program after some special operation is carried out. Other uses for bit patterns are listed below here:

1) Messages sent between devices in a complex operating environment use bits for efficiency

2) Serially transmitted data

3) Handling 'bit planes' in screen memory (raster ports).

4) Performing fast arithmetic in simple cases

Programmers who are interested in performing bit operations often work in hexadecimal because every hexadecimal digit conveniently handles four bits in one go (16 is two to the power four). See Chapter 23 for details about hexadecimal constants.

Flags, Registers and Messages

A register is a place inside a computer processor chip, where data are worked upon in some way.

A status register is a register which is used to return information to a programmer about the operations which took place in other registers. Status registers contain flags which give yes or no answers to questions concerning the other registers.

In advanced programming, there may be call for 'pseudo-registers' in addition to 'real' ones. A pseudo-register is merely a register which is created by the programmer in computer memory (it does not exist inside a processor).

Messages are just like pseudo status registers – they are collections of flags which signal special information between different devices and/or different programs in a computer system. Messages do not necessarily have fixed locations, they may be passed a parameters. Messages are an excellentand compact way of passing information to low-level functions in a program.

Flags, registers, pseudo-registers and messages are all treated as bit patterns. A program which makes use of them must therefore be able to assign these objects to C variables for use. A bit pattern would normally be declared as a character or some kind of integer type in C, perhaps with the aid of a typedef statement.

```
typedef char byte;

typedef int bitpattern;

bitpattern variable;

byte message;
```

The flags or bits in a register/message have the values one or zero, depending upon whether they are 'on' or 'off' ('set' or 'cleared'). A program can test for this by using combinations of the operators which C provides.

Bit Operators and Assignments

C provides the following operators for handling bit patterns:

Operator	Description
<<	Bit shift left (a specified number or bit positions)
>>	Bit shift right (a specified number of bit positions)
|	Bitwise Inclusive OR
^	Bitwise Exclusive OR
&	Bitwise AND
~	Bitwise one's complement

Operator	Description
&=	AND assign (variable = variable & value)
|=	Exclusive OR assign (variable = variable | value)
^=	Inclusive OR assign (variable = variable ^ value)
>>=	Shift right assign (variable = variable >> value)
<<=	Shift left assign (variable = variable << value)

The meaning and the syntax of these operators is given next.

The Meaning of Bit Operators

Bitwise operations are not to be confused with logical operations (&& || (AND, OR) and so on) A bit pattern is made up of zeros and ones and bitwise operators operate individually upon each bit in the operand. Every zero or one undergoes the operations individually.

Bitwise operators (AND, OR) can be used in place of logical operators (&& ||) but they are less efficient, because logical operators are designed to reduce the number of comparisons made in an expression, to the optimum. As soon as the truth or fallacy of an expression is known, a logical comparison operator quits. A bitwise operator would continue operating to the last before the final result were known.

Below is a brief summary of the operations which are performed by the above operators on the bits of their operands.

Shift Operations

Imagine a bit pattern as being represented by the following group of boxes. Every box represents a bit and the numbers inside represent their values. The values written over the top are the common integer values which the whole group of bits would have, if they were interpreted collectively as an integer.

```
128  64  32  16  8   4   2   1
--------------------------------
| 0 | 0 | 0 | 0 | 0 | 0 | 0 | 1 |   = 1
--------------------------------
```

Shift operators move whole bit patterns left or right by shunting them between boxes. The syntax of this operation is:

```
value << number of positions
value >> number of positions
```

So for example, using the boxed value (1) just mentioned:

```
1 << 1
```

would have the value two, because the bit pattern would have been moved one place the the left:

```
128  64  32  16  8   4   2   1
---------------------------------
| 0 | 0 | 0 | 0 | 0| 0 | 1 | 0 |   = 2
---------------------------------
```

Similarly:

```
1 << 4
```

has the value 16 because the original bit pattern is moved by four places:

```
128  64  32  16  8   4   2   1
---------------------------------
| 0 | 0 | 0 | 1 | 0 | 0 | 0 | 0 |   = 16
---------------------------------
```

and:

```
6 << 2 == 12:

128  64  32  16  8   4   2   1
---------------------------------
| 0 | 0 | 0 | 0 | 0 | 1 | 1 | 0 |   = 6
---------------------------------
```

Shift left two places:

```
128  64  32  16  8   4   2   1
---------------------------------
| 0 | 0 | 0 | 0 | 1 | 1 | 0 | 0 |   = 12
---------------------------------
```

Notice that every shift left multiplies by two and that every shift right would divide by two, integerwise. If a bit reaches the edge of the group of boxes then it falls out and is lost forever. So:

```
1 >> 1 == 0
2 >> 1 == 1
2 >> 2 == 0
n >> n == 0
```

A common use of shifting is to scan through the bits of a bit pattern one by one in a loop. This is done by using 'masks'.

Truth Tables and Masking

The operations AND, OR (inclusive OR) and XOR/EOR (exclusive OR) perform comparisons or 'masking' operations between two bits. They are binary, or dyadic, operators. Another operation called *complement* is a unary operator. The operations performed by these bit wise operators are best summarised by 'truth tables'. Truth tables indicate what the results of all possible operations are between two single bits. The same operation is then carried out for all the bits in the variables which are operated upon.

Complement (~)

This operator works on a single value

The complement of a number is the 'logical opposite' of the number. C provides a 'one's complement' operator which simply changes all ones into zeros and vice versa.

~1 has the value 0 (for each bit)
~0 has the value 1

As a 'truth table' this would be summarised as follows:

~value	==	result
0		1
1		0

AND (&):

This works between two values, eg, one and zero:

value 1	&	value 2	==	result
0		0		0
0		1		0
1		0		0
1		1		1

Both value one AND value two have to be one in order for the result to be one.

OR (|):

This works between two values, eg, one | zero:

value 1	|	value 2	==	result
0		0		0
0		1		1
1		0		1
1		1		1

The result is one if one OR the other OR both of the values is one.

XOR/EOR (^):

Operates on two values, eg, one ^ zero:

value 1	^	value 2	==	result
0		0		0
0		1		1
1		0		1
1		1		0

The result is one if one OR the other (but not both) of the values is one.

An extremely common use for logic operators is to make masks. A mask is thought of as a thing which fits over a bit pattern and modifies the result, usually to cover up part of a bit pattern. This is particularly pertinent for handling flags, where a programmer wishes to know if one particular flag is set or not set and does not care about the values of the others. This is done by deliberately inventing a value which only allows the particular flag of interest to have a non-zero value, and then ANDing that value with the flag register. For example, in *symbolic language*:

```
MASK = 00000001

VALUE1 = 10011011
VALUE2 = 10011100

MASK & VALUE1 == 00000001
MASK & VALUE2 == 00000000
```

The zeros in the mask 'mask off' the first seven bits and leave only the last one to reveal its true value. Alternatively, masks can be built up by specifying several flags:

```
FLAG1 = 00000001
FLAG2 = 00000010
FLAG3 = 00000100

MESSAGE = FLAG1 | FLAG2 | FLAG3

MESSAGE == 00000111
```

It should be emphasised that these expressions are only written in symbolic language. It is not possible to use binary values in C. The programmer must convert to hexadecimal, octal or denary first (see the appendices for conversion tables).

A simple example helps to show how logical masks and shift operations can be combined. The first program gets a denary number from the user and converts it into binary. The second program gets a value from the user in binary and converts it into hexadecimal.

Listing 24.1. Bit manipulation #1.

```
/**********************************************/
/*                                            */
/* Bit Manipulation #1                        */
/*                                            */
/**********************************************/
        /* Convert denary numbers into binary */
        /* Keep shifting i by one to the left */
        /* and test the highest bit. This does*/
        /* NOT preserve the value of i        */

        #include <stdio.h>

        #define numberofbits  8

/***********************************************/

        main ()
        {    short i,j,bit,;
             short MASK = 0x80;

        printf ("Enter any number less than 128: ");
        scanf ("%h", &i);

        if (i > 128)
             {
             printf ("Too big\n");
             return (0);
             }

        printf ("Binary value = ");

        for (j = 0; j < numberofbits; j++)
             {
             bit = i & MASK;
             printf ("%1d",bit/MASK);
             i <<= 1;
             }

        printf ("\n");
        }
                          /* end */
```

Example Output

```
Enter any number less than 128: 56
Binary value = 00111000

Enter any value less than 128: 3
Binary value = 00000011
```

Listing 24.2. Bit manipulation #2.

```
/***********************************************/
/*                                             */
/* Bit Manipulation #2                         */
/*                                             */
/***********************************************/
      /* Convert binary numbers into hex       */

      #include <stdio.h>

      #define numberofbits 8

/***********************************************/

      main ()

      {   short j,hex = 0;
          short MASK;
          char binary[numberofbits];

      printf ("Enter an 8-bit binary number: ");

      for (j = 0; j < numberofbits; j++)
          {
          binary[j] = getchar();
          }

      for (j = 0; j < numberofbits; j++)
          {
          hex <<= 1;

          switch (binary[j])
              {
              case '1' : MASK = 1;
                         break;
              case '0' : MASK = 0;
                         break;
              default  : printf("Not binary\n");
```

```
                        return(0);
                }
        hex |= MASK;
        }

    printf ("Hex value = %lx\n",hex);
    }
                                /* end */
```

Example Output

```
Enter any number less than 128: 56
Binary value = 00111000

Enter any value less than 128: 3
Binary value = 00000011
```

Questions:

1) What distinguishes a bit pattern from an ordinary variable? Can any variable be a bit pattern?

2) What is the difference between an inclusive OR operation and an exclusive OR operation?

3) If you saw the following function call in a program, could you guess what its parameter was?

```
OpenWindow (BORDER | GADGETS | MOUSECONTROL | SIZING);
```

4) Find out what the denary (decimal) values of the following operations are:

a) 7 & 2
b) 1 & 1
c) 15 & 3
d) 15 & 7
e) 15 & 7 & 3

Try to explain the results. (Hint: draw out the numbers as binary patterns, using the program listed.)

5) Find out what the denary (decimal) values of the following operations are:

a) 1 | 2
b) 1 | 2 | 3

6) Find out the values of:

a) 1 & (~1)
b) 23 & (~23)
c) 2012 & (~2012)

(Hint: write a short program to work them out. Use 'short' type variables for all the numbers.)

25 : Files and Devices

Advanced Input/Output
Writing to a Printer

Files are places for reading data from or writing data to. This includes disc files and it includes 'pseudo devices' such as the printer or the monitor of a computer. All information which enters or leaves a C program has to do so by means of a file. Most commonly, these files are stdin and stdout (see Chapter 15) but more sophisticated programs need to be able to read or write to files which are found on a disc or to the printer and so on.

An operating system allows a program to see files in 'the outside world' by providing a number of 'portals' ('inlets and outlets') to work through. In order to examine the contents of a file or to write information to a file, a program has to 'open' one of these portals. The reason for this slightly indirect method of working is that these 'portals' hide the irrelevant details of filing from the programmer. A program which writes information does no more than pass that information to one of these portals and the operating system's file-manager does the rest. A program which reads data, simply reads values from its file 'portal' and does not have to worry about how they got there. This is extremely simple to work in practice.

In order to use a file, a program has to go through the three steps of the following routine:

1) Open a file for reading or writing. (Reserve a portal and locate the file on disc or whatever.)

2) Read or write to the file using file handling functions provided by the standard library.

3) Close the file to free the operating system 'portal' for use by another program or file.

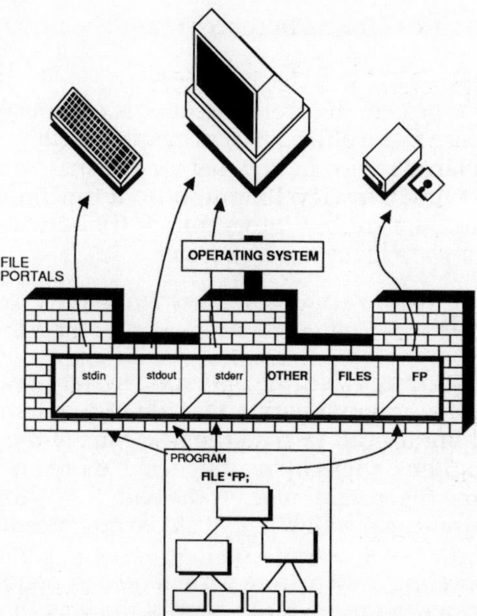

Figure 25.1. Files to and from a program.

A program opens a file by calling a standard library function and is returned a file pointer, by the operating system, which allows a program to address that particular file and to distinguish it from all the others.

Files Generally

C provides two levels of file handling, high-level and low-level. High-level files are all treated as text files. In fact, the data which go into the files are exactly what would be seen on the screen, character by character, except that they are stored in a file instead. This is true whether a file is meant to store characters, integers, floating point types or whatever. Any file, which is written to by high-level file handling functions, ends up as a text file which could be edited by a text editor.

High-level text files are also read back as character files, in the same way that input is acquired from the keyboard. All this means that high-level file functions are identical in concept to keyboard/screen input/output.

The alternative to these high-level functions, is obviously low-level functions. These are more efficient, in principle, at filing data, as they can store data in large lumps in raw memory format, without converting to text first. Low-level input/output functions have the disadvantage that they are less 'programmer friendly' than the high-level ones, but they are likely to work faster.

File Positions

When data are read from a file, the operating system keeps track of the current position of a program within that file so that it only needs to make a standard library call to 'read the next part of the file'. The operating system then obliges by reading some more and advancing its position within the file, until it reaches the end. Each single character which is read causes the position in a file to be advanced by one.

Although the operating system does a great deal of hand holding as regards file positions, a program can control the way in which that position changes using functions such as ungetc if need be. In most cases it is not necessary and it should be avoided, since complex movements within a file can cause complex movements of the disc drive mechanism, which in turn can lead to wear and tear of discs and the occurrence of errors.

High-level File Handling Functions

Most of the high-level input/output functions which deal with files are easily recognisable in that they start with the letter 'f'. Some of these functions will appear strikingly familiar. For instance:

fprintf()
fscanf()
fgets()
fputs()

These are all 'file versions' of the standard input/output library. They work with generalised files, as opposed to the specific files, stdin and stdout, which printf and scanf use. The file versions differ only in that they need an extra piece of information – the file pointer to a particular portal. This is passed as an extra parameter to the functions. They process data in an identical way to their standard input/output counterparts.

Other filing functions will not look so familiar. For example:

fopen()
fclose()
getc()
ungetc();
putc()
fgetc()
fputc()
feof()

Before any work can be done with high-level files, these functions need to be explained in some detail.

Opening Files

A file is opened by a call to the library function, fopen(). This is available automatically when the library file 'stdio.h' is included. There are two stages to opening a file. First, a file 'portal' must be found so that a program can access information from a file at all. Second, the file must be physically located on a disc or as a device or whatever. The fopen() function performs both of these services and if the file it attempts to open does not exist, that file is created anew. The syntax of the fopen() function is:

```
FILE *returnpointer;
returnpointer = fopen("filename","mode");
```

or:

```
FILE returnpointer;
char *fname, *mode;

returnpointer = fopen(fname,mode);
```

The filename is a string which provides the name of the file to be opened. Filenames are *system dependent*, so the details should be found in your operating system manual. The operation mode is also a string, chosen from one of the following:

"r"	Open file for reading
"w"	Open file for writing
"a"	Open file for appending
"rw"	Open file for reading and writing (some systems)

This mode string specifies the way in which the file will be used. Finally, returnpointer is a pointer to a FILE structure – which is the whole object of calling this function. If the file (which was named) opens successfully when fopen() is called, returnpointer is a pointer to the file portal. If the file could not be opened, this pointer is set to the value NULL. This should be tested for, because it doesn't make sense to attempt to write to a file which could not be opened or created, for whatever reason.

A 'read only' file might be opened, for example, with some program code such as:

```
FILE *fp;

if ((fp = fopen ("filename","r")) == NULL)

      {
      printf ("File could not be opened\n");
      error_handler();
      }
```

A question which springs to mind is: what happens if the user has to type in the name of a file while the program is running? The solution to this problem is quite simple. Recall the function filename() which we came accross in Chapter 21:

```
/***************************************************************/

      char *filename()                      /* return  filename */

      {    static char *filenm = ".........................";

      do
           {
           printf ("Enter filename :");
           scanf ("%24s",filenm);
```

```
        skipgarb();
        }
    while (strlen(filenm) == 0);

    return (filenm);
    }

/**********************************************************/
```

This function makes file opening simple. The programmer would now write something like:

```
    FILE *fp;
    char *filename();

    if ((fp = fopen (filename(),"r")) == NULL)
        {
        printf ("File could not be opened\n");
        error_handler();
        }
```

and the user would automatically be prompted for a filename.

When a file has been opened, it can be read from or written to using the other library functions, such as fprintf and fscanf, and finally the file has to be closed again.

Closing a File

A file is closed by calling the function fclose. The syntax for fclose is as follows:

```
    int returncode;
    FILE *fp;

    returncode = fclose (fp);
```

fp is a pointer to the file which is to be closed and returncode is an integer value which is zero if the file was closed successfully. fclose prompts the file manager to finish off its dealings with the named file and to close the portal which the operating system reserved for it.

When closing a file, a program needs to do something like the following:

```
if (fclose(fp) != 0)

     {
     printf ("File did not exist.\n");
     error_handler();
     }
```

fprintf

This is the highest level function which writes to files. Its name is meant to signify 'file-print-formatted' and it is almost identical to its stdout counterpart, printf. The form of the fprintf statement is as follows:

```
fprintf (fp,"string",variables);
```

where fp is a file pointer, string is a control string (which is to be formatted), and the variables are those which are to be substituted into the blank fields of the format string. For example, assume that there is an open file, pointed to by fp:

```
int i = 12;
float x = 2.356;
char ch = 's';
fprintf (fp, "%d %f %c", i, x, ch);
```

The conversion specifiers are identical to those for printf. In fact fprintf is related to printf in a very simple way: the following two statements are identical:

```
printf ("Hello world %d", 1);
fprintf (stdout,"Hello world %d", 1);
```

fscanf

The analogue of scanf is fscanf and, as with fprintf, this function differs from its standard I/O counterpart only in one extra parameter – a file pointer. The form of an fscanf statement is:

```
FILE *fp;
int n;
n = fscanf (fp,"string",pointers);
```

where n is the number of items matched in the control string and fp is a pointer to the file which is to be read from. For example, assuming that fp is a pointer to an open 'read' file:

```
int i = 10;
float x = -2.356;
char ch = 'x';
fscanf (fp, "%d %f %c", &i, &x, &ch);
```

The remarks which were made about scanf also apply to this function – fscanf is a 'dangerous' function in that it can easily get out of step with the input data, unless the input is properly formatted.

skipfilegarb ?

Do programs need a function such as skipgarb to deal with instances of badly formatted input data?

A program can assume a bit more about files which are read into a program from disc file than it can assume about the user's typed input. A disc file will presumably have been produced by the same program which generated it, or will be in a format which the program expects. Is a function like skipgarb necessary then? The answer is, probably not. This does not mean to say that a program does not need to check for 'bad files', or files which do not contain the data they are alleged to contain. On the other hand, a programmer is at liberty to assume that any file which does not contain correctly formatted data is just nonsense – he or she does not have to try to make sense of it with a function like skipgarb, the program could simply return an error message like 'BAD FILE' or whatever, and recover in a sensible way. It would probably not make sense to use a function like skipgarb for files.

For comparison alone, skipfilegarb is written as follows:

```
skipfilegarb(fp)

FILE *fp;

{
while (getc(fp) != '\n')
      {
      }
}
```

Single Character I/O

There are commonly four functions/macros which perform single character input/output to or from files. They are analogous to the functions/macros:

getchar and putchar

for the standard I/O files, and they are called:

getc
ungetc
putc
fgetc
fputc

getc/fgetc

The difference between getc and fgetc will depend upon a particular system. It might be that getc is implemented as a macro, whereas fgetc is implemented as a function or vice versa. One of these alternatives may not be present at all in a library. Check the manual, to be sure! Both getc and fgetc fetch a single character from a file:

```
FILE *fp;
char ch;

/* open file */

ch = getc (fp);
ch = fgetc (fp);
```

These functions return a character from the specified file if they operated successfully, otherwise they return EOF to indicate the end of a file or some other error. Apart from this, these functions/macros are quite unremarkable.

ungetc

ungetc is a function which 'un-gets' a character from a file. That is, it reverses the effect of the last 'get' operation. This is not like writing to a file, but it is like stepping back one position within the file. The purpose of this function is to leave the input in the correct place for other functions in a program when other functions go too far in a file. An example of this would be a program which looks for a word in a text file and processes that word in some way.

```
while (getc(fp) != ' ')
     {
     }
```

The program would skip over spaces until it found a character and then it would know that this was the start of a word. However, having used getc to read the first character of that word, the position in the file would be the second character in the word! This means that if another function wanted to read that word from the beginning, the position in the file would not be correct, because the first character would already have been read. The solution is to use ungetc to move the file position back a character:

```
int returncode;
returncode = ungetc(fp);
```

The returncode is EOF if the operation was unsuccessful.

putc/fputc

These two functions write a single character to the output file, pointed to by fp. As with getc, one of these may be a macro. The form of these statements is:

```
FILE *fp;
char ch;
int returncode;

returncode = fputc (ch,fp);
returncode =  putc (ch,fp);
```

The returncode is the ASCII code of the character sent, if the operation was successful, otherwise it is EOF.

fgets and fputs

Just as gets and puts fetched and sent strings to standard input/output files stdin and stdout, so fgets and fputs send strings to generalised files.

The form of an fgets statement is as follows:

```
char *strbuff,*returnval;
int n;
FILE *fp;

returnval = fgets (strbuff,n,fp);
```

strbuff is a pointer to an input buffer for the string and fp is a pointer to an open file. Returnval is a pointer to a string: if there was an error in fgets this pointer is set to the value NULL, otherwise it is set to the value of 'strbuff'. No more than n-1 characters are read by fgets so the programmer has to be sure to set n equal to the size of the string buffer (one byte is reserved for the NULL terminator).

The form of an fputs statement is as follows:

```
char *str;
int returnval;
FILE *fp;

returnval = fputs (str,fp);
```

Where str is the NULL terminated string which is to be sent to the file pointed to by fp. Returnval is set to EOF if there was an error.

feof

This function returns a true or false result. It tests whether or not the end of a file has been reached and if it has, it returns 'true' (which has any value except zero); otherwise the function returns 'false' (which has the value zero). The form of a statement using this function is:

```
FILE *fp;
int outcome;

outcome = feof(fp);
```

Most often feof will be used inside loops or conditional statements. For example, consider a loop which reads characters from an open file, pointed to by fp. A call to feof is required in order to check for the end of the file.

```
while (!feof(fp))

          {
          ch = getc(fp);
          }
```

Roughly translated this code reads: 'while NOT end of file, ch equals get character from file'. To explain fully, the loop continues to fetch characters as long as the end of the file has not been reached. Notice the logical NOT operator (!) which stands before feof.

Switching Output Files: Printer Output

Any serious application program has to be in full control of the output of a program. For instance, it may need to redirect output to the printer so that data can be made into hard copies. To do this, one of three things must be undertaken:

1) stdout must be redirected so that it sends data to the printer device

2) A new 'standard file' must be used (not all C compilers use this method)

3) A new file must be opened in order to write to the printer device

The first method is not generally satisfactory for applications programs, because the standard files stdin and stdout can only easily be redirected from the operating system command line interpreter (when a program is run by typing its name). Examples of this are:

```
type file > PRN
```

or alternatively:

```
type > PRT: file
```

which send a text file to the printer device. The second method is reserved for only a few C implementations, in which another 'standard file' is opened by the local operating system and is available for sending data to the printer stream. This file might be called 'stdprn' or 'standard printer file' and data could be written to the printer by switching writing to the file like this:

```
fprintf (stdprn,"string %d...", integer);
```

The final method of writing to the printer is to open a file to the printer. To do this, a program has to give the 'filename' of the printer device. This could be something like 'PRT:' or 'PRN' or 'LPRT' or whatever. The filename (referred to as a pseudo-device name), is used to open a file in precisely the same way as any other file is opened, ie, by using a call to fopen(). fopen() then returns a pointer to file (which is effectively 'stdprn') and this is used to write data to a computer's printer driver. The program code to do this should look something like the following:

```
FILE *stdprn;

if ((stdprn = fopen("PRT:","w")) == NULL)
     {
     printf ("Printer busy or disconnected\n");
     error_handler;
     }
```

Listing 25.1 is an example program which reads a source file (for a program, written in C, Pascal or whatever), and lists it, along with its line numbers. This kind of program is invaluable for debugging. The program provides the user with the option of sending the output to the printer. The printer device is assumed to have the filename 'PRT:'. Details of how to convert the program for other systems is given at the end.

Listing 25.1. Program file utility.

```
/*************************************************************/
/*                                                           */
/* LIST : program file utility                               */
/*                                                           */
/*************************************************************/
   /* List a source file with line numbers attached. Like */
   /* TYPE only with lines numbers too.                   */
```

```
    #include <stdio.h>

    #define code   0
    #define size   255
    #define on     1
    #define off    0
    #define true   1
    #define false
    FILE *fin;
    FILE *fout = stdout;        /* where output goes to */

/**************************************************************/
/* Level 0                                                    */
/**************************************************************/

    main ()

    {    char strbuff[size],*filename();
         int Pon = false;
         int line = 1;

    printf ("Source Program Lister V1.0\n\n");

    if ((fin = fopen(filename(),"r")) == NULL)
         {
         printf ("\nFile not found\n");
         exit (code);
         }

    printf ("Output to printer? Y/N");

    if (yes())
         {
         Pon = Printer(on);
         }

    while (!feof(fin))
         {
         if (fgets(strbuff,size,fin) != strbuff)
              {
              if (!feof(fin))
                   {
                   printf ("Source file corrupted\n");
                   exit (code);
                   }
              }

              fprintf (fout,"%4d %s",line++,strbuff);
         }
    CloseFiles(Pon);
    }
```

```
/**********************************************************/
/* Level 1                                                */
/**********************************************************/

     CloseFiles(Pon)                          /* close & tidy */

     int Pon;
     {

     if (Pon)
          {
          Printer(off);
          }

     if (fclose(fin) != 0)
          {
          printf ("Error closing input file\n");
          }
     }

/**********************************************************/

     Printer (status)                /* switch printer file */

     int status;
     {

     switch (status)
          {

          case on:   while ((fout = fopen("PRT:","w")) == NULL)
               {

               printf ("Printer busy or disconnected\n");
               printf ("\n\nRetry? Y/N\n");

               if (!yes())
                    {
                    exit(code);
                    }
               }

               break;
          case off:  while (fclose(fout) != 0)
                    {
                    printf("Waiting to close printer stream\r");
                    }
          }
     }

/**********************************************************//*
```

```
Toolkit                                                   ` */
/**************************************************************/

      char *filename()                    /* return  filename */
      {    static char *filenm = "........................";

      do
           {
           printf ("Enter filename :");
           scanf ("%24s",filenm);
           skipgarb();
           }
      while (strlen(filenm) == 0);

      return (filenm);
      }

/**************************************************************/

      yes ()         /* Get a yes/no response from the user */

      {    char ch;

      while (true)
           {
           ch = getchar();
           skipgarb();

           switch (ch)
                {
                case 'y' : case 'Y' : return (true);
                case 'n' : case 'N' : return (false);
                }
           }
      }

/**************************************************************/

      skipgarb()               /* skip garbage corrupting input */
      {
      while (getchar() != '\n')
           {
           }
      }

                              /* end */
```

Program Output

Here is a sample portion of the output of this program as applied to one of the example programs in chapter 30.

```
 1 /*********************************************************/
 2 /*                                                       */
 3 /*  C programming utility : variable referencer          */
 4 /*                                                       */
 5 /*********************************************************/
 6
 7                    /* See section 30 */
 8
 9 #include "stdio.h"
10 #include "ctype.h"
11
12 #define true         1
13 #define false        0
14 #define dummy        0
15 #define maxstr     512
16 #define maxIDsize   32
```

Converting the Example

The example program could be altered to work with a standard printer file 'stdprn' by changing the following function:

```
Printer (status)                  /* switch printer file */
int status;
{

switch (status)
     {
     case on:   fout = stdprn;
                break;
     case off:  fout = stdout;
     }
}
```

Filing Errors

The standard library provides an error function/macro which returns a true/false result according to whether or not the last filing function call returned an error condition. This is called ferror(). To check for an error in an open file, pointed to by fp:

```
FILE *fp;

if (ferror(fp))
   {
   error_handler();
   }
```

This function/macro doesn't shed any light upon the cause of errors, only whether errors have occurred at all. A detailed diagnosis of what went wrong generally is only possible by means of a deeper level call to the disc operating system (DOS).

Other Facilities for High-level Files

Files which have been opened by fopen can also be handled with the following additional functions:

fread
fwrite

ftell
fseek
rewind
fflush

These functions provide facilities to read and write whole blocks of characters in one operation, as well as further facilities to locate and alter the current focus of attention within a file. They offer, essentially, low-level filing operations for files which have been opened for high-level use!

fread and fwrite

These functions read and write whole blocks of characters at a time. The form of fread is as follows:

```
FILE *fp;
int  noread,n,size;
char *ptr;

noread = fread (ptr,size,n,fp);
```

The parameters in brackets provide information about where the data will be stored when read from a file. Fp is a pointer to an open file; ptr is a pointer to the start of a block of memory which is to store the data when it is read; size is the size of a 'block' of data in characters; n is the number of blocks of data to be read. Finally, 'noread' is a return value which indicates the number of blocks which were actually read during the operation. It is important to check that the number of blocks expected is the same as the number received, in case something went wrong with the reading process. For example, the disc might be corrupted, or the file might have been altered in some way.

fwrite has an identical call structure to fread:

```
FILE *fp;
int  nowritten,n,size;
char *ptr;

nowritten = fread (ptr,size,n,fp);
```

This time the parameters in brackets provide information about where to find the data which are to be written to a file. Fp is a pointer to an open file; ptr is a pointer to the start of a block of memory at which the data are stored. Size is the size of a data 'block' in characters and n is the number of blocks of data to be read. Finally, 'nowritten' is a return value which indicates the actual number of blocks which was written. Again, this should be checked.

A caution about these functions – each of these 'block transfer' routines makes an important assumption about the way in which data is stored in the computer system. It is assumed that the data are stored 'contiguously' in the memory, that is, side by side, in sequential memory locations. In some systems this can be difficult to arrange (in multi-tasking systems in particular) and almost impossible to guarantee. Memory which is allocated in C programs by the function 'malloc()' does not guarantee to find contiguous portions of memory on successive calls. This should be noted carefully when developing programs which use these calls.

File Positions: ftell and fseek

ftell tells a program its position within a file, opened by fopen. fseek seeks a specified place within a file, opened by fopen.

Normally high-level read/write functions perform as much management over positions inside files as the programmer wants, but if they are insufficient, ftell and fseek can be used. The form of them function calls is:

```
long int pos;
FILE *fp;

pos = ftell(fp);
```

fp is an open file, which is in some state of being read or written to. The long integer value, pos, describes the position in terms of character number from the beginning of the file.

Aligning a file 'portal' with a particular place in a file is more sophisticated than simply taking note of the current position. The call to fseek looks like this:

```
long int pos;
int mode,returncode;
FILE *fp;

returncode = fseek (fp,pos,mode);
```

The parameters have the following meanings. Fp is a pointer to a file opened by fopen. Pos is some way of describing the position required within a file. Mode is an integer which specifies the way in which pos is to be interpreted. Finally, returncode is an integer whose value is zero if the operation was successful, and minus one if there was an error.

Mode values are as follows:

Mode	Action
0	Pos is an offset measured relative to the beginning of the file
1	Pos is an offset measured relative to the current position
2	Pos is an offset measured relative to the end of the file

Some examples help to show how this works in practice:

```
long int pos = 50;
int mode = 0,returncode;
FILE *fp;

if (fseek (fp,pos,mode) != 0) /* find 50th character */
    {
    printf("Error!\n");
    }

fseek(fp,0L,0);                  /* find beginning of file */
fseek(fp,2L,0);                  /* find the end of a file */

if (fseek (fp,10L,1) != 0)       /* move 10 char's forward */
    {
    printf("Error!\n");
    }
```

The 'L's indicate 'long' constants.

rewind

rewind is a macro, based upon fseek, which resets a file position to the beginning of the file. For example:

```
FILE *fp;

rewind(fp);

fseek(fp,0L,0);                /* = rewind() */
```

fflush

This is a macro/function which can be used on files which have been opened for writing or appending. It 'flushes' the output buffer by forcing the characters in the output buffer to be written to the file. If used on files which are open for reading, it causes the input buffer to empty (assuming that this is allowed at all). For example:

```
FILE *fp;

fflush(fp);
```

Low-level Filing Operations

Normally a programmer can get away with using the high-level input/output functions, but there may be times when C's predilection for handling all high-level input/output as text files becomes a nuisance. A program can then use a set of low-level I/O functions which are provided by the standard library. These are:

open
close
creat
read
write
rename
unlink/remove
lseek

These low-level routines work on the operating system's end of the file 'portals'. They should be regarded as advanced features because they are dangerous routines for bug-ridden programs. The data which they deal with are *untranslated*, that is, no conversion from characters to floating point, integers or any type at all takes place. Data are treated as a raw stream of bytes. Low-level functions should not be used on any file at the same time as high-level routines, as high-level file handling functions often make calls to the low-level functions.

Working at the low-level, programs can create, delete and rename files but they are restricted to the reading and writing of untranslated data – there are no functions such as fprintf() or fscanf() which make type conversions. As well as the functions mentioned, a local operating system will doubtless provide special function calls which enable a programmer to make the most of the facilities offered by the particular operating environment. These will be documented in your compiler manual or operating system manual, depending on the system concerned. (They might concern special graphics facilities or windowing systems or provide ways of writing special system dependent data to disc files, such as date/time stamps and so on.)

File Handles

At the low-level, files are not handled using file pointers but with integers known as *file handles* or *file descriptors*. A file handle is essentially the number of a particular 'file portal' in an array. In other words, for all the different terminology, they describe the same thing. For example:

```
int fileportal;
```

would declare a file 'handle,' or 'descriptor', or 'portal', or whatever it is to be called.

open()

Open() is the low-level file open function. The form of this function call is as follows:

```
int fileportal, mode;
char *filename;

fileportal = open (filename,mode);
```

where filename is a string which holds the name of the file concerned, mode is a value which specifies what the file is to be opened for and fileportal is either a number used to distinguish the file from others, or minus one if an error occurred.

A program can give more information to this function than it can to fopen in order to define exactly what open will do. The integer 'mode' is a message, or a pseudo register, which passes the necessary information to open, by using the following flags (See Chapter 24 for information on flags):

O_RDONLY	Read access only
O_WRONLY	Write access only
O_RDWR	Read/write access

and on some compilers:

O_CREAT	Create the file if it does not exist
O_TRUNC	Truncate the file if it does exist
O_APPEND	Find the end of the file before each write
O_EXCL	Exclude. Force create to fail if the file exists.

The macro definitions of these flags will be included in a library file – find out which one and #include it in the program.

The normal procedure is to open a file using one of the first three modes. For example:

```
#define failed -1

main()

{    char *filename();
     int fileportal;

fileportal = open(filename(), O_RDONLY);

if (fileportal == failed)
     {
     printf ("File not found\n");
     error_handler (failed);
     }
}
```

This program will open up a 'read only' file for low-level handling, with error checking.

Some systems allow a more flexible way of opening files. The four appended modes are values which can be bit-wise ORed with one of the first three, in order to get more mileage out of open. The bit-wise OR operator is the split vertical bar '|'. For example, to emulate the fopen function, a program could opt to create a file if it did not already exist:

```
fileportal = open (filename(), O_RDONLY | O_CREAT);
```

open sets the file position to zero, if the file is opened successfully.

close

close releases a file portal for use by other files and brings a file completely up to date with regard to any changes that have been made to it. Like all other filing functions, it returns the value zero if it performs successfully, and the value minus one if it fails. For example:

```
#define failed -1

if (close(fileportal) == failed)
     {
     printf ("ERROR!");
     }
```

creat

This function creates a new file and prepares it for access using the low-level file handling functions. If a file which already exists is created, its contents are discarded. The form of this function call is:

```
int fileportal, pmode;
char *filename;

fileportal = creat (filename,pmode);
```

Filename must be a valid filename, pmode is a flag which contains access-privilege mode bits (system specific information about allowed access) and fileportal is a returned file handle. In the absence of any information about pmode, this parameter can be set to zero.

read

This function gets a block of information from a file. The data are loaded directly into memory as a sequence of bytes. The user must provide a place for them, either by making an array, or by using malloc to reserve space. Read keeps track of file positions automatically, so it actually reads the next block of bytes from the current file position. The following example reads 'n' bytes from a file:

```
int returnvalue, fileportal, n;
char *buffer;

if ((buffer = malloc(size)) == NULL)
     {
     puts ("Out of memory\n");
     error_handler ();
     }

returnvalue = read (fileportal,buffer,n);
```

The return value should be checked. Its values are defined as follows:

returnvalue	Description
0	End of file
-1	Error occurred
?	The number of bytes actually read. If all went well this should be equal to n

write

This function is the opposite of read. It writes a block of n bytes from a contiguous portion of memory to a file which was opened by open. The form of this function is:

```
int returnvalue, fileportal, n;
char *buffer;

returnvalue = write (fileportal,buffer,n);
```

The return value should, again, be checked for errors:

Returnvalue	Description
-1	error
?	number of bytes written

fseek

Low-level file handing functions have their equivalent of fseek for finding a specific position within a file. This is almost identical to fseek except that it uses the file handle rather than a file pointer as a parameter and has a different return value . The constants should be declared long int, or simply 'long':

```
#define failed  -1L

long int pos,offset,fileportal;
int mode,returncode;

if ((pos = fseek (fileportal,offset,mode)) == failed)
     {
     printf("Error!\n");
     }
```

pos gives the new file position if successful and -1 (long) if an attempt was made to read past the end of the file.

The values which mode can take are:

Mode	Action
0	Offset measured relative to the beginning of the file.
1	Offset measured relative to the current position.
2	Offset measured relative to the end of the file.

unlink/remove

These functions delete a file from disc storage. When deleted, files are usually irretrievable. They return minus one if the action failed:

```
#define failed -1

int returnvalue;
char *filename;

if (unlink (filename) == failed)
     {
     printf ("Can't delete %s\n",filename);
     }

if (remove (filename) == failed)
     {
     printf ("Can't delete %s\n",filename);
     }
```

filename is a string containing the filename concerned. This function can fail if a file concerned is protected, if it isn't found or if it is a device. It is impossible to delete the printer!

rename

This function renames a file. The programmer specifies two filenames – the old filename and a new filename. As usual, it returns the value minus one if the action fails. An example illustrates the form of the rename call:

```
#define failed -1
char *old,*new;
if (rename(old,new) == failed)
     {
     printf ("Can't rename %s as %s\n",old,new);
     }
```

rename can fail because a file is protected or it may be in use, or because one of the filenames given was not valid.

The example program in listing 25.2 strings together some low-level filing actions so as to illustrate their use in a real program. The idea is to present a kind of file or 'project' menu for creating, deleting and renaming files. A rather feeble text-editor allows the user to enter 255 characters of text which can be saved.

Listing 25.2. Low-level file handling.

```
/***********************************************************/
/*                                                         */
/* LOW-LEVEL FILE HANDLING                                 */
/*                                                         */
/***********************************************************/

      #include <stdio.h>
      #include <ctype.h>
      #include <fcntl.h>            /* defines O_RDONLY etc.. */

      #define code    0
      #define size    255
      #define fnmsize 30             /* Max size of filenames */
      #define true    1
      #define false   0
      #define failed  -1

      #define clrscrn() putchar('\f')
      #define newline() putchar('\n')

      int fileportal;

/**********************************************************/
/* Level 0                                                */
/**********************************************************/

      main ()

      {    char *data,getkey(),*malloc();
```

```
        if ((data = malloc(size)) == NULL)
            {
            puts ("Out of memory\n");
            return (code);
            }

            while (true)
                {
                menu();

                switch (getkey())
                    {
                    case 'l' : LoadFile(data);
                               break;
                    case 's' : SaveFile(data);
                               break;
                    case 'e' : Edit(data);
                               break;
                    case 'd' : DeleteFile();
                               break;
                    case 'r' : RenameFile();
                               break;
                    case 'q' : if (sure())
                                   {
                                   return (code);
                                   }
                               break;
                    }
                }
            }

/**************************************************************/
/* Level 1                                                    */
/**************************************************************/

        menu ()

        {
        clrscrn();
        printf (" ---------------------------------\n");
        printf ("|              MENU                |\n");
        printf ("|              ~~~~~~              |\n");
        printf ("|                                  |\n");
        printf ("|          L) Load File            |\n");
        printf ("|          S) Save File            |\n");
        printf ("|          E) Edit File            |\n");
        printf ("|          D) Delete File          |\n");
        printf ("|          R) Rename File          |\n");
        printf ("|          Q) Quit                 |\n");
        printf ("|                                  |\n");
        printf ("|      Select Option and RETURN    |\n");
        printf ("|                                  |\n");
```

```
    printf (" ---------------------------------- \n");
    newline();
    }

/***************************************************************/

    LoadFile(data)                          /* Low level load */

    char *data;

    {   char *filename(),getkey();
        int error;

    fileportal = open(filename(), O_RDONLY);

    if (fileportal == failed)
        {
        printf ("File not found\n");
        return (failed);
        }

    error = read (fileportal,data,size);

    if (error == failed)
        {
        printf ("Error loading file\n");
        wait();
        }

    else
        {

        if (error != size)
            {
            printf ("File was corrupted\n");
            wait();
            }
        }

    close (fileportal,data,size);
    return (error);
    }

/***************************************************************/

    SaveFile(data)                          /* Low Level save */

    char *data;

    {   char *filename(),getkey(),*fname;
        int error,fileportal;
```

```
fileportal = open ((fname = filename()), O_WRONLY);

if (fileportal == failed)
     {
     printf ("File cannot be written to\n");
     printf ("Try to create new file? Y/N\n");

     if (yes())
          {
          if ((fileportal = CreateFile(fname)) == failed)
               {
               printf ("Cannot create file %s\n",fname);
               return (failed);
               }
          }

     else
          {
          return (failed);
          }
     }
error = write (fileportal,data,size);

if (error < size)
     {
     printf ("Error writing to file\n");

     if (error != failed)
          {
          printf ("File only partially written\n");
          }
     }

close (fileportal,data,size);
wait();
return (error);
}

/**********************************************************/

Edit(data)                      /* primitive text editor */

char *data;

{    char *ptr;
     int ctr = 0;

printf ("Contents of file:\n\n");

for (ptr = data; ptr < (data + size); ptr++)
     {
```

```
          if (isprint(*ptr))
               {
               putchar(*ptr);

               if ((ctr++ % 60) == 0)
                    {
                    newline();
                    }
               }
          }

     printf ("\n\nEnter %1d characters:\n",size);
     for (ptr = data; ptr < (data + size); ptr++)
          {
          *ptr = getchar();
          }

     skipgarb();
     }

/**********************************************************/

     DeleteFile()          /* Delete a file from current dir */

     {    char *filename(),getkey(),*fname;

     printf ("Delete File\n\n");

     fname = filename();
     if (sure())
          {
          if (remove(fname) == failed)
               {
               printf ("Can't delete %s\n",fname);
               }
          }
     else
          {
          printf ("File NOT deleted!\n");
          }

     wait();
     }

/**********************************************************/

     RenameFile()
     {    char old[fnmsize],*new;

     printf ("Rename from OLD to NEW\n\nOLD: ");
     strcpy (old,filename());
```

```
        printf ("\nNEW: ");
        new = filename();

        if (rename(old,new) == failed)
            {
            printf ("Can't rename %s as %s\n",old,new);
            }

        wait();
        }

/**********************************************************/
/* Level 2                                                */
/**********************************************************/

        CreateFile (fname)

        char *fname;

        {    int fileportal;

        if ((fileportal = creat(fname,0)) == failed)
            {
            printf ("Can't create file %s\n",fname);
            return (failed);
            }

        return (fileportal);
        }

/**********************************************************/
/* Toolkit                                                */
/**********************************************************/

        char *filename()                    /* return  filename */
        {    static char statfilenm[fnmsize];

        do
            {
            printf ("Enter filename :");
            scanf ("%24s",statfilenm);
            skipgarb();
            }
        while (strlen(statfilenm) == 0);
        return (statfilenm);
        }

/*********************************************************/

        sure ()                          /* is the user sure ? */
        {
        printf ("Are you absolutely certain? Y/N\n");
```

```
      return(yes());
      }

/*********************************************************/

      yes()

      {   char getkey();

      while (true)
          {
          switch(getkey())
              {
              case 'y' : return (true);
              case 'n' : return (false);
              }
          }
      }

/*********************************************************/

      wait()

      {   char getkey();
      printf ("Press a key\n");
      getkey();
      }

/*********************************************************/

      char getkey()           /* single key + RETURN response */

      {   char ch;

      ch = getchar();
      skipgarb();
      return((char)tolower(ch));
      }

/*********************************************************/

      skipgarb()             /* skip garbage corrupting input */

      {
      while (getchar() != '\n')
          {
          }
      }
                              /* end */
```

Questions:

1) What are the following?

a) filename
b) file-pointer
c) file-handle

2) What is the difference between high and low-level filing?

3) Write a statement which opens a high-level file for reading.

4) Write a statement which opens a low-level file for writing.

5) Write a program which checks for illegal characters in text files. Valid characters are ASCII codes 10,13,and 32..126. Anything else is illegal for programs.

6) What statement performs formatted writing to text files?

7) Print out all the header files on your system so that you can see what is defined where!

26 : Structures & Unions

Grouping Data and Tidying Up Programs

Tidy programs are a blessing to programmers. Likewise, tidy data are just as important.

As programs become increasingly complex, their data also grows in complexity and they can no longer manage with single, independent variables or arrays. In this situation, a program rapidly becomes faced with the need for a data structure. This is where a new type of variable comes in – it is called a 'struct' type, or in other languages, a record. 'Struct' types or 'structures' are accompanied by a special type called a 'union'.

Organisation: Black Box Data

What is the relationship between a program and its data? A program can often be thought of as being a giant operator which operates on the memory of the computer. Local data are operated upon inside sealed function capsules, where they are protected from the reach of certain parts of a program. Global data are wide open to alteration by any part of a program. If a program were visualised schematically, what would it look like? A traditional flow diagram? No. A computer program only looks like a flow diagram at the machine code level and that is too primitive for C programmers. One way of visualising a program is illustrated by figure 26.1. This shows a program as a kind of society of sealed function capsules which work together like a beehive of activity on a honeycomb of program data. This imaginative idea of a computer program is not quite complete. A program has to manipulate data – it has to look at it, move it around and copy it from place to place. All of these things would be very difficult if data were scattered about liberally, with no particular structure. For this reason C has within it the facility to make sealed capsules – not of program code – but of program data, so that all of these actions very simply by grouping variables together in convenient packages for handling. These capsules are called structures.

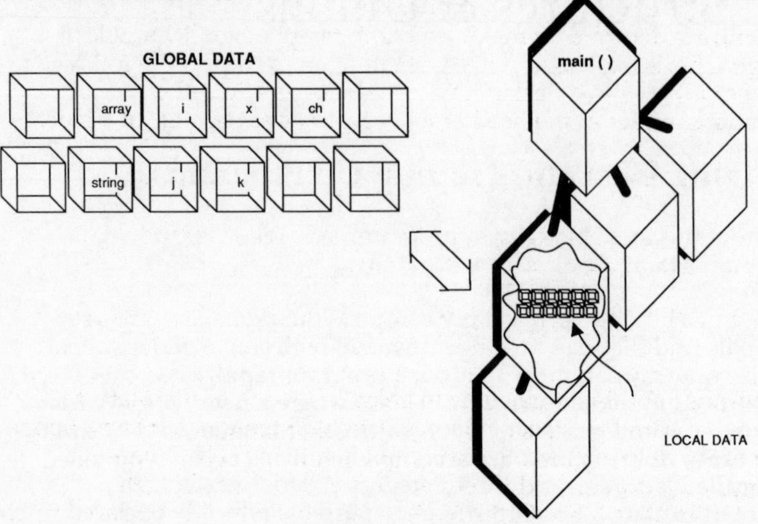

Figure 26.1. The program is a "society" of functions operating on a data structure

struct

A 'structure' is a package of one, or preferably more, variables grouped under a single name. Structures are not like arrays as a structure can hold any mixture of different data types. Structures can even hold arrays of different types. A structure can be as simple or as complex as the programmer desires.

The word 'struct' is a reserved word in C and it represents a new data type, called an aggregate type. It is not any single type – the purpose of structures is to offer a tool for making whatever shape or form of variable package a programmer wishes. Any particular structure type is given a name, called a structure name and the variables (called *members*) within a structure type are also given names. Finally, every variable declared to be a particular structure type has a name of its own too. This plethora of names is not as complicated as it sounds.

Declarations

A structure is declared by making a blank template for a variable package. This is explained with the help of an example. The following statement is actually a declaration, so it belongs with other declarations, either at the head of a program or at the start of a block...

```
struct PersonalData

      {
      char name[namesize];
      char address[addresssize];
      int YearOfBirth;
      int MonthOfBirth;
      int DayOfBirth;
      };
```

This purpose of this statement is to create a model, or template, to define what variable 'struct PersonalData' will look like. It says, define a type of variable which collectively holds a string called 'name', a string called 'address' and three integers called 'YearOfBirth', 'MonthOfBirth' and 'DayOfBirth'. Any variable which is declared to be 'struct PersonalData' type will be made up of parts like these. The list of variable components making up the structure are called the *members* of the structure. The names of the members are not the names of variables, but are a way of naming the parts which make up a structure variable. (Note: a variable which has been declared to be of type 'struct something' is usually called a 'structure' rather than a 'structure variable'. The distinction is maintained here in places where confusion might arise.) The names of members are held separate from the names of other identifiers in C, so it is quite possible to have variable names and struct member names which are the same. Unfortunately, older compilers did not support this luxury.

At this stage, no storage has been given over to a variable, nor has any variable been declared – only a type has been defined. Having defined this type of structure the programmer can declare variables to be of this type. For example:

```
struct PersonalData x;
```

declares a variable called x to be of type 'struct PersonalData'. 'x' is certainly not a very good name for any variable which holds a person's personal data, but it contrasts well with all the other names which abound and so it serves its purpose for now.

Before moving on to consider how structures can be used, it is worth pausing to show the different ways in which structures can be declared. The method just looked at is probably the most common, however there are two other methods of achieving the same thing.

A variable can be declared immediately after the template definition:

```
struct PersonalData

     {
     char name[namesize];
     char address[addresssize];
     int YearOfBirth;
     int MonthOfBirth;
     int DayOfBirth;
     }
     x;         /* variable identifier follows type */
```

Alternatively, 'typedef' can be used to cut down on typing in the long term. This type definition is made when at the head of the program and then subsequent declarations are made by using the new name:

```
typedef struct

     {
     char name[namesize];
     char address[addresssize];
     int YearOfBirth;
     int MonthOfBirth;
     int DayOfBirth;
     }

PersonalData;
```

then declare:

```
PersonalData x;
```

Any one of these methods will do.

Scope

Both structure types and structure variables obey the rules of scope, that is, a structure type declaration can be local or global, depending on where the declaration is made. Similarly, if a structure type variable is declared locally, it is only valid inside the block brackets in which it was originally defined:

```
main ()

{ struct ONE
     {
     int a;
     float b;
     };

struct ONE x;
}

function ()

{ struct ONE x;       /* This line is illegal, since ONE */
                      /* is a local type definition      */
                      /* Defined only in main()          */
}
```

Using Structures

How does a program use the variables which are locked inside these structures?

The whole point about structures is that they can be used to group data into sensible packages which can then be treated as single objects. Early C compilers, some of which still exist, placed very severe restrictions on what a program could do with structures. Essentially, the members of a structure could be assigned values, and pointers to individual structures could be found. Although this sounds highly restrictive, it did account for the most frequent uses of structures. Modern compilers allow more flexible use. Programs can assign one structure variable to another structure variable (provided the structures match in type). Structure variables can be passed whole as parameters to functions and functions can return structure values. This makes structures extremely powerful data objects to have in a program.

A structure is assigned to another structure by the following statements:

```
struct Personal x,y;

x = y;
```

The whole bundle of members is copied in one statement!

Structures are passed as parameters in the usual way:

```
function (x,y);
```

The function then has to be declared:

```
function (x,y)

struct PersonalData x,y;
{
}
```

Finally, a function which returns a structure variable such as:

```
{ struct PersonalData x,function();

x = function();
}
```

would be declared in the following way:

```
struct PersonalData function ()

{
}
```

Notice that the return type of such a function must also be declared in the function. You will begin to see that structure names account for a good deal of typing! The typedef statement is a very good way of reducing this burden.

The members of a structure are accessed with the dot character (.). This is a structure 'member operator'. Consider the structure variable x, which has the type 'struct PersonalData'. The members of x could be assigned by the following program:

```
main ()
{ struct PersonalData x;

FillArray ("Some name", x.name);
FillArray ("Some address", x.address);
x.YearOfBirth = 1987;
x.MonthOfBirth = 2;
x.DayOfBirth = 19;
}
```

Where FillArray is a hypothetical function which copies the string in the first parameter to the array in the second parameter. The dot between the variable, and the names which follow, implies that the statements in this brief program are talking about the members in the structure variable x, rather than the whole collective bundle. Members of actual structure variables are always accessed with this dot operator. The general form of a member reference is:

```
<structure variable>.<member name>
```

This applies to any type of structure variable, including those accessed by pointers. Whenever a program needs to access the members of a structure, this dot operator can be used. C provides a special member operator for pointers, however, because they are used so often in connection with structures. This new operator is described shortly.

Arrays of Structures

Just as arrays of any basic type of variable are allowed, so are arrays of a given type of structure. Although a structure contains many different types, the compiler never gets to know this information because it is hidden away inside a sealed structure capsule. It can thus believe that all the elements in the array have the same type, even though that type is made up of lots of different types! An array would be declared in the usual way as follows:

```
int i;
struct PersonalData x,array[size];
```

The members of the arrays would then be accessed by statements like the following examples:

```
array[i] = x;
array[i] = array[j];
array[i].YearOfBirth = 1987;
i = array[2].MonthOfBirth;
```

This listing uses a structure type which is slightly different to 'PersonalData', in that string pointers are used instead of arrays. This allows more convenient handling of real-life strings.

Listing 26.1. Structures demo #1.

```
/*********************************************************/
/*                                                       */
/* Structures Demo                                       */
/*                                                       */
/*********************************************************/
   /* Simple program to initialize some structures */
   /* and to print them out again. Does no error   */
   /* checking, so be wary of string sizes etc..   */

      #include <stdio.h>

      #define namesize     30
      #define addrsize     80
      #define noofpersons  20
      #define newline()    putchar('\n');

/*********************************************************/

      typedef struct

           {
           char *Name;
           char *Address;
           int YearOfBirth;
           int MonthOfBirth;
           int DayOfBirth;
           }
      PersonDat;

/*********************************************************/

      main ()                        /* Make some records */

      {    PersonDat record[noofpersons];
           PersonDat PersonalDetails();
           int person;
```

```
    printf ("Birth Records For Employees");
    printf ("\n---------------------------");
    printf ("\n\n")
;
    printf ("Enter data\n");

    for (person = 0; person < noofpersons; person++)
         {
         record[person] = PersonalDetails();
         newline();
         }

    DisplayRecords (record);
    }

/*********************************************************/

    PersonDat PersonalDetails() /* No error checking! */

    {    PersonDat dat;
         char strbuff[addrsize], *malloc();

    printf ("Name :");
    dat.Name = malloc(namesize);
    strcpy (dat.Name,gets(strbuff));

    printf ("Address :");
    dat.Address = malloc(addrsize);
    strcpy (dat.Address,gets(strbuff));

    printf ("Year of birth:");
    dat.YearOfBirth = getint (1900,1987);
    printf ("Month of birth:");
    dat.MonthOfBirth = getint (1,12);

    printf ("Day of birth:");
    dat.DayOfBirth = getint(1,31);

    return (dat);
    }

/**********************************************************/

    DisplayRecords (rec)

    PersonDat rec[noofpersons];
    {    int pers;

    for (pers = 0; pers < noofpersons; pers++)
         {
         printf ("Name : %s\n", rec[pers].Name);
         printf ("Address : %s\n", rec[pers].Address);
```

```
          printf("Date of Birth: %1d/%1d/%1d\n", rec[pers]
                 .DayOfBirth,  rec[pers].MonthOfBirth,
                                     rec[pers].YearOfBirth);

          newline();
          }
     }
/***********************************************************/
/* Toolkit                                                 */
/***********************************************************/

     getint (a,b)           /* return int between a and b */

     int a,b;
     {    int  p, i = a - 1;

     for (p=0;  ((a > i)  ||  (i > b)); p++)
          {
          printf ("? : ");
          scanf ("%d",&i);

          if (p > 2)
               {
               skipgarb();
               p = 0;
               }
          }
     skipgarb();
     return (i);
     }
/***********************************************************/

     skipgarb()  /* Skip input garbage corrupting scanf */
     {
     while (getchar() != '\n')
          {
          }
     }
```

Structures of Structures

Structures are said to 'nest'. This means that structure templates can contain other structures as members. Consider the two following structure types:

```
struct first_structure
    {
    int value;
    float number;
    };
```

and:

```
struct second_structure
    {
    int tag;
    struct first_structure fs;
    }

x;
```

These two structures are of different type, yet the first of the two is included in the second! The second structure would be initialised by the following assignments. The structure variable name is x:

```
x.tag = 10;
x.fs.value = 20;
x.fs.number = 30.0;
```

Notice the way the member operator '.' can be used over and over again. Note also that no brackets are necessary, because the reference which is calculated by this operator is worked out from left to right. This nesting can, in principle, go on many times though some compilers might place restrictions upon this nesting level. Statements such as:

```
variable.tag1.tag2.tag3.tag4 = something;
```

are probably OK although they aren't good programming. Structures should nest safely a few times.

A word of caution is in order here. There is a problem with the aforementioned scheme which hasn't been considered yet. It is this: What happens if a structure contains an instance of itself? For example:

```
struct Regression

    {
    int i;
    struct Regression tag;
    };
```

There is simply no way that this kind of statement can make sense, unless the compiler's target computer has an infinite supply of memory! References to this type of variable would go on for ever and an infinite amount of memory would be needed for every variable. For this one reason, it is forbidden for a structure to contain an instance of itself. What is not forbidden, however, is for a structure to contain an instance of a pointer to its own type. This is because a pointer is not the same type as a structure, it is merely a variable which holds the address of a structure. Pointers to structures are quite invaluable for building data structures such as linked lists and trees. These extremely valuable devices are described below.

Pointers to Structures

A pointer to a structure type variable is declared by a statement like:

```
struct Name *ptr;
```

Ptr is then, formally, a pointer to a structure of type 'Name' only. It can be assigned to any other pointer of similar type and it can be used to access the members of a structure. It is in the second of these actions that a new structure operator is revealed.

According to the rules which have been described so far, a structure member could be accessed by pointers with the following statements:

```
struct PersonalData *ptr;

(*ptr).YearOfBirth = 20;
```

This says, let the member 'YearOfBirth' of the structure pointed to by ptr, have the value 20. Notice that *ptr by itself means the contents of the address which is held in ptr. Notice too that the brackets around this statement avoid any confusion about the precedence of these operators.

There is a better way to write the above statement using a new operator: '->'. This is an arrow made out of a minus sign and a 'greater than' symbol. It is used in the following way:

```
struct PersonalData *ptr;

ptr->YearOfBirth = 20;
```

This statement is identical in every way to the first version, but as this kind of access is required so frequently when dealing with structures, C provides this special operator to make the operation clearer.

It is assumed that ptr has been assigned to the address of some pre-assigned structure: for example, by means of a statement such as:

```
ptr = &x;
```

where x is a pre-assigned structure.

Listing 26.2. Structures demo #2.

```
/*********************************************************/
/*                                                       */
/* Structures Demo #2                                    */
/*                                                       */
/*********************************************************/
   /* This is the same program, using pointer references */
   /* instead of straight variable references. i.e. this */
   /* uses variable parameters instead of value params   */

     #include <stdio.h>

     #define namesize    30
     #define addrsize    80
     #define noofpersons 20

     #define newline()   putchar('\n');

/*********************************************************/

     typedef struct

         {
         char *Name;
         char *Address;

         int YearOfBirth;
         int MonthOfBirth;
         int DayOfBirth;
         }

     PersonDat;

/*********************************************************/

     main ()                        /* Make some records */
```

```
     {    PersonDat record[noofpersons];
          int person;

     printf ("Birth Records For Employees");
     printf ("\n---------------------------");
     printf ("\n\n");

     printf ("Enter data\n");

     for (person = 0; person < noofpersons; person++)
          {
          PersonalDetails(&(record[person]));
          newline();
          }

     DisplayRecords (record);
     }

/*******************************************************/

     PersonalDetails(dat)           /* No error checking! */

     PersonDat *dat;

     {    char strbuff[addrsize], *malloc();

     printf ("Name :");
     dat->Name = malloc(namesize);
     strcpy (dat->Name,gets(strbuff));

     printf ("Address :");
     dat->Address = malloc(addrsize);
     strcpy (dat->Address,gets(strbuff));

     printf ("Year of birth:");
     dat->YearOfBirth = getint (1900,1987);

     printf ("Month of birth:");
     dat->MonthOfBirth = getint (1,12);

     printf ("Day of birth:");
     dat->DayOfBirth = getint(1,31);
     }

/*******************************************************/

     DisplayRecords (rec)

     PersonDat rec[noofpersons];
```

```
{    int pers;

for (pers = 0; pers < noofpersons; pers++)
     {
     printf ("Name : %s\n", rec[pers].Name);
     printf ("Address : %s\n", rec[pers].Address);
     printf("Date of Birth: %1d/%1d/%1d\n",
rec[pers].DayOfBirth,
                rec[pers].MonthOfBirth, rec[pers].
                                          YearOfBirth);

     newline();
     }
}

/*********************************************************/
/* Toolkit                                               */
/*********************************************************/

                 /* As before */
```

Pre-initialising Static Structures

In Chapter19 it was shown how static and external type arrays could be initialised with values at compile time. Static and external structures can also be pre-assigned by the compiler so that programs can set up options and starting conditions in a convenient way.

A static variable of type PersonDat (as in the example programs) could be declared and initialised in the same statement:

```
#define namesize 20
#define addresssize 22

struct PersonDat

     {
     char *name;
     char *address;
     int YearOfBirth;
     int MonthOfBirth;
     int DayOfBirth;
     };

main ()
```

```
{ static struct PersonalData variable =
      {
      "Alice Wonderment",
      "Somewhere in Paradise",
      1965,
      5,
      12
      };
/* rest of program */
}
```

The items in the curly braces are matched to the members of the structure variable, and any items which are not initialised by items in the list are filled out with zeros.

Creating Memory for Dynamical Struct Types

Probably the single most frequent use of struct type variables is in the building of dynamical data structures. Dynamical (or usually just 'dynamic') data is created explicitly by a program using a scheme of memory allocation and pointers. Normal program data, which is reserved space by the compiler are static data structures because they do not change during the course of a program – an integer is always an integer and an array is always an array. Their sizes cannot change while the program is running.

A dynamical structure is built using the memory allocation function:

```
malloc()
```

and pointers. The idea is to create the memory space for a new structure as and when it is needed, and to use a pointer to access the members of that structure, using the '->' operator.

malloc was described in Chapter 20 in connection with strings. It allocates a fixed number of bytes of memory and returns a pointer to that data. For instance, to allocate 10 bytes, you would write something like this:

```
char *malloc(), *ptr;

ptr = malloc(10);
```

ptr is then a pointer to the start of that block of 10 bytes.

When a program wants to create the space for a structure, it has a template for that structure, which was used to define it. However, it does not generally know in advance, how many bytes long a structure is. In fact, it is seldom possible to know this information, as a structure may occupy more memory than the sum of its parts. How then does a program know how much space to allocate? The C compiler comes to the rescue here, by providing a compile time operator called:

```
sizeof ()
```

which calculates the size of an object while a program is compiling. For example:

sizeof(int)   Works out the number of bytes occupied by the type 'int'

sizeof(char) Works out the number of bytes occupied by a single character. This equals one in fact

sizeof(struct PersonalData) works out the number of bytes needed to store a single structure variable. Obviously this tool is very useful for working with malloc. The memory allocation statement becomes something like:

```
ptr = malloc(sizeof(type_name));
```

There is a problem with this statement though – malloc is declared as a function which returns a type 'pointer to character' whereas here, the programmer is interested in pointers of type 'pointer to struct Something'. malloc has to be forced to produce a pointer of the correct type then and this is done by using the cast operator to mould it into shape. The cast operator casts pointers with a general form:

```
(type *) <value>
```

Consider the following example of C source code which allocates space for a structure type called 'SomeStruct', and creates a correctly aligned pointer to it, called ptr:

```
struct SomeStruct *ptr;
char *malloc();
ptr = (struct SomeStruct *) malloc(sizeof(struct
Somestruct));
```

This rather laboured statement provides both the memory and the location of that memory in a legal and type-sensical way.

The next chapter discusses what a programmer can do with dynamically allocated structures.

Unions

A union is like a structure in which all the members are stored at the same address. Only one member can be stored in such an object at any one time, as it would be overwritten by another. Otherwise unions behave like specially-sized storage containers which can hold many different types of data. A union can hold any one of its members, but only at different times. The compiler arranges that a union type variable is big enough to handle the job.

Declaration

A union is declared in the same way as a structure. It has a list of members, which are used to mould the type of object concerned:

```
union IntOrFloat

      {
      int ordinal;
      float continuous;
      };
```

This declares a type template. Variables are then declared as:

```
union IntOrFloat x,y,z;
```

At different times the program is to treat x,y and z as being either integers or float types. When the variables are referred to as:

```
x.ordinal = 1;
```

the program sees 'x' as being an integer type. At other times, when x is referred to as x.continuous, it takes on another aspect – its alter ego, the float type. Notice that x by itself does not have a value, only its members have values. X is just a box for the different members to share.

Using Unions

Unions are used in just the same ways as structures. The dot operator selects the different members for variable and the arrow selects different values for pointers. The form of such statements is:

```
union_variable.member;
union_pointer->member;
```

Unions are seldom very useful in programs, as a program has no automatic way of knowing what type of member is currently stored in the union type. One way to overcome this is to keep a variable which signals the type currently held in the variable. This is done very easily with the aid of enumerated data.

Consider the following kind of union:

```
union WhichType
    {
    int ordinal;
    float continuous;
    char letter;
    };
```

This could be accompanied by an enumerate declaration such as:

```
enum Types
    {
    INT,
    FLOAT,
    CHAR
    };
```

Variables could then go in pairs:

```
union WhichType x;
enum Types x_status;
```

which would make union type-handling straight forward:

```
switch (x_status)
    {
    case INT   : x.ordinal = 12;
                 break;
    case FLOAT : x.continuous = 12.23;
                 break;
```

```
        case CHAR   : x.letter = '*';
        }
```

These variables could even be grouped into a structure:

```
struct Union_Handler
    {
    union WhichType x;
    enum Types x_status;
    }
var;
```

which would then require statements such as:

```
var.x.ordinal = 2;
ptr->x.ordinal = 2;
var.x_status = CHAR;
```

Questions:

1) What is the difference between a structure and a union?

2) What is a member?

3) If x is a variable, how would you find out the value of a member called 'mem'?

4) If ptr is a pointer to a structure, how would you find out the value of a member called 'mem'?

5) A union is a group of variables in a single package. True or false?

27 : Data Structures

Uses for struct Variables and Structure Diagrams

This section is advanced. Beginners may wish to omit it on first reading.

Data structures are organised patterns of data. The purpose of building a data structure is to create a pattern of information which models a particular situation clearly and efficiently. Take the simplest kind of data structure, the array. Arrays are good for storing patterns of information which look like arrays, or share the same structure. For example, a chess board looks like a two-dimensional array, so a chess game would naturally use a two-dimensional array to store the positions of pieces on the board. The aim of a data structure is to model real life patterns with program data.

Most application programs require more complex data structures than C variables can offer – often arrays are not suitable structures for a given application. To see this, consider an application example in which a program stores a map of the local countryside. This program has to store information about individual towns and it has to be able to give directions to the user about how to get to particular towns from some reference point. In real life, all of this information is most easily conveyed by means of a map, with towns' vital statistics written on it (see figure 27.1). The diagram shows such a simplified map of the surrounding land. This sort of map is ideally, just what a computer ought to be able to store. The handicap is that the map does not look very computerish. If the map is ever going to be stored in a computer, it will need to look more mechanical. A transformation is needed. In order to make the map into a more computer-like picture, it must be drawn as a *structure diagram*.

A structure diagram is a picture which shows how something is connected up. Most often a structure diagram shows how a problem is 'connected up' by relating all the parts which go together to make it up.

In this case, the structure diagram just shows how program data are related to one another.

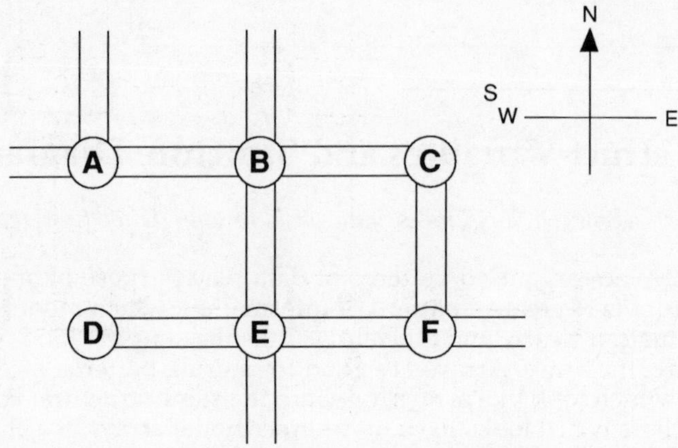

27.1. A conceptual diagram.

Data Structure Diagrams

Now examine figure 27.2. This diagram is a data structure diagram. It demonstrates how boxes of data must relate to one another in order to solve the problem of the towns map. It has been drawn, quite deliberately, in a way which is intended to conjure up some particular thoughts. The arrows tend to suggest that pointers will play a role in the data structure. The blocks tend to suggest that sealed capsules or 'struct' type data will also play a role. Putting these two together creates the idea of a 'town structure' containing pointers to neighouring villages which lie on roads to the north, south, east and west of the town, as well as the information about the town itself. This town structure might look something like this:

```
struct Town
    {
    struct Town *north;
    struct Town *south;
    struct Town *east;
    struct Town *west;
    struct LocalInfo help;
    };
```

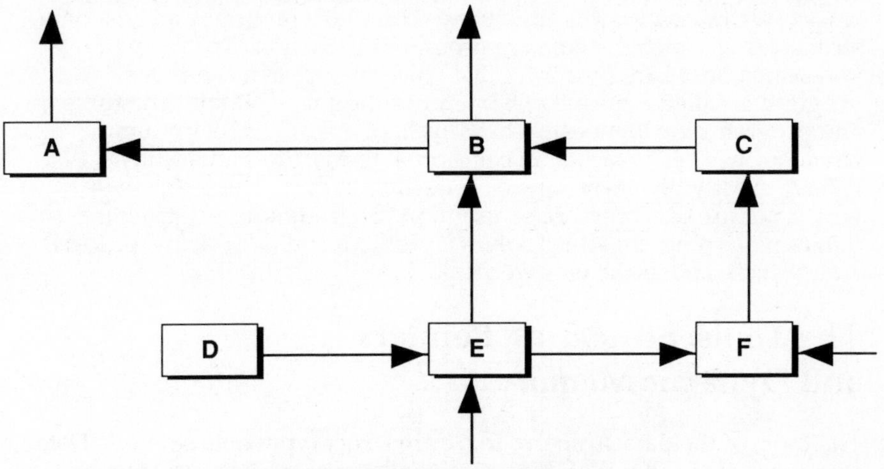

Figure 27.2.Mechanised diagram.

Assume for now that LocalInfo is a structure which contains all the information about a town required by the program. This part of the information is actually irrelevant to the structure of the data because it is hidden inside the sealed capsule. It is the pointers which are the main items of concern, because these contain information that enables a program to find its way around the map very quickly. If the user of this imaginary application program wished to know about the town to the north of one particular place, the program would only have to refocus its attention on the new structure which was pointed to by the struct member 'north' and similarly for other directions.

A data structure is built up, like a model, by connecting struct type variables together with pointers: these are the building blocks.

By thinking of struct types and pointers in terms of pictures, you begin to understand how structures can be fashioned, in computer memory to look exactly like the problems which they represent.

There is an interesting point to be made about data structure diagrams. It's worth remarking about the way in which these data structure diagrams resemble the structure diagrams of C programs, which were drawn in Chapter 7, and will be drawn again in the next chapter. There is a simple reason for this similarity – computer programs are just data structures in which the data are program instructions and the pointers and sealed boxes are function calls. The structure of a computer program is called a hierachy. Sometimes the shape of data structures and programs are identical. When this happens, a kind of optimum efficiency has been reached in conceptual terms. Programs which behave exactly like their data, operate very simply. This is the reason why structure diagrams are so useful in programming – a structure diagram is a diagram which solves a problem and does so in a pictorial way, which models the way we think.

The Tools: Structures, Pointers and Dynamic Memory

The tools of the data structure trade are struct types and pointers. Data structures are built out of dynamically allocated memory, so storage places do not need names - all a program needs to do is to keep a record of a pointer to a particular storage space, and the computer will be able to find it at any time after that. Pointers are the keys which unlock a program's data. The reader might object to this by saying that a pointer has to be stored in some C variable somewhere, so does a program really gain anything from working with pointers? The answer is yes, because pointers in data structures are invariably chained together to make up the structure. To understand this, make a note of the following two terms:

Root This is a place where a data structure starts. Every chain has to start somewhere. The address of the root of a data structure has to be stored explicitly in a C variable.

Links A link is a pointer to a new struct type. Links are used to chain structures together. The address of the next element in a chain structure is stored inside the previous structure.

Data structures do not have to be linear chains and they are often not. Structures, after all, can hold any number of pointers to other structures, so there is the potential to branch out into any number of new structures. In the map example, there were four pointers in each structure, so the chaining was not linear, but more like a lattice.

Programmers should be concerned about where and how data structures are going to be stored. Remember that pointers alone do not create any storage space – they are only a way of finding out the contents of storage space which already exists. In fact, a program must create its own space for data structures, in the same way in which space had to be allocated for strings in Chapter 20. The key phrase is *dynamic storage*: a program makes space for structures as new ones are required and deletes space which it does not require. The functions which perform this memory allocation and release are:

malloc and free

There are some advantages which go with the use of dynamic storage for data structures and they are summarised by the following points:

1) Since memory is allocated as it is needed, the only restriction on data size is the memory capacity of the computer.

2) Using pointers to connect structures means that they can be re-connected in different ways as the need arises. For example, data structures can be sorted.

3) Data structures can be made up of lots of 'lesser' data structures, each held inside struct type storage. Limitations are few.

The remaining parts of this chapter aim to provide you with a basic plan or formula for putting data structures together in C. This is done with recourse to two example structures, which become two example programs in the next chapter.

Programme for Building Data Structures

In writing programs which centre around their data, such as wordprocessors, accounts programs or database managers, it is extremely important to plan data structures *before* any program code is written. Changes in program code do not affect data structure, but alterations to a data structure imply drastic changes to program code.

Only in some numerical applications does a data structure actually assist an algorithm rather than vice versa.

The steps which a programmer would undertake in designing a data structure follow a basic pattern:

1) Group all the data, which must be stored, together and define a struct type to hold them.

2) Think of a pattern which reflects the way in which the data are connected and add structure pointers to the struct definition to connect them.

3) Design the programming algorithms to handle the memory allocation, link pointers and data storage.

Setting Up a Data Structure

When the basic mould has been cast for the building blocks, a program actually has to go through the motions of putting all the pieces together, by connecting structures together with pointers and filling them up with information. The data structure is set up by repeating the following actions as many times as is necessary.

1) Define a struct type. For example:

```
struct Town

      {
      struct Town *north;
      struct Town *south;
      struct Town *east;
      struct Town *west;
      struct LocalInfo help;
      };
```

2) Declare two pointers to this type:

```
struct Town *ptr,*root;
```

One of these is used to hold the root of the data structure and the other is used as a current pointer.

3) Allocate memory for one structure type:

```
root = (struct Town *) malloc(sizeof(struct Town));
```

Be careful to check for errors. Root will be NULL if no memory could be allocated.

4) Initialise the members of the structure with statements such as:

```
root->north = NULL;
root->south = NULL;
root->help.age = 56;   /*if age is a member*/
                      /*of struct LocalInfo*/
```

This sets the pointers 'north' and 'south' to the value NULL, which conventionally means that the pointer actually does not point anywhere.

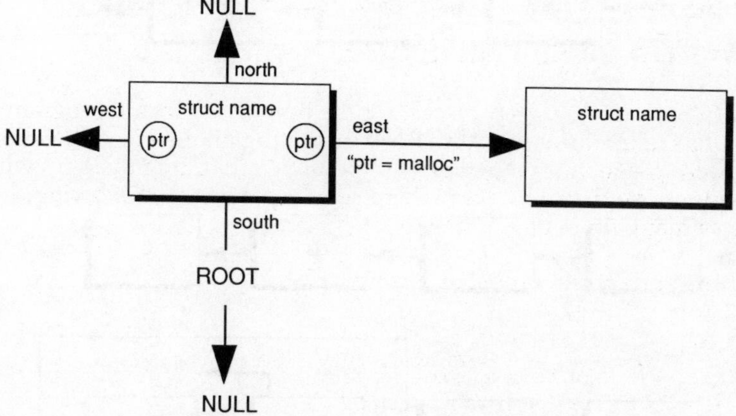

Figure 27.3. Connecting data with pointers.

5) When other structures have been created, the pointers can be assigned to them:

```
ptr = (struct Town *) malloc(sizeof(struct Town));
ptr->north = NULL;
ptr->south = NULL;
/* etc.. initialize members */
root->north = ptr;
```

> This last statement connects the new structure onto the north branch of root.

NULL pointer assignments tell the program handling the data structure when it has come to the edge of the structure: that is when it has found a pointer which doesn't lead anywhere.

Example Structures

There are two data structures which are so common that it is almost hard to write applications which do not use them! These two are called the 'linked list' and the 'binary tree', and both work on the principles just outlined. They are just different manifestations of the same thing.

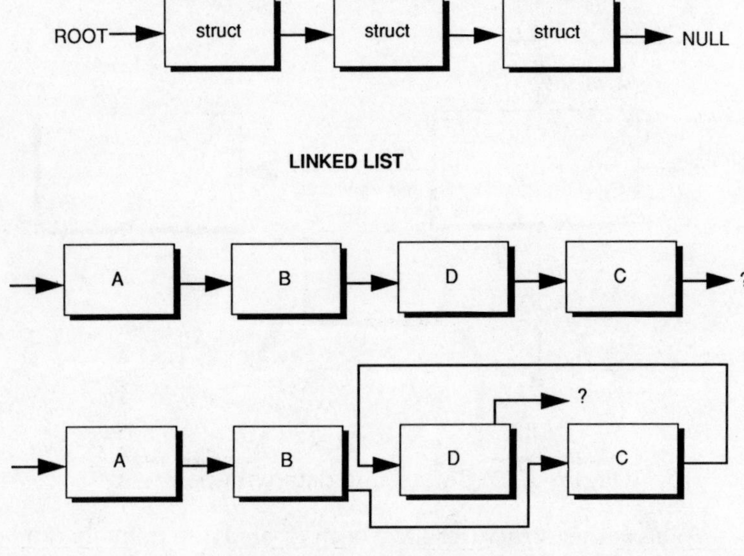

Figure 27.4. A Linked List.

A linked list is a 'linear' sequence of structures joined together by pointers. If a structure diagram were drawn of a linked list, all the storage blocks in it would lie in a straight line, without branching out:

```
struct list

      {
      double value;
      struct list *succ;
      };
```

A linked list has only a single pointer per structure, which points to the successor in the list. If the blocks were labelled A, B, C, D, E... then B would be the successor of A, C would be the successor of B and so on.

Linked lists have two advantages over one-dimensional arrays – they can be sorted easily and they can be made any length at all.

A binary tree is a sequence of structures, each of which branches out into two new ones:

```
struct BinaryTree

      {
      /* other info */
      struct BinaryTree *left;
      struct BinaryTree *right;
      }

      *tree = NULL;
```

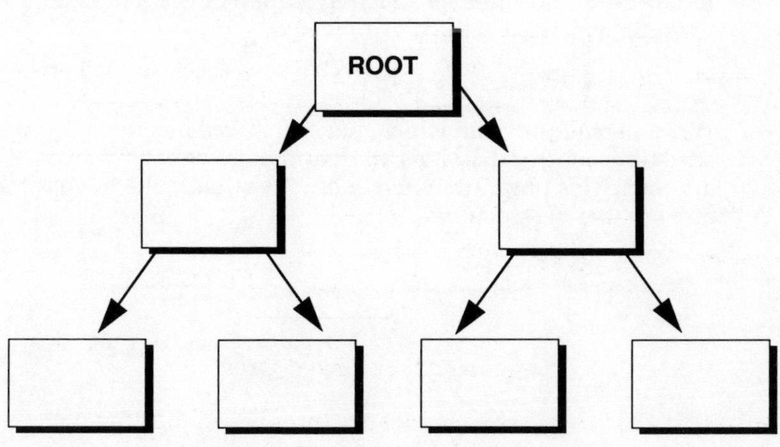

Figure 27.5. Binary tree pointers.

A binary tree structure has two pointers per struct type. This is useful for classifying data on a greater than/less than basis. Right and left branches are taken to mean 'greater than' and 'less than' respectively.

The programs which handle these data structures are written in the form of complete, usable application programs. They are simple by professional standards, but they are long by book standards so they are explained in a chapter by themselves, along with their accompanying programmers' documentation. See Chapter 30.

Questions:

1) What is a structure diagram?

2) How are data linked together to make a data structure?

3) Every separate struct type in a data structure has its own variable name. True or false?

4) How are the members of structures accessed in a data structure?

5) Write a statement which creates a new structure of type 'struct BinaryTree' and finds its address. Store that address in a variable which is declared as follows:

```
struct BinaryTree *ptr;
```

6) Write a small program which makes a linked list, three structures long and assigns all their data to be zero. Can you automate this program with a loop? Can you make it work for any number of structures?

28 : Recursion

The Demon Which Swallowed Its Tail

This section is advanced. First time readers may wish to omit it on first time reading.

This section is about program structures which can talk about themselves. Examine the function below:

```
Well_Function ()

{
/* ... other statements ... */

Well_Function ();
}
```

Well_Function is said to be a recursive function. It is defined in terms of itself: it contains itself and it calls itself. It swallows its own tail! The act of self-reference is called recursion. What happens to such a function when it is called in a C program? In the simple example above, something dramatic and fatal happens. The computer naturally begins executing the statements in the function, inside the curly braces. This much is only normal – programs are designed to do this and the computer could do no more and no less. Eventually the program comes upon the statement 'Well_Function;' and it makes a call to that function again. It then begins executing statements in Well_function, from the beginning, as though it were a new function, until it comes upon the statement 'Well_Function' and then it calls the function again, and again...

This kind of function-calling scenario is doomed to continue without end, as, each time the function is called, it is inevitably called again. The computer becomes totally consumed with the task of calling 'Well_Function' over and over. It is apparently doomed to repeat the same procedure for ever. Or is it?

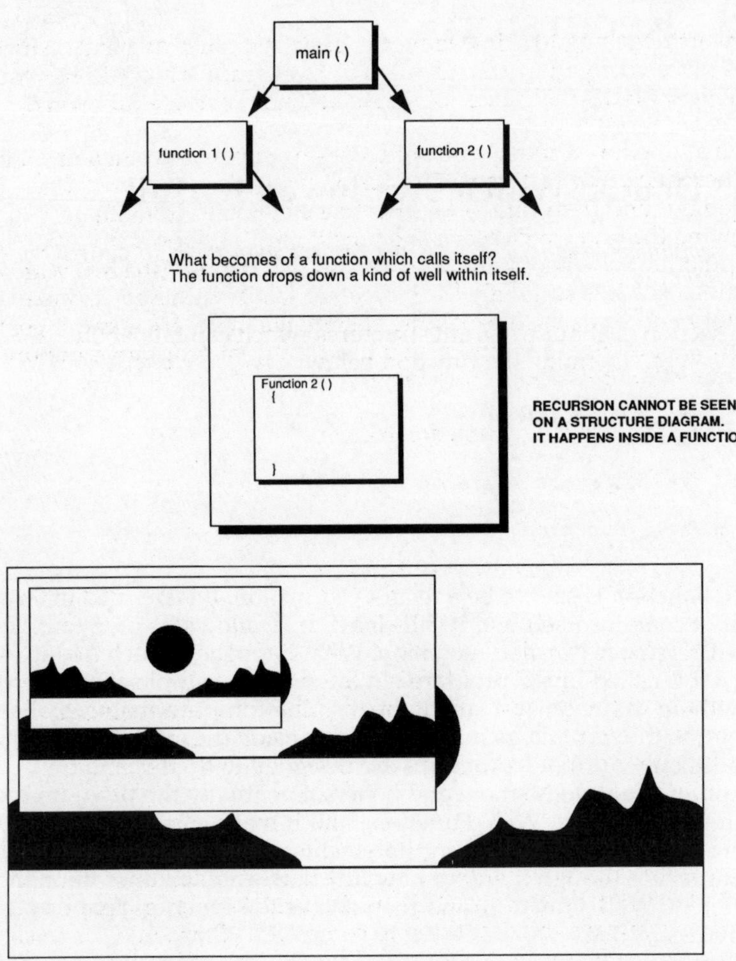

Figure 28.1 Recursion: Things inside themselves.

Functions and The Stack

It is worth pausing to think about the exact sequence of events which takes place when a function is called in a program. This will help to cast some light on the mechanics of recursion and recursive functions.

When a function is called, control passes from one place in a program to another place. The statements in this new region of the program are carried out and then control returns to a statement immediately following the one which made the function call. But how does the computer know where it must go back to when it has finished with a function call? It is suddenly thrown into a wildly different region of the memory and finds itself executing statements there. How can it get back again? A diagram does not answer this question: program structure diagrams hide this detail from view:

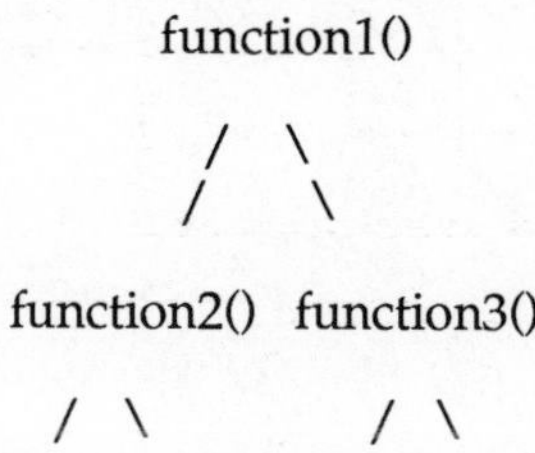

The answer to this puzzle is that the computer keeps a record of the addresses of the places to which it must return, no matter how many times functions are called. It does this by building a special data structure called a 'stack'.

A stack is quite literally a data pile, organised in the memory. Information is placed on top of a stack and taken from the top. It is called a 'last in/first out' structure because the last thing to go on the top of a stack is always the first thing to come off it. C organises a stack structure when it runs a program and uses it for storing local variables and for keeping track of where it has to return to. When it calls a function, it leaves itself a reminder, on the top of its program stack, which tells it where it has to go to when it has finished executing that function. C management makes sure that it does not put anything else on top of that reminder to spoil the flow of control. When a function is finished, the program takes the first message from the top of the stack and carries on executing statements at the place specified by the message. Normally this method works perfectly, without any problems at all. Functions are called and they return again; the stack grows and shrinks and all is well.

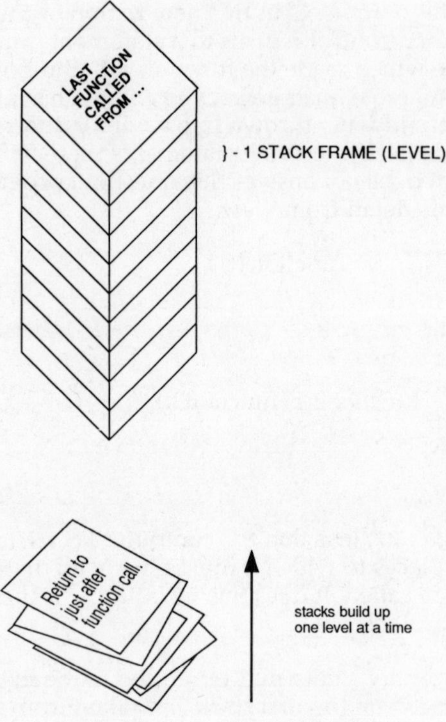

Figure 28.2. The Stack.

What happens when a recursive function, like 'Well_Function' calls itself? The system works as normal. C makes a note of the place it has to return to and puts that note on top of the stack. It then begins executing statements. When it comes to the call 'Well_Function' again, it makes a new note of where it has to come back to and deposits it on top of the stack. It then begins the function again and when it finds the function call, it makes a new note and puts on the top of the stack. As this process continues, the memory gets filled up with the program's messages to itself and the stack of messages gets larger and larger. As the function has no chance of returning control to its caller, the messages never get taken off the stack and it just builds up. Eventually the computer runs out of memory and the computer crashes or interrupts the program with a fatal error message.

Levels and Wells

A stack is made up of frames or levels. Each time a function is called, the program is said to drop down a level. This is the reason for structure comments like:

```
/*************************************************/
/* Level 1                                       */
/*************************************************/
```

in the programs in this book. The main function is at level zero because it is the root of the program. If main calls any functions at all, control drops down to level one. When a level one function returns, it hands control back to level zero. These level numbers actually count the height of the program stack at any point in a program. The level number is the number of messages or reminders on the stack.

A function like 'Well_Function' digs itself a well of infinite depth. It punches a great hole in a program; it has no place in a levelled structure diagram. The function is 'sick' because it causes the stack to fill up the computer's memory. A better name for this function would be:

```
StackOverflow()  /* Causes stack to grow out of control */

{
StackOverflow();
}
```

Tame Recursion and Self-Similarity

Recursion does not have to be so dramatically disastrous as the example given. If recursion is tamed, it provides a powerful way of handling certain kinds of problem in programming, particularly those concerning data structures.

In Chapter 27 it was remarked that programs and data structures aim to model the situation they deal with as closely as possible. Some problems are made up of many levels of detail (see the introduction to this book), and the details are identical at all levels. As recursion is about functions which contain themselves at all levels, this tends to suggest that recursion would be useful for dealing with these self-similar problems. Data structures are prime candidates for this because they are made up of identical structure types, connected together in a way which make them look like programs connected up by function calls.

Recursive functions can be tamed by making sure that there is a safe exit for them, so that recursion only happens under particular circumstances. The aim is to control the number of times that recursion takes place by making a decision about what happens in the function: the decision about whether a function calls itself or not. For example, it is easy to make 'Well_Function' recurse four times only, by making a test as folows:

```
Well_Function(nooftimes)

int nooftimes;
{

if (nooftimes == 0)
     {
     return (0);
     }

else
     {
     Well_Function(nooftimes-1);
     }
}
```

A call of Well_Function(4) would make this function drop down four stack levels and then return. Notice the way in which the if...else statement shields the program from the recursion when 'nooftimes' equals zero. It effectively acts as a safety net, stopping the program from plunging down the level well infinitely.

Simple Example Without a Data Structure

A standard example of controlled recursion is the factorial (or gamma) function. This is a mathematical function which is important in statistics. (Mathematicians also deal with recursive functions; computer programs are not alone in this.)

The factorial function is defined to be the 'product' (multiplication) of all the natural (unsigned integer) numbers from one to the parameter of the function. For example:

```
factorial(4) == 1 * 2 * 3 * 4             == 24
factorial(6) == 1 * 2 * 3 * 4 * 5 * 6     == 720
```

Formally, the factorial function is defined by two mathematical statements:

```
factorial (n) = n * factorial(n-1)
```

and also:

```
factorial (0) = 1
```

The first of these statements is recursive, because it defines the value of factorial(n) in terms of the factorial function of (n-1). This strange definition seems to want to lift itself by its very boot-straps! The second statement saves it, by giving it a reference value. The factorial function can be written down immediately, as a controlled recursive function:

```
factorial (n)

unsigned int n;
{

if (n == 0)
     {
     return (1);
     }

else
     {
     return (n * factorial(n-1));
     }
}
```

To see how this works, try following it through for n equals three. The following statement:

```
factorial (3);
```

causes a call to be made to 'factorial'. The value of n is set to three. factorial then tests whether n is zero (which it is not), so it takes the alternative branch of the if...else statement. This instructs it to return the value of:

```
3 * factorial(3-1)
```

In order to calculate that, the function has to call factorial recursively, passing the value (3-1) or two to the new call. The new call takes this value, checks whether it is zero (it is not) and tries to return the value 2 * factorial(1). In order to work this out, it needs to call factorial again, which checks that n is not zero (it is not), and so tries to return 1 * factorial(0). Finally, it calls factorial(0) which *does not* call factorial any more, but starts unloading the stack and returning the values. The expression goes through the following steps below before finally being evaluated:

```
factorial (3) == 3 * factorial(2)
              == 3 * (2 * factorial(1))
              == 3 * (2 * (1 * factorial(0)))
              == 3 * (2 * (1 * 1)))

              == 3 * 2 * 1 * 1
```

Try to write this function without using recursion and compare the two.

Simple Example With a Data Structure

A data structure earns the name recursive if its structure looks identical at every point within it. The simplest recursive structure is the linked list. At every point in a linked list, there are some data of identical type and one pointer to the next structure. The next simplest structure is the binary tree. This structure splits into two at every point. It has two pointers, one which branches left and one which branches to the right. Neither of these structures goes on for ever, so it seems reasonable to suppose that they might be handled easily using controlled recursive functions. Examples are presented in Chapter 29 on Toolkits. Here is one of them, examined in detail.

Deletetoend is a function which releases the dynamic memory allocated to a linked list in one go. The problem it faces is this: if it deletes the first structure in the list, it will loose information about where the rest of the list is, because the pointer to the successor of a structure is held in its predecessor. It must therefore make a note of the pointer to the next structure in the list, before it deletes that structure or it will never be able to get beyond the first structure in the list. The solution is to delete the list backwards from last to first using the following recursive routine:

```
/* structure definition */

      struct list
          {
          /* some other data members */
          struct list *succ;
          };

/************************************************************/

      struct list *deletetoend (ptr)
      struct list *ptr;
      {

      if (ptr != NULL)
          {
          deletetoend (ptr->succ);
          releasestruct (ptr);
          }
      return (NULL);
      }

/************************************************************/

      releasestruct (ptr)       /* release memory back to pool */
      struct list *ptr;
      {

      if (free((char *) ptr) != 0)
          {
          printf ("DEBUG [Z0/TktDtStrct] memory release
              failure\n");
          }
      }
```

The user supplies a pointer to the place he/she would like the list to end. This need not be the beginning – it could be any place in the list. The function then eliminates all structures after that point, up to the end of the list. It does assume that the programmer has been careful to ensure that the end of the list is marked by a NULL pointer! This is the conventional way of denoting a pointer which does not point anywhere. If the pointer supplied is already NULL then this function does nothing.

If it is not NULL, then it executes the statements enclosed by the 'if' braces. Notice that deletetoend calls itself immediately, passing its successor in the list as a parameter (ptr->succ). The function keeps doing this until it finds the end on the list. The very last-called deletetoend then reaches the statement releasestruct, which frees the memory taken up by the last structure and hands it back to the free memory pool. That function consequently returns and allows the second-last deletetoend to reach the releasestruct statement, releasing the second last structure (which is now on the end of the list). This, in turn, returns and the process continue until the entire list has been deleted. The function returns the value NULL at each stage, so that when called, deletetoend offers a very elegant way of deleting part or all of a linked list:

```
struct list *newlast;

newlast->succ = deletetoend (newlast->succ);

ptr = deletetoend (ptr);
```

newlast then becomes the new end of the list, and its successor is NULLified in a single statement.

Advantages and Disadvantages of Recursion

But why should programmers want to clutter up programs with techniques as mind-boggling as recursion at all?

The great advantage of recursion is that it makes functions very simple and allows them to behave just like the data structure they are attempting to model. Unfortunately there are few situations in which recursion can be employed in a practical way. The major disadvantage of recursion is the amount of memory required to make it work. Don't forget that the program stack grows each time a function call is made. If a recursive function buried itself a thousand levels deep, a program would almost certainly run out of memory. There is also the slight danger that a recursive function will go out of control if a program contains bugs.

Recursion and Global Variables

Global variables and recursion do not mix well. Most recursive routines only work because they are sealed capsules, and what goes on inside them can never affect the outside world. The only time that recursive functions should attempt to alter global storage, is when the function concerned operates on a global data structure, as in the previous example. To appreciate the danger, consider a recursive function, in which a second function alterGLOBAL accidentally alters the value of GLOBAL in the middle of the function:

```
int GLOBAL = -2;

recursion ()
{

if (++GLOBAL == 0)
        {
     return (0);
     }

alterGLOBAL();   /* another function which alters GLOBAL */

recursion();
}
```

This function is treading a fine line between safety and digging its own recursive grave. If alterGLOBAL makes GLOBAL more negative, as fast as ++ can make it more positive, then GLOBAL will never be able to satisfy the condition of being zero. It will go on making recursive calls, never returning. If alterGLOBAL makes the mistake of setting GLOBAL to a positive value, then the ++ operator in recursion can only make GLOBAL larger. It will never be able to satisfy the condition that GLOBAL equals zero, and so again the function would never be able to return. The stack would fill up the memory and the program would plunge down a bottomless recursive well.

If global variables and parameters are used instead, this difficulty can be controlled much more easily. AlterGLOBAL cannot alter a variable in recursion by accident, if only local variables are used, because it only works with its own local copies of parameters and variables which are locked away in a sealed capsule, out of harm's way.

Questions:

1) What is a recursive function?

2) What is a program 'stack' and what is it for?

3) State the major disadvantage of recursion.

29 : Toolkits

A toolkit is a set of functions which can be used over and over again in programs. Toolkits are created by programmers when they come upon particular functions, or sets of functions, which can be used in other programs. Experienced programmers learn to be aware of this possibility and to recognise programming tasks which are general, or have been used before, and separate off those parts. A strict set of program structuring rules (as described in Appendix A) can help with this. Toolkits are then created automatically.

The point about toolkits is not necessarily that they have to be used without modification in every program, but that they form a basic set of 'customisable commands' which cut down the amount of work needed in programming. Ideally, a program should try to make the best of each program individually. Functions in a toolkit can always be altered to suit a particular application. Most of the functions listed below have proven to be useful in writing the programs for this book.

The toolkits provided here contain routines in the following areas of programming:

1) Linked list data structure
2) Console output
3) Console input
4) Complex numbers

The salient points of these functions are described below:

```
/**************************************************************/
/* Toolkit Linked List                                        */
/**************************************************************/
     /* The following functions require a defintion like...*/

       struct list
           {
           /* some other data members */
```

```
        struct list *succ;
        };

/************************************************************/

    #define true        1
    #define false       0
    #define off         0
    #define set         1

    struct list *ROOT,*ptr;
```

ROOT is a GLOBAL variable of type 'struct list' which points to the start of a linked list.

```
/************************************************************/
```

Find the end of a linked list by looking for a NULL pointer. The linked list structure must contain a member called 'succ' for successor which points to the next item in the list.

```
    struct list *eolist()
    {    struct list *ptr,*p = NULL;

    for (ptr = ROOT; ptr != NULL; ptr = ptr->succ)
         {
         p = ptr;
         }
    return (p);
    }

/************************************************************/

    struct list *startfrom (i)    /* Find ith node in list */
    int i;
    {    struct list *ptr,*p = NULL;
         int j = 0;

    for (ptr=ROOT; (ptr != NULL) && (j++ != i); ptr=ptr->succ)
         {
         p = ptr;
         }
    return (p);
    }

/************************************************************/
```

Install a new structure on the end of a linked list. This function can not insert a structure in the middle of a linked list, because it does not take care to reconnect pointers in the correct way.

```
struct list *install (ptr)

{    struct list *thispos, *newstruct();

if ((thispos = newstruct()) == NULL)
     {
     warning();
     printf ("DEBUG **: Free memory pool is empty");
     exit(0);
     }

if (ROOT = NULL)
     {
     ROOT = thispos;
     ROOT = true;
     }

else
     {
     ptr->succ = thispos;
     }

thispos->secs = t;
thispos->rate = r;
thispos->succ = NULL;

return (thispos);
}
```

/***/

Delete from ptr to the end of a linked list. In other words, make this structure pointed to be ptr the new end of the list.

```
struct list *deletetoend (ptr)
struct list *ptr;

{
if (ptr != NULL)
     {
     deletetoend (ptr->succ);
     releasestruct (ptr);
     }
return (NULL);
}
```

```
/****************************************************************/
```

Obtain memory for a new dynamic structure of type 'struct list'.

```
struct list *newstruct ()

{     char *malloc();
return ((struct list *) malloc(sizeof(struct list)));
}
```

```
/****************************************************************/
```

Free the memory, previously allocated by newstruct() which is pointed to by ptr and hand it back to the free memory pool where it can be used by other data structures, other programs or whatever.

```
releasestruct (ptr)

struct list *ptr;
{

if (free((char *) ptr) != 0)
      {
      printf ("DEBUG [Z0/TktDtStrct] memory release
            faliure\n");
      }
}
```

```
/****************************************************************/
/* Toolkit CONSOLE Output                                       */
/****************************************************************/
```

These functions perform very basic output facilities. Most of the functions in this section could also be implemented as macros. For example:

```
#define clrscrn()      putchar('\f')
#define blankline()    printf ("\r           \r")
```

```
/****************************************************************/
```

Clears the user's screen.

```
clrscrn ()
{
putchar ('\f');
}
```

```
/****************************************************************/
```

Makes the current line on the screen blank by printing spaces over it and leaves the cursor at the start of the line. There must be enough spaces to cover the whole line, but not so many that the line spills over onto the next line.

```
blankline ()

{
printf ("\r                                              \r");
}
```

```
/****************************************************************/
```

This mimics pressing RETURN. It prints a blank line on the screen.

```
newline ()

{
putchar ('\n');
}
```

```
/****************************************************************/
```

This function makes a beep, or makes a warning signal to the user.

```
warning ()

{
putchar ('\7');
}
```

```
/****************************************************************/
```

Pause briefly. A very short gap. The limit on x can be altered to make the gap longer or shorter.

```
pause ()

{   int x;
for (x=0; x <= 50000; x += 1);
}
```

```
/****************************************************************/
/* TOOLKIT Console Input                                        */
/****************************************************************/
```

This function is useful when a program user opts to finish a section by selecting a 'quit' option. The program could verify the quit option by writing the following:

```
if (wantout(carefully))
     {
     /* really quit:  exit() or return() etc. */
     }
```

If a programmer writes wantout(fast), the function simply returns 'true'. The function serves only a decorative purpose. Note that this function calls another function yes() in this toolkit.

```
#define fast      false       /* parameters for wantout */
#define carefully true

wantout (becareful)           /* quit a program section */
int becareful;
{

if (becareful)
     {
     printf ("Really quit? (Y/N)\n");
     return (yes());
     }
return (true);
}
```

```
/**********************************************************/
```

Here are some functions which have been used extensively during the course of this book. They are listed here for completeness, in the 'proper' toolkit.

```
yes ()                      /* boolean response Y/N query */

{
while (true)
     {
     switch (getkey())
          {
          case 'y' : case 'Y' : return (true);
          case 'n' : case 'N' : return (false);
          }
     }
}
```

```
/**********************************************************/
```

This function, in particular, can be altered from system to system. Most micros support a 'getcharacter' function in which the character value is returned immediately, without the user having to press RETURN. This is normally called getch and is implemented as part of the standard input output library.

```
char getkey ()                  /* single key press response */
                                /* user must press RETURN    */
{    char ch;
scanf ("%c",&ch);
skipgarb();
return (ch);
}
```

/**/

This function waits to get an integer from the user, which lies between the values a and b (b should be greater than a). If the value is not valid, the program re-prompts the user with a question mark, until a valid value has been found. Note that this function calls skipgarb.

```
getint (a,b)                    /* return int between a and b */

int a,b;
{    int  p, i = a - 1;

for (p=0; ((a > i) || (i > b)); p++)
     {
     printf ("?");
     scanf ("%d",&i);

     if (p > 3)
          {
          skipgarb();
          p = 0;
          }
     }

skipgarb();
return (i);
}
```

/**/

As above, for floating point values. When converting this to double or long float types, remember to use the '%lf' conversion specifier in place of '%f'.

```
float getfloat (a,b)   /* return float between a and b */
float a,b;

{    short p;
     float  x = a - 1.0;

for (p=0; ((a > x) || (x > b)); p++)
     {
     printf ("? ");
     scanf ("%f",&x);
     if (p > 3)
          {
          skipgarb();
          p = 0;
          }

     }
skipgarb();
return (x);
}
```

/**/

Skip garbage up to the end of the current line.

```
skipgarb ()
{

while (getchar() != '\n')
     {
     }
}
```

```
/*************************************************************/
/* Toolkit : Complex Arithmetic                              */
/*************************************************************/
```

Define the complex structure type. Programmers who already know about complex numbers will appreciate the relevance of this toolkit. Programmers who do not, will never need to worry about them!

```
typedef struct
     {
     long float x,y;
     }
complex;
```

/***/

```
complex add (a,b)
```

```
complex a,b;

{ complex z;

z.x = a.x + b.x;
z.y = a.y + b.y;

return(z);
}
/************************************************************/

complex subtract (a,b)

complex a,b;

{     complex z;
z.x = a.x - b.x;
z.y = a.y - b.y;
return (z);

}

/************************************************************/

complex multiply (a,b)
complex a,b;

{    complex z;
z.x = (a.x * b.x) - (a.y * b.y);
z.y = (a.y * b.x) + (a.x * b.y);

return (z);
}
/************************************************************/

complex divide (a,b)
complex a,b;

{    complex z;

long float denominator;
denominator = (b.x * b.x  +  b.y * b.y);

z.x = (a.x * b.x + a.y * b.y)/denominator;
z.y = (b.x * a.y - a.x * b.y)/denominator;

return (z);
}
```

30 : Example Programs

The aim of this chapter is to provide two substantial examples of C, which use the data structures described in Chapter 27.

Example 1. Statistical Data Handler

The first program is a utility which allows the user to type sets of floating point data into an editor, and to calculate the mean, standard deviation and so on. The program is capable of loading and saving the data to disc, as well as being able to handle several sets of data at once. The editor works in insert or overwrite modes.

The program is menu-driven and its operation should be reasonably self-explanatory, so it is presented with rather sparse documentation.

The Editor

A simple machine-independent editor is provided for entering data. The editor first asks the user whether the current number of sets of data is to be altered. The default value is zero so, when data is typed in for the first time, this should be set up, by responding Y for 'yes'. Up to 20 independent sets of data can be used. This number is set at the start and it is held in the memory and saved to disc with data files. If the number of sets is reduced at any time, the top sets are 'cut off' from the calculations. They are not lost forever, provided the number is changed back to include them before they are saved to disc, as the number of sets is used as an upper bound in a for loop: it does not actually alter the memory. More sets can be added at any time by making this value larger.

Insert/Overwrite

A project file can be edited in either insert mode or overwrite mode. Files which contain no data can only be edited in insert mode. The editor senses this and selects the mode automatically. In *insert mode* the user is prompted for values. Type 0.0 in place of an entry to get out of this mode.

In overwrite mode the user is offered each entry in turn. If a non-digit character is typed in (such as a . (dot), a - (dash) and so on, the value of an entry is not altered. However, if a new value is entered, the new value will replace the old one. By default, the values are offered in turn from one to the final value. But on selecting *overwrite mode,* the user is prompted for a starting value, and the values are offered from the starting number to the end. This is to avoid the rather tedious process of working through all the entries which are not required in a system independent way.

Quitting Sections

When quitting sections in which the user is supposed to enter data, the convention is that typing a zero value (0.0 for a time, 0 in any other instance), is a signal to break out of a section. Typing 0.0 while editing in insert mode causes the editor to quit.

The Program Listing

The program includes three library files, which are used for the following purposes:

#include "stdio.h"	standard header file
#include "ctype.h"	contains character ID macros
#include "math.h"	includes math function declarations

The flow of program logic is most easily described by means of a program structure diagram. The diagram shows the structure of function calls within the program and this can be related to the listing.

The general scheme of the program is this:

1) Various flags concerning the data structure are cleared.

2) A menu is printed and the program cycles through the options.

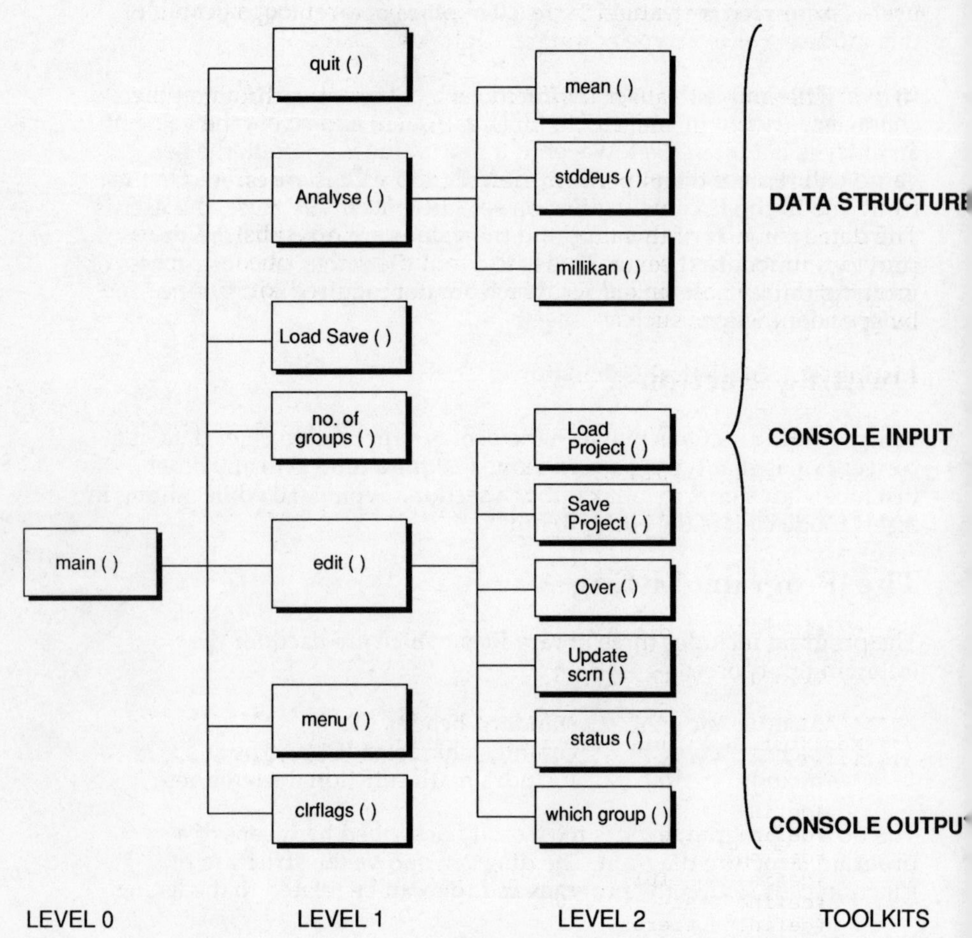

Figure 30.1. The structure of STAT.C

3) The editor determines the data group to be edited, updates the screen with the data in the current group and loops through insert or overtype editing until the user quits.

4) The analysis calls custom functions which scan through the data structure calculating the relevant quantities.

5) Various toolkits perform run-of-the-mill activities.

The data structure of this program is an array of linked lists. The array provides the roots of several independent linked lists: one for each group of data. These linked lists are attended to by toolkit routines and by special functions such as 'over()'.

Listing 30.1. Statistical Calculator.

```
/***********************************************************/
/*                                                         */
/* Statistical Calculator                                  */
/*                                                         */
/***********************************************************/
    /****************************************/
    /* Include some library files for linking */
    /****************************************/

      #include "stdio.h"
      #include "ctype.h"
      #include "math.h"

/**********************************************************/
/** Manifest Constants / Macros / Static Variables      **/
/**********************************************************/

      #define true        1
      #define false       0
      #define grps        20 /* No grps which can be handled */
      #define carefully   1
      #define fast        0
      #define notzero     1
      #define endmark     -1.1
      #define notendmark  0
      #define bignum      1e300

      int   DATSETS = 0;
      short DATATHERE = false;                  /* list data */
      char  *FSP = "........................";  /* project
                                                     name */
```

```
/*********************************************************/
/** STRUCTURES                                          **/
/*********************************************************/

    struct list
        {
        double value;
        struct list *succ;
        };

    struct Vlist
        {
        struct list *datptr;
        int datathere;
        }
    Data[grps];

/*********************************************************/
/**  LEVEL 0 : Main Program                             **/
/*********************************************************/

    main ()

        {    char getkey();
        clrflags();

        while (true)
            {
            Menu();
            switch (getkey())
                {
                case '1' : edit(noofgroups());
                           break;
                case '2' : LoadSave();
                           break;
                case '3' : Analyse();
                           break;
                case 'q' : if (wantout(carefully)) quit();
                }
            }
        }

/*********************************************************/
/**  LEVEL 1                                            **/
/*********************************************************/

    clrflags()               /* Initialize a virtual list */
    {    short i;

    for (i=1; i<=grps; i++);
        {
        Data[i].datathere = false;
```

```
        Data[i].datptr = NULL;
        }
    }

/*************************************************************/

    Menu ()

    {
    clrscrn();
    printf ("\nStatistical Calculator V1.0\n\n\n");

    printf ("1 : Edit Data Files\n\n");
    printf ("2 : Project Files\n\n");
    printf ("3 : Analyse Files\n\n");
    printf ("q : Quit\n\n");
    printf ("\nEnter Choice and RETURN : ");
    }

/*************************************************************/

    edit (no_grps)                      /* Edit a linked list */
    int no_grps;

    {   char s,status(),getkey();
        int i,stop = false,ctr;
        void saveproject();
        double over(),t,correct,getfloat();
        struct list *ptr,*here,*eolist(),
                *install(),*startfrom();

    while (true)
        {
        i = whichgroup();
        switch (s = status(i))
            {
            case 'i':

                for (here = eolist(i,&ctr); true; ctr++)
                    {
                    updatescrn (i,s);
                    printf("%d:",ctr);

                    if ((t = getfloat ()) == 0) break;
                    here = install (here,t,i);
                    }
                printf ("\n\nFile closed\n\n");
                break;

            case 'o':
                for (ptr=startfrom(&ctr,i);
```

```
                  ptr != NULL; ptr = ptr->succ)
                      {
                      if (ctr % 4 == 1) updatescrn (i,s);
                          correct = over(ctr++,ptr->value);
                          ptr->value = correct;
                      }
                      break;

              case 's': saveproject();
                      break;

              case 'l': loadproject();
                      break;

              case 'q': stop = wantout(fast);
              }

          if (stop) break;
          }
      }

/**********************************************************/

      noofgroups ()                 /* Check no. of data groups */

      {   char ch,getkey();

      printf ("Project currently holds %d groups\n\n",DATSETS);
      printf ("Alter groups or Edit? (A/E)");

      ch = getkey();

      switch (tolower(ch))
          {
          case 'a': printf ("\nHow many groups for this file?
                                (0..%d)\n\n",grps);
                  return (DATSETS = getint(0,grps));

          case 'e':return (DATSETS);
          }
      }

/**********************************************************/

      LoadSave ()                            /* Project options */

      {   char ch,getkey();

      clrscrn();

      printf ("\nCurrent Project %s\n\n\n", FSP);
```

```
     printf ("Load new project or Save current one (L/S/Quit)
                                                    ?\n\n");
     ch = getkey();

     switch (tolower(ch))
          {
          case 'l' : if (sure())
                    {
                    DATATHERE = loadproject ();
                    }
                    break;

          case 's' : if (sure())
                    {
                    saveproject ();
                    }

          case 'q' :
          }
     }

/**********************************************************/

     Analyse ()         /* Work out some typical quantities */

     {    char getkey();
          double mean(), mn, millikan();
          int i;

     printf ("Analysis of Data\n\n");

     for (i = 1; i <= DATSETS; i++)
          {
          mn = mean(i);
          printf ("Mean value of group %2d : %f\n",i,mn);

          stddevs(mn);

          printf ("Millikan value %d %lg:\n",i,millikan(i));
          newline();
          }

     getkey();
     }

/**********************************************************/

     quit ()                              /* Quit program & tidy */
     {    short i;
          struct list *deletetoend();
```

```
        for (i = 0; i <= DATSETS; i++)
              {
              deletetoend (Data[i].datptr);
              }

        exit(0);
        }

/************************************************************/
/* LEVEL 2                                                  */
/************************************************************/

        void saveproject ()
        {     FILE *dfx;
              char *filename(),ch,getkey();
              struct list *ptr;
              int i;

        if ((dfx = fopen (filename(),"w")) == 0)
              {
              printf ("Cannot write to file\nPress a key\n");
              ch = getkey();
              return;
              }

        fprintf (dfx,"%ld\n",DATSETS);

        for (i=1; i <= DATSETS; i++)
              {
              for (ptr = Data[i].datptr;
                          ptr != NULL; ptr = ptr->succ)
                    {
                    fprintf (dfx,"%lf \n",ptr->value);
                    }

              fprintf (dfx,"%f\n",endmark);
              fprintf (dfx,"%d\n",Data[i].datathere);
              }

        while (fclose (dfx) != 0)
              {
              printf ("Waiting to close ");
              }

        blankline ();
        return;
        }

/************************************************************/

        loadproject ()          /* Load new list & delete old */
```

```
{    FILE *dfx;
     char *filename(),ch,getkey();
     int   r,i;
     double t = 1.0;
     struct list *ptr,*install(),*deletetoend();

if ((dfx = fopen(filename(),"r")) == NULL)
     {
     printf ("File cannot be read\nPress any key\n");
     ch = getkey();
     return (0);
     }

fscanf (dfx,"%ld",&DATSETS);

for (i = 1; i <= DATSETS; i++)
     {
     t = notendmark;
     Data[i].datptr = deletetoend(Data[i].datptr);
     Data[i].datathere = false;

     for (ptr = Data[i].datptr; t != endmark;)
          {
          fscanf (dfx,"%lf",&t);
          if (t != endmark)
               {
               ptr = install (ptr,t,i);
               }
          }
     fscanf (dfx,"%ld",&r);
     Data[i].datathere = r;
     }

while (fclose(dfx) != 0)
     {
     printf ("Waiting to close file");
     }

blankline();
return (true);
}

/**********************************************************/

whichgroup ()

{    int n = 0;

printf ("\n\nEdit account number: ");
n = getint (0,DATSETS);

if (n == 0)
```

```
          {
          printf ("Quit!\n");
          }
     return (n);
     }

/*********************************************************/
     char status (i)
     int i;
     {    char stat;

     if (i==0)
          {
          stat = 'q';
          }

     else
          {

          if (Data[i].datathere)
               {
               printf ("Insert/Overwrite/Load/Save/Quit?");
               stat = getkey();
               stat = tolower(stat);
               }
          else
               {
               stat = 'i';
               }
          }
     return (stat);
     }

/*********************************************************/

     updatescrn (grp,status)       /* Update editor screen */

     int grp;
     char status;

     {    int ctr=0;
          struct list *ptr;
     clrscrn();
     printf ("\nStatistical Editor V1.0\n\n");
     printf ("\nThis project file contains %d
groups.\n",DATSETS);

     for (ptr = Data[grp].datptr; (ptr != NULL); ptr=ptr->succ)
          {
          if ((ctr % 3) == 0) newline();
          printf (" (%2d) %12g ",ctr+1,(ptr->value));
```

```
        ctr++;
        }
    printf ("\n\nEditing Group %d. Contains %d entries  **
                                                   ",grp,ctr);

    switch (tolower(status))
        {
        case 'i' : printf ("INSERT MODE  **\n"); break;
        case 'o' : printf ("OVERWRITE MODE  **\n");
        }
    newline();
    }

/**********************************************************/

    double over (n,old)             /* Edit overtype mode */

    int n;
    double old;

    {   double correct = 0;

    printf ("Entry %-2d : ",n);
    scanf("%lf",&correct);
    skipgarb();

    if (correct == 0)
        {
        return (old);
        }
    else
        {
        return(correct);
        }
    }

/************************************************************/

    double mean (i)                     /* find mean average */

    int i;

    {   struct list *ptr;
        double sum;
        int num;

    sum = num = 0;

    for (ptr = Data[i].datptr; ptr != NULL; ptr=ptr->succ)
        {
        sum += ptr->value;
```

```
          num ++;
          }
     return (sum/num);
     }

/*************************************************************/

     stddevs (mean,i)          /* find variance/std deviation */

     double mean;
     int i;

     {    double sum,num,var;
          struct list *ptr;

     sum = num = 0;

     for (ptr = Data[i].datptr; ptr != NULL; ptr=ptr->succ)
          {
          sum += (ptr->value - mean) * (ptr->value - mean);
          num ++;
          }

     var = sum/num;                          /* "biased" value */

     printf ("Variance %d = %f\n",i,var);
     printf ("Std deviation %d = %f\n",i,sqrt(var));
     }

/*************************************************************/

     double millikan (i) /* smllest diffnce between 2 data */

     int i;

     {    double temp,record = bignum;
          struct list *ptr1,*ptr2;

     for (ptr1 = Data[i].datptr; ptr1 != NULL;
                                    ptr1 = ptr1->succ)
          {

          for (ptr2=Data[i].datptr; ptr2 !=ptr1;
                                    ptr2 = ptr2->succ)
               {
               temp = (ptr1->value) - (ptr2->value);

               if (abs(temp) < record)
                    {
                    record = abs(temp);
                    }
               }
```

```
        }
    return(record);
    }

/**********************************************************/
/* LEVEL 3                                                */
/**********************************************************/

    char *filename ()
    {

    do
        {
        printf ("Enter filename : ");
        scanf ("%s",FSP);
        skipgarb();
        }
    while (strlen(FSP) == 0);

    return (FSP);
    }

/**********************************************************/
/* Toolkit data structure                                 */
/**********************************************************/

    struct list *eolist(i,c)  /* Seek end of linked Vlist */

    int i,*c;

    {   struct list *ptr,*p = NULL;
    *c = 1;

    for (ptr = Data[i].datptr; ptr != NULL; ptr = ptr->succ)
        {
        ++(*c);
        p = ptr;
        }
    return (p);
    }

/**********************************************************/

    struct list *startfrom (ctr,i)/* Find ith node in list */

    int *ctr,i;

    {   struct list *ptr,*p = NULL;
        int j = 0;

    printf ("Overtype starting from which entry");
    *ctr = getint(1,99);
```

```
    for (ptr=Data[i].datptr; (ptr != NULL) && (j++ != *ctr);
                                              ptr=ptr->succ)
        {
        p = ptr;
        }
    return (p);
    }

/***********************************************************/

    struct list *install (ptr,t,i)  /* install at thispos */
    struct list *ptr;

    double t;
    int i;

    {   struct list *thispos, *newstruct();

    if ((thispos = newstruct()) == NULL)
        {
        warning();
        printf ("DEBUG **: Free memory pool is empty");
        exit(0);
        }

    if (!Data[i].datathere)
        {
        Data[i].datptr = thispos;
        Data[i].datathere = true;
        }
    else
        {
        ptr->succ = thispos;
        }

    thispos->value = t;
    thispos->succ = NULL;
    return (thispos);
    }

/***********************************************************/

    struct list *deletetoend (ptr)  /* RECURSIVE WELL - */
    /* returns NULL for easy deletion of  call ptr */

    struct list *ptr;
    {

    if (ptr != NULL)
        {
        deletetoend (ptr->succ);
        releasestruct (ptr);
```

```
          }
       return (NULL);
       }

/*********************************************************/

       struct list *newstruct ()/* Allocate space for new item */

       {    char *malloc();
       return ((struct list *) malloc(sizeof(struct list)));
       }

/*********************************************************/

       releasestruct (ptr)  /* release memory back to pool */
       struct list *ptr;
       {

       if (free((char *) ptr) != 0)
          {
          printf ("DEBUG [Z0/TktDtStrct] memory release
                                                    faliure\n");
          }
       }

/*********************************************************/
/* Toolkit CONSOLE Output                               */
/*********************************************************/

       clrscrn ()
       {
       printf ("\f");
       }

/*********************************************************/

       newline ()
       {
       printf ("\n");
       }

/*********************************************************/

       blankline ()
       {
       printf ("                                          \r");
       }

/*********************************************************/

       warning ()
```

```
      {
      putchar('\7');
      }

/*********************************************************/
/*** Toolkit CONSOLE Input                             **/
/*********************************************************/

      wantout (becareful)            /* Exit from a section */
      int becareful;

      {
      if (becareful)
            {
            printf ("Really quit? (Y/N)\n");
            if (yes()) return (true); else return (false);
            }
      return (true);
      }

/**********************************************************/
      sure (becareful)              /* Are you sure : boolean */

      int becareful;
      {

      if (becareful)
            {
            printf ("Are you sure? (Y/N)\n");
            if (yes()) return (true); else return (false);
            }
      return (true);
      }

/*********************************************************/

      yes ()                   /* boolean response Y/N query */

      {
      while (true)
            {
            switch (getkey())
                  {
                  case 'y' : case 'Y' : return (true);
                  case 'n' : case 'N' : return (false);
                  }
            }
      }

/*********************************************************/
```

```
    char getkey ()               /* get single character */

    {    char ch;
    scanf ("%c",&ch);
    skipgarb();
    return (ch);
    }

/**********************************************************/

    getint (a,b)           /* return int between a and b */

    int a,b;
    {    int  p, i = a - 1;

    for (p=0; ((a > i) || (i > b)); p++)
         {
         printf ("?");
         scanf ("%d",&i);

         if (p > 3)
              {
              skipgarb();
              p = 0;
              }
         }
    skipgarb();
    return (i);
    }

/**********************************************************/

    double getfloat ()               /* return long float */

    {    double x = 0;
    printf ("? ");
    scanf ("%lf",&x);
    skipgarb();
    return (x);
    }

/***********************************************************/

    skipgarb()    /* Skip input garbage corrupting scanf */
    {
    while (getchar() != '\n');
    }
                        /* end */
```

End of Listing 30.1. Statistical Calculator.

Example 2. Variable Cross Referencer

A variable cross referencer is a utility which produces a list of all the identifiers in a C program (variables, macros, functions and so on), and lists the line numbers of those identifiers within the source file. This is sometimes useful for finding errors and for spotting variables, functions and macros which are never used, since they show up clearly as identifiers which have only a single reference. The program is listed here, with its line numbers, using the file utility written in Chapter 25 and its output (applied to itself), is supplied afterwards for reference. Readers should note that the line numbers are supplied for convenience. They should *not* be typed in. The structure diagram illustrates the operation of the program.

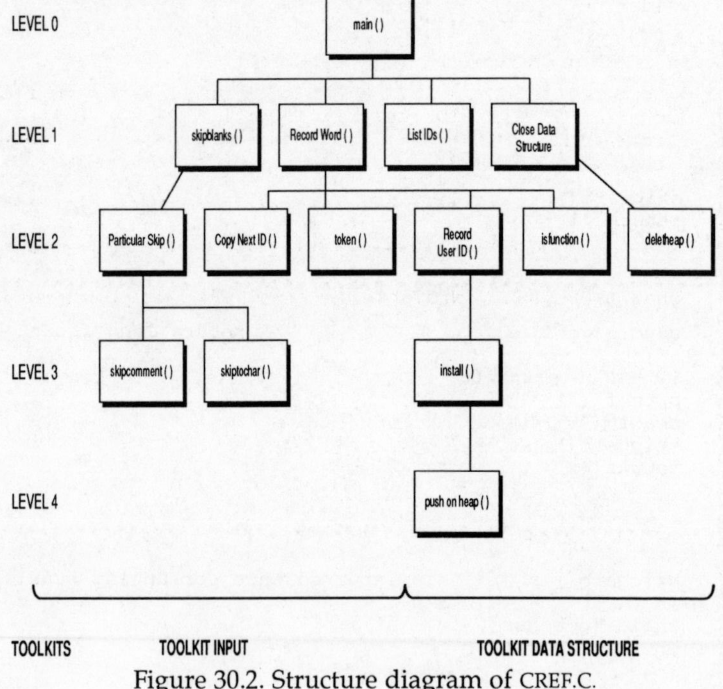

Figure 30.2. Structure diagram of CREF.C.

Listing 30.2. Cref.C.

```
/**********************************************************/
/*                                                        */
/*  C programming utility : variable referencer           */
/*                                                        */
/**********************************************************/

                    /* See notes above */

  #include "stdio.h"
  #include "ctype.h"

  #define true        1
  #define false       0
  #define dummy       0
  #define maxstr      512
  #define maxIDsize   32
  #define WrdTable    33

  int   LINECOUNT = 1;      /* Contains line no. in file */
  char  BUFFER[maxIDsize];  /* Input BUFFER for IDs      */
  char  CH;                 /* Current input character   */
  char  SPECIALCHAR;        /* macro/pointer flag        */

/**********************************************************/
/* TABLE                                                  */
/**********************************************************/

 char *WORDTABLE [WrdTable] =    /* Table of resvd words */

      {
      "auto"    ,
      "break"   ,
      "case"    ,
      "char"    ,
      "const",
      "continue",
      "default" ,
      "do"      ,
      "double"  ,
      "else"    ,
      "entry"   ,
      "enum"    ,
      "extern"  ,
      "float"   ,
      "for"     ,
      "goto"    ,
      "if"      ,
      "int"     ,
```

```
        "long"    ,
        "register",
        "return"  ,
        "short"   ,
        "signed"  ,
        "sizeof"  ,
        "static"  ,
        "struct"  ,
        "switch"  ,
        "typedef" ,
        "union"   ,
        "unsigned",
        "void"    ,
        "volatile",
        "while"   ,
        };

/**********************************************************/
/** STRUCTURES                                          **/
/**********************************************************/

  struct heap

        {
        short num;
        char spec;
        struct heap *next;
        };

/***********************************************************/

   struct BinaryTree

        {
        char *name;
        struct heap *line;
        struct BinaryTree *left;
        struct BinaryTree *right;
        }

        *tree = NULL;

/**********************************************************/
/* LEVEL 0 : main program                                 */
/**********************************************************/

  main ()

    { FILE *fp;
        char *filename();
        struct BinaryTree *CloseDataStruct();

```

```
    printf ("\nIdentifier Cross Reference V 1.0\n\n");
    if ((fp = fopen (filename(),"r")) == NULL)
       {
       printf ("Can't read file .. Aborted!\n\n");
       exit(0);
       }
    CH = getc(fp);

    while (!feof(fp))
       {
       SkipBlanks (fp);
       RecordWord (fp);
       }

    listIDs (tree);
    CloseDataStruct(tree);
    printf ("\n%d lines in source file\n",LINECOUNT);
    }

/**********************************************************/
/* LEVEL 1                                                */
/**********************************************************/

    SkipBlanks (fp)         /* Skip irrelevant characters */

    FILE *fp;

    {

    while (!feof(fp))

       {
       if (iscsymf(CH))
               {
               return(dummy);
               }
       else
               {
               ParticularSkip(fp);
               }
       }
    }

/**********************************************************/

    RecordWord (fp) /* get ID in buffer & tube it to data */

    FILE *fp;

    { int tok;

    CopyNextID (fp);
```

```

    if ((tok = token()) == 0)          /* if not resved word */
       {
       RecordUserID(isfunction(fp));
       }

    SPECIALCHAR = ' ';
    }

/*********************************************************/

    listIDs (p)                            /* List Binary Tree */

    struct BinaryTree *p;

    { struct heap *h;
       int i = 0;

    if (p != NULL)
       {
       listIDs (p->left);
       printf ("\n%-20s",p->name);

       for (h = p->line; (h != NULL); h = h->next)
                {
                printf ("%c%-5d",h->spec,h->num);
                if ((++i % 8) == 0)
                    {
                    printf ("\n                    ");
                    }
                }

       printf ("\n");
       listIDs (p->right);
       }
    }

/*********************************************************/

    struct BinaryTree *CloseDataStruct (p)  /* Recursive! */

    struct BinaryTree *p;

    {
    if (p->left != NULL)
       {
       CloseDataStruct(p->left);
       }
    else if (p->right != NULL)
       {
       CloseDataStruct(p->right);
       }
```

```

   deleteheap(p->line);
   releasetree(p);
   return (NULL);
   }

/**********************************************************/
/* LEVEL 2                                                */
/**********************************************************/

   ParticularSkip (fp)   /* handle particular characters */

   FILE *fp;

   { char c;

   switch (CH)

      {
      case '/' : if ((c = getc(fp)) == '*')
                    {
                    skipcomment (fp);
                        }
                    else
                        {
                        CH = c;
                        return (dummy);
                        }
                    break;

      case '"' : if (skiptochar (fp,'"') > maxstr)
                        {
                        printf ("String too long or unterminated ");
                        printf ("at line %d\n",LINECOUNT);
                        exit (0);
                        }
                    break;

      case '\'': if (skiptochar (fp,'\'') == 1)
                        {
                        if (CH=='\'') CH = getc(fp);;
                        }
                    break;

      case '#' : skiptochar(fp,' ');
                    SPECIALCHAR = '#';
                    break;

      case '\n': ++LINECOUNT;
      default  : CH = getc(fp);
                    SPECIALCHAR = ' ';
```

```
    }
  }
/********************************************************/
  CopyNextID (fp)    /* Put next identifier into BUFFER */
  FILE *fp;
  { int i = 0;
  while (!feof(fp) && (iscsym (CH)))
      {
      BUFFER[i++] = CH;
      CH = getc (fp);
      }
  BUFFER[i] = '\0';
  }
/********************************************************/
  token ()                       /* Token: pos in WORDTABLE */
  { int i;
  for (i = 0; i < WrdTable; i++)
      {
      if (strcmp(&(BUFFER[0]),WORDTABLE[i]) == 0)
              {
              return(i);
              }
      }
  return(0);
  }
/********************************************************/
 RecordUserID (fnflag) /* check ID type & install data */
 int fnflag;
 { char *strcat();
     struct BinaryTree *install();
 if (fnflag)
     {
     strcat (BUFFER,"()");
     tree = install (tree);
     }
 else
     {
```

```
        tree = install (tree);
        }
  }

/*******************************************************/

  isfunction (fp)            /* returns true if ID is a fn */

  FILE *fp;

  {
  while(!feof(fp))
        {
        if (!(CH == ' ' || CH == '\n'))
                {
                break;
                }
        else if (CH == '\n')
                {
                ++LINECOUNT;
                }
        CH = getc(fp);
        }

  if (CH == '(')
        {
        return (true);
        }
  else
        {
        return (false);
        }
  }

/*******************************************************/

  deleteheap (h)      /* Release back to free memory pool */

  struct heap *h;

  { struct heap *temp = h;

  while (h!=NULL && temp!=NULL)
        {
        temp = h->next;
        releaseheap(h);
        h = temp;
        }
  }

/*******************************************************/
```

```
/** LEVEL 3                                                  **/
/*************************************************************/

 skipcomment (fp)              /* skip to char after comment */

 FILE *fp;

 { char cs = ‘x’;

 for (CH = getc(fp); !feof(fp); CH = getc(fp))
      {
      switch (CH)
              {
              case ‘\n’: ++LINECOUNT;
                      break;
              case ‘/’ : if (cs == ‘*’)
                      {
                      CH = getc(fp);
                      return(dummy);
                      }
              }
      cs = CH;
      }
 }

/*************************************************************/

 skiptochar (fp,ch)                /* skip to char after ch */

 FILE *fp;
 char ch;

 { int c=0;

 while (((CH =getc(fp)) != ch) && !feof(fp))
      {
      if (CH == ‘\n’)
              {
              ++LINECOUNT;
              }
      c++;
      }

 CH = getc(fp);
 return (c);
 }

/*************************************************************/

 struct BinaryTree *install (p)  /* install ID in tree */

 struct BinaryTree *p;
```

```

{ struct heap *pushonheap();
    struct BinaryTree *newtree();
    char *stringin();
    int pos;

if (p == NULL)                              /* new word */
    {
    p = newtree();
    p->name = stringin(BUFFER);
    p->line = pushonheap (NULL);
    p->left = NULL;
    p->right = NULL;
    return (p);
    }

if ((pos = strcmp (BUFFER,p->name)) == 0) /* found word*/
    {
    p->line = pushonheap(p->line);
    return (p);
    }

if (pos < 0)                          /* Trace down list */
    {
    p->left = install(p->left);
    }
else
    {
    p->right = install(p->right);
    }

return (p);
}

/*********************************************************/
/* LEVEL 4                                               */
/*********************************************************/

struct heap *pushonheap (h)  /* push nxt ln no.to heap */

struct heap *h;

{ struct heap *hp,*newheap();

hp = newheap();
hp->num  = LINECOUNT;
hp->spec = SPECIALCHAR;
hp->next = h;

return (hp);
}

```

```
/***********************************************************/
/* TOOLKIT file input                                      */
/***********************************************************/

 backone (ch,fp)                  /* backspace one in file */

 char ch;
 FILE *fp;

 {
 if (ungetc(ch,fp) != ch)
      {
      printf ("\nDebug: Toolkit file input: backone() failed\n");
      exit(0);
      }
 }

/***********************************************************/
/* TOOLKIT stdin                                           */
/***********************************************************/

 char *filename ()

 { static char *fsp = "..................................";

 do
      {
      printf ("Enter filename of source program: ");
      scanf ("%33s",fsp);
      skipgarb ();
      }
 while (strlen(fsp) == 0);
 return (fsp);
 }

/***********************************************************/

 skipgarb ()           /* skip garbage upto end of line */

 {
 while (getchar() != '\n');
 }

/***********************************************************/
/* TOOLKIT data structure                                  */
/***********************************************************/

 char *stringin (array)     /* cpy str in arry to ptr loc*/

 char *array;

```

```
{ char *malloc(),*ptr;
    int i;
ptr = malloc (strlen(array)+1);
for (i = 0; array[i] != '\0'; ptr[i] = array[i++]);
ptr[i] = '\0';
return(ptr);
}
/*****************************************************/
struct heap *newheap ()
{ char *malloc ();
return ((struct heap *) malloc(sizeof(struct heap)));
}
/*****************************************************/
struct BinaryTree *newtree ()
{ char *malloc ();
return ((struct BinaryTree *) malloc(sizeof(struct
BinaryTree)));
}
/*****************************************************/
releaseheap (ptr)
struct heap *ptr;
{
if (free((char *) ptr) != 0)
    {
    printf ("TOOLKIT datastruct: link release failed\n");
    }
}
/*****************************************************/
releasetree (ptr)
struct BinaryTree *ptr;
{
if (free((char *) ptr) != 0)
    {
    printf ("TOOLKIT datastruct: link release failed\n");
    }
```

```
}
                        /* end */


```

End of Listing 30.2. Cref.C.

Output of Cross Referencer

```
Identifier Cross Reference V 1.0
Enter filename of source program: Cref.c

                    568
BUFFER              427   420   303   284   273   269   20

BinaryTree          557   536   536   533   413   410   408
                    299   194   192   166   99    86    85
                    82
CH                  402   395   393   380   376   370   368
                    368   332   329   325   321   321   270
                    269   267   254   245   245   230   221
                    133   107   21
CloseDataStruct()   203   199   192   116   99
CopyNextID()        261   152
FILE                470   388   364   316   263   217   148
                    126   97
LINECOUNT           456   397   372   327   253   238   117
                    19
NULL                423   422   421   417   350   350   208
                    201   197   176   171   102   89
ParticularSkip()    215   139
RecordUserID()      294   156
RecordWord()        146   112
SPECIALCHAR         457   255   250   159   22
SkipBlanks()        124   111
WORDTABLE           284   28
WrdTable            282   28   #17
array               518   518   517   512   510
backone()           467
c                   403   399   391   230   224   219
ch                  473   473   469   467   393   389   386

cs                  380   374   366
deleteheap()        344   206
dummy               377   231   135   #14
exit()              476   239   105
false               338  #13
feof()              393   368   319   267   130   109
filename()          484   102   98
fnflag              301   296   294
fopen()             102
fp                  473   470   467   402   393   393   388
                    386   376   368   368   368   364   362
                    329   319   316   314   270   267   263
                    261   254   249   245   243   235   226
```

	224	217	215	156	152	148	146
	139	130	126	124	112	111	109
	107	102	97				
free()	560	546					
fsp	495	494	491	486			
getc()	402	393	376	368	368	329	270
	254	245	224	107			
getchar()	503						
h	458	451	449	354	353	352	350
	348	346	344	178	178	176	176
	176	176	168				
heap	543	528	528	525	453	451	449
	412	348	346	168	84	75	72
hp	460	458	457	456	455	453	
i	519	518	518	518	518	515	286
	284	282	282	282	280	273	269
	265	179	169				
install()	439	435	408	308	304	299	
iscsym()	267						
iscsymf()	133						
isfunction()	314	156					
left	435	435	422	199	197	173	85
line	429	429	421	206	176	84	
listIDs()	186	173	164	115			
main()	95						
malloc()	536	535	528	527	517	514	
maxIDsize	20	#16					
maxstr	235	#15					
name	427	420	174	83			
newheap()	525	455	453				
newtree()	533	419	413				
next	458	352	176	75			
num	456	178	73				
p	442	439	439	435	435	430	429
	429	427	424	423	422	421	420
	419	417	410	408	207	206	203
	201	199	197	194	192	186	176
	174	173	171	166	164		
pos	433	427	415				
printf()	563	549	490	475	238	237	185
	181	178	174	117	104	101	
ptr	560	557	555	546	543	541	520
	519	518	517	514			
pushonheap()	449	429	421	412			
releaseheap()	541	353					
releasetree()	555	207					
right	439	439	423	203	201	186	86
scanf()	491						
skipcomment()	362	226					
skipgarb()	500	492					
skiptochar()	386	249	243	235			
spec	457	178	74				
strcat()	303	298					
strcmp()	427	284					
stringin()	510	420	414				
strlen()	517	494					
temp	354	352	350	348			
tok	154	150					
token()	278	154					
tree	308	308	304	304	116	115	89
true	334	#12					

```
ungetc()              473

568 lines in source file
```

Comments

This simplified program could be improved in a number of ways. Here are some suggestions for improvement:

The program could determine whether an identifier was of type pointer or not and, if so, label the line number with a *, eg, *123 342 *1234.

At present the program only marks macros with a # symbol on the line at which they are defined. It could be made to mark them at every line, so that #undef-ined symbols and variables were clearly distinguished.

31 : Errors & Debugging

Mistakes!

Debugging can be a difficult process. A compiler manual should give detailed explanations of errors. However, in many cases compiler errors are not generated because of an actual error which was present, but because the compiler got out of step. Often the error messages give a completely misleading impression of what has gone wrong. It is useful therefore to build up your own list of errors and probable causes. The examples in this chapter should help beginners get started and perhaps give some insight into the way C works.

Compiler Trappable Errors

Missing semicolon

A missing semicolon (;) is easily trapped by the compiler. Every statement must end with a semicolon. A compound statement which is held in curly braces seldom needs a semicolon.

```
statement;
```

but:

```
{
};
```

This semicolon is only needed if the curly braces enclose a type declaration or an initialiser for static array/structure and so on.

Missing closing brace }

This error is harder to spot and may lead to a host of incorrect errors after the missing brace. Count braces carefully. One way to avoid this is to always fill braces in before the statements are written inside them. So write the following:

```
{
}
```

and fill in the statements afterwards. Often this error will generate a message like 'unexpected end of file' because it is particularly difficult for a compiler to diagnose.

Mistyping upper/lower case

C distinguishes between small and capital letters. If a program fails at the linking stage because it has found a reference to a function which had not been defined, this is often the cause.

Missing quote

If a quote is missed out of a statement containing a string then the compiler will usually signal this with a message like 'String too long or unterminated'.

Variable not declared or scope wrong

This means that a variable has been used which was not first declared, or that a variable was outside of its sealed capsule. (See Chapter 12 on scope.)

Missing & in scanf

See Appendix B.

Using a function or assignment inside a macro

If abs (x) is a macro and not a function then the following are most probably incorrect:

```
abs (function());
abs (x = function());
```

Only a single variable can be substituted into a macro. This error might generate something like 'lvalue required'.

Forgetting to declare a function which is not type int

All functions return values of int by default. If it is required that they return another type of variable, this must by declared in two places: in the function which calls the new function, along with the other declarations. For example:

```
CallFunction ()

{ char ch, function1(), *function2();
}
```

The function1 is type char; function2 is type pointer to char. This must also be declared where the function is defined:

```
char function1 ()

{
}
```

and:

```
char *function2()

{
}
```

This error might result in the message 'type mismatch' or 'external variable/function type/attribute mismatch'.

Type mismatch in expressions

In C all maths operations have to be performed with long variables. These are:

```
int
long int

double
long float
```

The result is also a long type. If you forget this and try to use short, C automatically converts it into long form. The result cannot therefore be assigned to a short type afterwards or the compiler will complain that there is a type mismatch. So the following is wrong:

```
short i,j = 2;

i = j * 2;
```

If a short result is required, the cast operator has to be used to cast the long result to be a short one.

```
short i,j = 2;

i = (short) j * 2;
```

Errors not Trapable by a Compiler
Run Time Errors

Confusion of = and ==

A statement such as:

```
if (a = 0)
     {
     }
```

is valid C, but notice that = is the assignment operator and *not* the equality operator, ==. It is legal to put an assignment inside the if statement (or any other function), and the value of the assignment is the value being assigned! So writing the above would always give the result zero (which is 'false' in C), so the contents of the braces { } would *never* be executed. To compare a to zero the correct syntax is:

```
if (a == 0)
     {
     }
```

Missing & in scanf

This error can often be trapped by a compiler, but not in all cases. The arguments of the scanf statement must be pointers or addresses of variables, not the contents of the variables themselves. Thus the following is wrong:

```
int i;
char ch;
scanf ("%c %d",ch,i);
```

and should read:

```
int i;
char;
scanf ("%c %d", &ch, &i);
```

Notice, however, that the & is not always needed if the identifier in the expression is already a pointer. The following is correct:

```
int *i;
char *ch;
scanf ("%c %d", ch, i);
```

Including the & now would be wrong. If this error is trapable then it will be something like 'variable is not a pointer'.

Confusing C++ and ++C

In many cases these two forms are identical. However, if they are hidden inside another statement, for example:

```
array [C++] = 0;
```

then there is a subtle difference. ++C causes C to be incremented by one before the assignment takes place, whereas C++ causes C to be incremented by one after the assignment has taken place. So if you find that a program is out of step by one, this could be the cause.

Unwarranted assumptions about storage of arrays/structures

C stores arrays in rows and, as far as the language is concerned, the storage locations are next to one another in one place up to the end of the array. In a multi-tasking environment this generally isn't true. A program will be loaded into one or more areas (where ever the operating system can find space), and new variable space will be found wherever it is available, but this will not generally be in whole blocks 'side by side' in the memory. So the following sort of construction, which is often used in C books, will not work:

```
char array[10];
*array = 0;
*(array + 1) = 0;
...
*(array + 10) = 0;
```

and may cause the program to crash. This is because (while it is true that the variable 'array' used without its square brackets is a pointer to the first element of the array) it is not true that the array will necessarily be stored in this way. Use:

```
char array[10];
array[0] = 0;
array[1] = 0;
...
array[10] = 0;
```

Also when finding a pointer to the third element for example, it cannot be assumed that:

```
array + 3
```

will be the location. Use:

```
&(array[3])
```

The same comments apply to structures, with one further remark: do not assume that the size of a structure is the sum of the sizes of its parts! There may be extra data inside for operating system use or for implementation reasons, like aligning variables with particular addresses for example.

The number of actual and formal parameters does not match

When passing values to a function, the compiler will not spot whether you have the wrong number of parameters in a statement – provided they are all of the correct type. The values which are assumed for missing parameters cannot be guaranteed. They are probably garbage and will spoil a program.

The conversion string in scanf/printf is wrong

Incorrect I/O is can be the result of poorly matched conversion strings in I/O statements. For example:

```
float x;                    float x;
```

should be :

```
scanf ("%d",&x);            scanf ("%f",&x);
```

or even:

```
double x;                   float x;
```

should perhaps be :

```
scanf  ("%f",&x);           scanf("%ld",&x);
```

Another effect which can occur, if the conversion specifier is selected as being long when it the variable is really short, is that neighbouring variables can receive the scanf values instead! For instance if two variables of the same type happen to be stored next to each other in the memory:

```
short i,j;
```

which might look like:

and the user tries to read into one with a long int value, scanf will store a long int value, which is the size of two of these short variables. Suppose the left-hand box were i and the right-hand box were j, and you wanted to input the value of i. Instead of getting:

```
----------------------
|  002345  |          |
----------------------
     i          j
```

scanf might store:

```
0000000000000002345
```

as:

```
 ---------------------------
 | 000000000 | 0000002345 |
 ---------------------------
       i          j
```

because the value was long. This would mean that the number would over-flow out of i into j. In fact j might get the correct value, and i would be set to zero!! Check the conversion specifiers!

Accidental confusion of int, short and char

Often when working with characters, you might also want to know their ASCII values. If characters/integers are passed as parameters it is easy to mistype char for int and so on. The compiler probably won't notice this because no conversion is needed between int and char. Characters are stored by their ASCII values. On the other hand if the declaration is wrong:

```
function (ch)

int (ch);
{
}
```

but the character is continually assumed to be a character by the program, a crash-worthy routine might be the result.

Arrays out of bounds

C does not check the limits of the programmers arrays. If an array is sized as follows:

```
type array[5];
```

and the programmer allows the program to write to array[6] or more, C will not complain. However, the computer might! In the worst case this could cause the program to crash.

Mathematical Errors

C does not necessarily signal mathematical errors. A program might continue regardless of the fact that a mathematical function has failed. (See Chapter 21: Special Library Functions and Macros)

Uncoordinated output using put/get I/O

Output which is generated by functions like putchar and puts is buffered. This means it will not be written to the screen until the buffer is either full, or is specifically emptied. This results in strange effects such as programs which produce no output until all the input is complete (short programs), or spontaneous bursts of output at uncoordinated intervals. One common cure is to use printf, terminated with a new-line '\n' character, which flushes the buffers on each write operation. Special functions such as getch may also suffer from this problem. Again the cure is to write:

```
printf ("\n");
ch = getch();
```

Global variables and recursion

Global variables and recursion should not be mixed. Most recursive routines work only because they are sealed capsules and their contents can never affect the outside world. The only time that recursive functions should alter global storage is when the function concerned operates on a global data structure. Consider a recursive function:

```
int GLOBAL;

recursion ()
{

if (++GLOBAL == 0)
     {
     return (0);
     }

alterGLOBAL();/* another function which alters GLOBAL */
recursion();
}
```

This function is treading a fine line between safety and digging its own recursive grave. All it would take to crash the program, would be the careless use of GLOBAL in the function 'alterGLOBAL', and the function would never be able to return. The stack would fill up the memory and the program would plunge down the unending recursive well.

Tracing Errors

Locating a problem

Complex bugs can be difficult to locate. Here are some tips for easy fault finding:

1) Try to use local variables, in preference to global ones, for local duties. Never rely on global variables for passing messages between functions

2) Check variable declarations and missing parameters

3) Check that the program has not run out of private memory. If it repeatedly crashes for no apparent reason, this could be a cause. Make the program stack size bigger if possible

4) Use statements like printf('program is now here') to map out the progress of a program, and to check that all function calls are made correctly

5) Use statements like 'ch = getchar' to halt a program in certain places and to find out the exact location where things go wrong

6) Try 'commenting out' lines of suspect code. In other words: put comment markers around lines that you would like to eliminate temporarily and then re-compile to pinpoint errors.

7) Check that the compiler disc has not been corrupted (make a new copy) – getting desperate now.

8) Try retyping the program, or using a filter which strips out any illegal characters which might have found their way into a program

9) Get some sleep! Hope the problem has gone away in the morning

Failing these measures, try to find someone who regularly programs in C on the computer system concerned.

Pathological problems

Problems which defy reasonable explanations are referred to as pathological or 'sick'. In most cases they will be the result of misconceptions about C functions, but occasionally they may be the result of compiler bugs, or operating system design peculiarities. Consider the following example which I encountered while writing the simple example in Chapter 25: Files and Devices, subsection 'Low -level File Handling'. A seemingly innocent macro defined by:

```
#define clrscrn() putchar('\f');
```

caused the C library functions 'creat' and 'remove' to fail in remarkable ways! The problem was that a single call to clrscrn at the start of the function DelFile, caused both of the library functions in very different parts of the program, to make recursing function calls function DelFile. The deletion of clrscrn cured the problem entirely!

In general, it is worth carefully checking the names of all functions within a program to be sure that they do not infringe upon library functions. For example, read and write are names which everyone wishes to use at some point, but they are the names of standard library functions, so they may not be used. Even capitalising (Read / Write) might not work. Beware that special operating system libraries have not already reserved these words as library commands.

It is almost impossible to advise about these errors. You can only hope to try to eliminate all possibilities in homing in on the problem. To misquote Sherlock Holmes: 'At the end of the day, when all else fails and the manuals are in the waste paper basket, the last possibility, however improbable, has to be the truth.'

Porting programs between computers

Programs written according to the style guidelines described in this book should be highly portable. Nevertheless, there are almost inevitably problems in 'porting' programs from one computer to another. The most likely area of incompatibility between compilers is filing operations, especially scanf. Programmers attempting to transfer programs between machines are recommended to look at all the scanf statements first, and to check all the conversion specifiers with a local compiler manual. Scanf is capable of producing a full spectrum of weird effects which have nothing to do with I/O.

Here are some common problems to look out for:

1) Assumptions about the size of data objects, such as int and float, can be risky

2) Check conversion characters in printf and scanf as some compilers choose slightly different conventions for these

3) The stack size and available memory is likely to vary between systems. This can cause errors at run time if a program runs out of space, even though there is nothing wrong with the code

4) Check for functions which rely on the speed of a particular computer. For example, pause or wait loops (See Chapter 29: Toolkits). Some computers may scarcely notice counting to 50000, whereas others may labour at it for some time!

5) Check for assumptions made about filenames. For example, limited/unlimited size, valid characters and so on

Questions:

1) Spot the errors in the following:

```
function (string,i)
{
char *string;
int i;
}
```

2)

```
while (a < b)
     {
     while (b == 0)
          {
          printf ("a is negative");
     }
```

3)

```
struct Name

    {
    int member1;
    int member2;
    }
```

32 : Summary of C

Reserved Words

auto	storage class specifier (declaration)
break	statement (escape from switch or loop)
case	option prefix within switch statement
char	typename
continue	statement (branch to start of next loop)
default	option in switch statement
do	statement
double	typename
else	statement
entry	(reserved for the future use)
extern	storage class specifier
float	typename
for	statement
goto	go to label
if	statement
int	typename
long	typename
register	storage class specifier
return	functional statement
short	typename
sizeof	compile time operator (see Chapter 27: Structures)
static	storage class specifier
struct	partial typename
switch	statement
typedef	statement
union	partial typename
unsigned	typename
while	statement

Also in some implementations:

enum partial typename: ordinal types only
voidtypename
conststorage class specifier (no storage allocated)
signedtypename
volatilestorage class specifier

Preprocessor Directives

#include	include file for linking
#define	define a pre-processor symbol/macro
#undef	un-define a previously defined symbol
#if	test for conditional compilation
#ifdef	test for conditional compilation
#ifndef	test for conditional compilation
#else	test for conditional compilation
#endif	test for conditional compilation
#line	debug tool
#error	debug tool

Header Files and Libraries

Header files contain macro definitions, type definitions and variable/function declarations which are used in connection with standard libraries. They supplement the object code libraries which are linked at compile time for standard library functions. Some library facilities are not available unless header files are included. Typical names for header files are:

stdio.h
ctype.h
math.h
dos.h

Constants

Integer	characters zero to nine only
Octal	Prefix 0 (zero) chars zero to seven only
Hexadecimal	Prefix 0x (zero ex) chars a to f, A to F, zero to nine
Explicit long	Integer/octal or hexadecimal types can be declared long by writing L immediately after the constant
Character	declared in single quotes: 'x' '\n'
Float	Characters 0...0 and one '.' May also use scientific notation exponents with e or E preceding them: 2.14E12 3.2e-2 for example
Strings	String constants are written in double quotes. For example "this is a string" and have type pointer to character

Primitive Data Types

char	holds any character
int	integer type
short int	integer no larger than int
long int	integer no smaller than int
float	floating point (real number)
long float	double precision float
double	double precision float
void	holds no value, uses no storage (except as a pointer)

Storage Classes

auto	local variable (redundant keyword)
const	no variable allocated, value doesn't change
extern	variable is defined in another file
static	value is preserved between function calls
register	stored in a register, if possible
volatile	value can be changed by agents outside the program

Identifiers

Idenitifiers may contain the characters:

0 to 9
A to Z
a to z
the underscore character (_)

Identifiers may not begin with a number. The compiler assumes that an object beginning with a number is a number.

Statements

A single statement is any valid string in C which ends with a semi-colon. For example:

```
a = 6;
printf ("I love C because...");
```

A compound statement is any number of single statements grouped together in curly braces. The curly braces do not end with a semi colon and stand in place of a single statement. Any pair of curly braces may contain local declarations after the opening brace. For example:

```
{
a = 6;
}

{ int a;

a;
printf ("I love C because...");
}
```

Summary of Operators and Precedence

The highest priority operators are listed first:

Operator	Operation	Evaluated
( )	parentheses	left to right
[]	square brackets	left to right
++	increment	right to left
--	decrement	right to left
(type)	cast operator	right to left
*	the contents of	right to left
&	the address of	right to left
-	unary minus	right to left
~	one's complement	right to left
!	logical NOT	right to left
*	multiply	left to right
/	divide	left to right
%	remainder (MOD)	left to right
+	add	left to right
-	subtract	left to right
>>	shift right	left to right
<<	shift left	left to right
>	is greater than	left to right
>=	greater than/equal to	left to right
<=	less than or equal to	left to right
<	less than	left to right

Operator	Operation	Evaluated
==	is equal to	left to right
!=	is not equal to	left to right
&	bitwise AND	left to right
^	bitwise exclusive OR	left to right
|	bitwise inclusive OR	left to right
&&	logical AND	left to right
||	logical OR	left to right
=	assign	right to left
+=	add assign	right to left
-=	subtract assign	right to left
*=	multiply assign	right to left
/=	divide assign	right to left
%=	remainder assign	right to left
>>=	right shift assign	right to left
<<=	left shift assign	right to left
&=	AND assign	right to left
^=	exclusive OR assign	right to left
|=	inclusive OR assign	right to left

Character Utilities

Function/Macro Description

Parameters are characters:

char ch;

isalpha(ch)	is alphabetic a to z, A to Z
isupper(ch)	is upper case
islower(ch)	is lower case
isdigit(ch)	is in the range zero to nine
isxdigit(ch)	is zero to nine, a to f or A to F
isspace(ch)	is white space character (space/new line/tab)
ispunct(ch)	is punctuation or symbolic
isalnum(ch)	is alphanumeric (alphabetic or number)
isprint(ch)	is printable on the screen (and space)
isgraph(ch)	if the character is printable (not space)

Function/Macro	Description
iscntrl(ch)	is a control character (not printable)
isascii(ch)	is in the range zero to 127
iscsym(ch)	is a valid character for a C identifier
toupper(ch)	converts character to upper case
tolower(ch)	converts character to lower case
toascii(ch)	converts character to ASCII (masks off top bit)

Special Control Characters

Control characters are invisible on the screen. They have special purposes usually to do with cursor movement and are written into an ordinary string or character by typing a backslash character (\), followed by some other character. These characters are listed below.

\b	backspace BS
\f	form feed FF (also clear screen)
\n	new line NL (like pressing RETURN)
\r	carriage return CR (cursor to start of line)
\t	horizontal tab HT
\v	vertical tab
\"	double quote
\'	single quote character (')
\\	backslash character (\)
\ddd	character ddd where ddd is an ASCII code given in octal or base eight. (See Appendix C)
\xdd	character dd where dd is a hexadecimal number formed from two characters. (See Appendix C)

Input/Output Functions

printf	formatted printing
scanf	formatted input analysis
getchar	get one character from stdin file buffer
putchar	put one charcter in stdout file buffer
gets	get a string from stdin
puts	put a string in stdout

fprintf	formatted printing to general files
fscanf	formatted input from general files
fgets	get a string from a file
fputs	put a string in a file
fopen	open/create a file for high-level access
fclose	close a file opened by fopen
getc	get one character from a file (macro?)
ungetc	undo last get operation
putc	put a character to a file (macro?)
fgetc	get a character from a file (function)
fputc	put a character from a file (function)
feof	end of file. Returns true or false
fread	read a block of characters
fwrite	write a block of characters
ftell	returns file position
fseek	finds a file position
rewind	moves file position to the start of file
fflush	empties file buffers
open	open a file for low-level use
close	close a file opened with open
creat	create a new file
read	read a block of untranslated bytes
write	write a block of untranslated bytes
rename	rename a file
unlink	delete a file
remove	delete a file
lseek	find file position

printf Conversion Specifiers

d	signed denary integer
u	unsigned denary integer
x	hexadecimal integer
o	octal integer
s	string
c	single character
f	fixed decimal floating point
e	scientific notation floating point
g	use f or e, whichever is shorter

The letter 'l' (el) can be prefixed before these for long types.

scanf Conversion Specifers

The conversion characters for scanf are not identical to those for printf.

d	denary integer (int or long int)
ld	long decimal integer
x	hexadecimal integer
o	octal integer
h	short integer
f	float type
lf	long float or double
e	float type
le	double
c	single character
s	character string

Maths Library

These functions require double parameters and return double values unless otherwise stated.

Function	**Description**
abs(x)	return absolute (unsigned) value. (Macro)
fabs(x)	return absolute (unsigned) value. (Function)
ceil(x)	rounds up a 'double' variable
floor(x)	rounds down (truncates) a 'double' variable.
exp(x)	find exponent
log(x)	find natural logarithm
log10(x)	find logarithm to base 10
pow(x,y)	raise x to the power y
sqrt(x)	square root
sin(x)	sine of (x in radians)
cos(x)	cosine of (x in radians)
tan(x)	tangent of (x in radians)
asin(x)	inverse sine of x in radians

Function	Description
acos(x)	inverse cosine of x in radians
atan(x)	inverse tangent of x in radians
atan2(x,y)	inverse tangent of x/y in radians
sinh(x)	hyperbolic sine
cosh(x)	hyperbolic cosine
tanh(x)	hyperbolic tangent

goto

This word is redundant in C and encourages poor programming style. For this reason it has been ignored in this book. For completeness, and for those who insist on using it (may their programs recover gracefully!), the form of the goto statement is as follows:

```
goto label;
```

'label' is an identifier which occurs somewhere else in the given function and is defined as a label by using the colon:

```
label : printf ("Ugh! You used a goto!");
```

For completely crazed programmers, many implementations of C provide program directives called 'longjump' for jumping across stack levels – out of one function, into another! These are totally unnecessary and diabolical style.

33 : The Amiga

C is the natural language to use for programming the Commodore Amiga. The Amiga reference manuals, and much of the software written for the Amiga, use C as the basic language of the machine. This is an appropriate choice of language for what is a particularly complicated operating system. Amiga C compilers make heavy use of struct type variables for building window displays and the linked list is the fundamental data structure used by the operating system.

System Peculiarities

The Commodore Amiga has two distinctive features. First, it multi-tasks – the system can run several programs at the same time, quite independently of one another. The second feature is a very deep-rooted windowing system which allows users to take full advantage of its multi-tasking capabilities and provides the programmer with a very powerful interface which is unlike any other, at the time of writing.

The Amiga's operating system (called Amiga-DOS), and the high-level user interface (called Intuition), present some peculiarities to C programmers. These peculiarites serve to place some minor restrictions on the input/output operations which can be controlled by the standard input/output library. The difficulties are not insurmountable, but they are not easily overcome either.

The most obvious restriction is due to the nature of the input/output system used by the Amiga. The operating system makes it almost impossible to receive keyboard data immediately the keys are pressed using standard library functions. Functions such as getch which are sometimes provided in libraries are not supported by the Amiga. The user must invariably press RETURN before any key presses are acknowledged by a program. This difficulty is quite ingrained, unless the programmer is willing to undertake some advanced device-handling quite beyond the scope of this book.

The second restriction concerns assumptions about the way memory is stored in the machine. As the Amiga can run several programs simultaneously, no one program has sole rights to the memory and when a memory request is put in by a program, the Amiga will find memory wherever it can get it. This may not be in solid, unbroken pieces, but scattered all over the memory. This information is vital to programmers who intend to use pointers for accessing arrays and strings, as the normal rule about arrays being stored row-wise in a solid block, will not necessarily apply.

A final remark. The Amiga will not tolerate sloppy programming. Do not expect to be able to get away with short-cuts and software 'tricks', which might work on simpler computers. A high standard of discipline is needed to make programs run smoothly. This is no problem, if programmers keep to the guidelines noted in this book and in the Amiga reference manuals.

Running C in the CLI

In order to be able to write programs effectively, the user has to be able to type commands into a CLI (Command Line Interpreter). This is a program which interprets a command language, as discussed in Chapter Four and provides the user with a relatively low-level interface to the computer. This is essential for programming, as all the programmers tools exist at this level. Since the Commodore Amiga is normally set up to run 'Workbench', whose sole purpose is to eliminate this kind of needless typing in application programs, programmer's must secure themselves a CLI window, or preferably two, for programming with. The Amiga can be prevented from starting up the Workbench program by altering the start-up file in directory 's' of the workbench. The simplest way to do this is to press:

```
CTRL D
```

as the Amiga starts up (when the window called 'AmigaDOS' first appears). This prevents Workbench from being loaded. The start-up file can then be altered by typing:

```
ed s/startup-sequence
```

Delete the 'LoadWb' and 'endcli' programs and replace them with 'newcli'. This leaves two CLI windows on the screen for programming in. It is useful to have two CLIs so that when one window is busy, commands can still be entered in the other. These CLI windows allow the user to type in the compiler commands:

```
execute cc program
```

for instance. Other useful commands are:

dir	to find out what is on the disc
ed <filename>	to invoke the screen editor
copy <> to <>	to copy one file to another

The full list of relevant commands is to be found in the elusive AmigaDOS documentation.

Special Features of the Amiga

The Amiga operating system is more like a mainframe operating system than a micro operating system. It is geared to the concept of multi-tasking, and so its operation is highly 'intelligent', and can interrupt programs before they go seriously wrong, know immediately when a disc is inserted into the machine, or is removed, work the mouse even when no mouse programs are loaded and so on. The list of capabilities is almost endless.

The mouse is a integral part of the Amiga system, even when Workbench is not loaded. It allows the user to re-size and move windows as well as push them behind others. More importantly, it allows the user to select the currently active window as far as keyboard input is concerned. This concept is unique to multi-tasking systems – which of the many programs running on the screen at one time is to recieve the data from the keyboard? It would not make sense for all programs to receive it at the same time. The user selects the current input route by clicking the mouse in the chosen window.

Programmers who want to do more than this with the mouse and windows must use Intuition, the Amiga windowing system, which is quite beyond the scope of this text. However, there is an example next about using graphics windows.

As a final word, programmers can rest assured that C allows them access to all the facilities which the machine offers.

Resources

The Amiga treats most of its hardware facilities as 'pseudo-devices'. A pseudo-device is a part of the operating system which relays information to a real device, after performing some extra service. Facilities such as windows, sound, the printer, serial and parallel ports are all represented as pseudo-devices on the Amiga. Most of those devices have 'pseudo-device names' – filenames for accessing those devices as C input/output files. The complete filename strings for the Amiga devices are:

'DFn:'	Disc file (drive) n, eg: "DF1:","DF0:"
'PRT:'	The printer device (controlled by Preferences)
'SER:'	The serial (port) device
'PAR:'	The parallel (port) device
'RAM:'	The RAM disc (silicon disc)
'RAW:'	A kind of window for passing untranslated I/O
'CON:'	A console window

These objects can be opened as files with the fopen function, in order to send, receive or exchange data with the appropriate device. All the data is passed through Amiga-DOS. An example program below shows how this can be done. Here are some notes on each device.

PRT:

The printer device is a pseudo-device which is controlled by Preferences (the option configuration program on Workbench). The printer may, in fact, be connected either to the parallel port or serial port – Preferences directs the information according to what the user has selected. If a program opens the file called 'PRT:', it opts to have its output channelled through Preferences, to either the serial device or to the parallel device. The program list.c in Chapter 25 is written for the Amiga in its default state. The printer is opened up for writing by the following:

```
FILE *fout;
fout = fopen ("PRT:","w");
```

PAR: and SER:

PAR: and SER: are filenames for the raw serial and parallel ports. As the printer must be connected to one of these, a program could opt to write directly to the devices in order to access the printer, instead of writing to the printer device 'PRT:'. If this is done, no translation or configuration would be performed by the Preferences program. Instead SER: and PAR: can be used to write data to other items connected to those ports at the default rates. The default serial rate in 9600 baud. Listing 33.1 shows how the Amiga could pass a text file to its serial port, perhaps to transfer to another machine.

Listing 33.1. Serial port demo.

```
/*************************************************************/
/*                                                           */
/* Serial Port Demo                                          */
/*                                                           */
/*************************************************************/
       /* Copy *fin to *fout character by character */

       #include "stdio.h"
       #include "ctype.h"

/************************************************************/

       main ()                        /* Copy ASCII file to SER: */

       { FILE *fin,*fout;
           char *filename(),ch;

       printf ("\nDumb Serial Transfer V1.0\n\n");

       if ((fin = fopen(filename(),"r")) == NULL)
           {
           printf ("File cannot be read\n");
           exit (0);
           }

       if ((fout = fopen("SER:","w")) == NULL)
           {
           printf ("Can't Open serial port\n");
           exit (0);
           }

       do
           {
           fscanf (fin,"%c",&ch);
```

```
        if (isascii(ch))
            {
            fprintf (fout,"%c",ch);
            printf ("%c",ch);
            }
        }
    while (!feof(fin));

    exit(0);
    }
/**************************************************************/

    char *filename ()
    { static char *fsp = "...................";

    do
        {
        printf ("Enter filename : ");
        scanf ("%s",fsp);
        skipgarb();
        }
    while (strlen(fsp) == 0);
    return (fsp);
    }

/*************************************************************/

    skipgarb ()          /* Skip Garbage corrupting scanf */

    {
    while (getchar() != '\n');
    }
```

CON: and RAW:

These two files are both ways of opening windows for text input and output. They take parameters for the size and position of windows:

```
CON:x/y/width/height/name
RAW:x/y/width/height/name
```

A CON: window receives translated character data. A RAW: window receives untranslated key number data, as the keys are pressed. Some considerable background knowledge is needed to operate these files fully, which is beyond the capacity of this book.

Listing 33.2. CON: Window demo.

```
/*********************************************************/
/*                                                       */
/* CON: window demo                                      */
/*                                                       */
/*********************************************************/

      #include <stdio.h>

/*********************************************************/

      main ()
      { FILE *fp;

      char ch;

      printf ("Opening CON:0/0/200/200/Demo\n");

      if ((fp = fopen("CON:0/0/200/200/Demo","r")) == NULL)
           {
           printf ("Can't open CON: window");
           }

      while ((ch = getc(fp)) != 'Q')   /* echo chars back */
           {
           printf("%c",ch);
           }
      }

           /* end */
```

Graphics

The Amiga is loaded with facilities for drawing or rendering graphics. All graphics are based upon the idea that the 'piece of paper' on the Amiga is the 'window'. Amiga windows are unlike windows on other computers, as they multi-task, but this is not all. The Amiga can also create multiple screens. Some terminology needs to be explained before this can be understood properly.

A screen is a viewing area, the full size of the computer monitor screen. A screen is the basic template which defines the number of colours and resolution of the objects displayed. When you switch on, there is a single medium resolution screen called the 'Workbench screen' in view. The Amiga has the ability to hold more than one type of screen in its memory, but only one full screen can be viewed at a time. Screens have 'drag bars' and 'depth gadgets' (see your Amiga manual), and they can be moved around like windows.

A window is a viewing area, which lives on the screen. A screen can hold any number of overlapping windows (memory permitting), and every window inherits the colours and resolution which are supported by that screen. Windows are treated as pixel grids, which have co-ordinates x,y. Note that the origin (0,0) is located at the top left-hand corner of any window.

A raster port is an area of memory which is used to store the contents of a window. Before multiple windows were conceived, only one raster port was needed for a computer display and programmers seldom had to know about such things. Now several are required – one for each window. Being a multi-tasking machine, the Amiga could be using several windows at one time and so programs must specify the window they are using when drawing graphics. This is done by using a pointer to a raster port. A raster port is found from a window structure. A window is opened with the OpenWindow function:

```
window = OpenWindow(&NewWdw);
```

and then a raster port pointer is found with:

```
rast = window->RPort;
```

See the example program for details.

Graphics 'Primitives'

There are many graphics command routines (or 'primitives'), supported by the Amiga! Here are some of the most common ones. The parameters have the following types, as defined on the Amiga:

```
short x,y,xp,yp,mode;
BYTE colour;
struct RastPort *rast;
```

SetAPen (rast,colour)

The 'A' pen defines the colour of foreground objects. Colour is a colour between zero and the macro 'numofcols' minus one. In the example below numofcols is 16.

SetOPen (rast,colour)

The 'O' Pen defines an outline colour which is searched for by the flood-fill routines. (Implemented as a macro.)

Move (rast,x,y)

Move to a point relative to top left-hand of window (which is 0,0), and rast is a pointer to the window raster port.

Draw (rast,x,y)

Draw from current position to x,y. Draw draws in the colour set by SetAPen.

WritePixel(rast,x,y)

Plot one pixel at x,y. WritePixel plots a single pixel in the colour specified by SetAPen.

RectFill(rast,x,y,x1,y1)

This draws and fills a rectangle with the colour set by SetAPen. The rectangle is specified by giving the co-ordinates of the top left-hand corner (x,y) and the bottom right-hand corner (x1,y1).

Flood (rast,mode,x,y)

This routine performs a flood fill. It has two modes of operation, colour fill and outline fill (modes 1 and 0 respectively). The two modes work as follows:

1) Outline fill begins at the point x,y and starts searching for a closed outline in the colour set by SetOPen. It fills the area bounded by that outline with the colour set by SetAPen.

2) Colour fill is a way of re-colouring certain areas of the display. This mode starts from x,y and makes a note of the colour of the pixel at that point. It then searches for neighbouring pixels of the same colour and re-colours them in the new colour set by SetAPen.

The example program below shows the simplest way to use these graphics primitives. It is split into two separate files, called:

```
graph0.c
graph1.c
```

graph1.c is a general toolkit zone for opening a graphics window and graph0.c is the actual program. Graph1.c is #included into the first file. It can also be included in other programs and customised as required.

Listing 33.3. Amiga graphics demo.

```
/***********************************************************/
/*                                                         */
/* AMIGA GRAPHICS DEMO (graph0.c)                          */
/*                                                         */
/***********************************************************/

      #include <stdio.h>
      #include <graph1.c>

/***********************************************************/
/**  LEVEL 0 : Main Program                               **/
/***********************************************************/

      main ()
      {
      open_graphics_window ();
      create_picture ();
      wait_for_window_close ();
      }

/***********************************************************/
/** LEVEL 1                                               **/
/***********************************************************/

      create_picture ()
```

```
{ short x,y;

SetAPen(rast,RED);

Move (rast,20,20);
Draw (rast,200,20);
Draw (rast,200,100);
Draw (rast,20,20);

SetOPen (rast,RED);
SetAPen (rast,BLUE);
Flood   (rast,OUTLNMODE,30,30);

SetAPen (rast,PINK);
RectFill (rast,100,100,130,130);

x = y = 10;

WritePixel (rast,x,y);
}

      /* end */
```

This 'zone' is a general-purpose file which can be included in any program in order to create a graphics window. Notice the use of pre-initialised structures for creating screens and windows. Notice also the use of flags and messages such as in the statement #define WINDOWGADGETS. These features are typical of the way in which screens and gadgetry are built up.

Listing 33.4. Open a graphic screen and window.

```
/*****************************************************************/
/*                                                               */
/*  graph1.c : GRAPHICS Open a graphics screen & window          */
/*                                                               */
/*                                                               */
/*****************************************************************/

      #include <types.h>
      #include <intuition.h>
      #include <graphics/gfxmacros.h>

      #define WINDOWGADGETS (WINDOWSIZING | WINDOWDRAG |
                              WINDOWDEPTH | WINDOWCLOSE)
      #define true            1
      #define OUTLNMODE       0
      #define COLMODE         1
```

```
       #define width          480
       #define height         160
       #define numofcols      16

       enum ScreenColours
           {
           BLACK,
           WHITE,
           GREY,
           RED,
           BLUE,
           PINK                          /* etc. */
           };

       extern struct Window *OpenWindow();
       extern struct Screen *OpenScreen();

       int IntuitionBase = NULL;
       int GfxBase = NULL;

       USHORT class;

/****************************************************************/
/** STRUCTURE ASSIGNMENTS                                     **/
/****************************************************************/

       struct NewWindow NewWdw =

           {
           20, 20,                         /* top left x,y */
           width, height,                  /* width,height */
           1, 2,
           MOUSEBUTTONS |
           CLOSEWINDOW,
           WINDOWSIZING | RMBTRAP |
           GIMMEZEROZERO | WINDOWGADGETS,
           NULL,
           NULL,
           "Graphics Window",              /* Title of window */
           NULL,
           NULL,
           50,40,200,100,
           CUSTOMSCREEN
           };

       struct NewScreen NewScr =
           {
           0,0,              /* top left x,y        */
           640,200,4,        /* width,height,type */
           1,0,
           HIRES,
           CUSTOMSCREEN,
```

```
        NULL,
        "Graphic Screen",
        NULL, NULL
        };

    struct Window *window;                      /* Global vars */
    struct Screen *Scr;
    struct RastPort *rast;

/*************************************************************/
/** LEVEL 0                                                 **/
/*************************************************************/

    open_graphics_window ()
    {
    GfxBase = OpenLibrary("graphics.library", 0);
    if (GfxBase == NULL)
        {
        printf("graphics library open failed\n");
        exit(0);
        }

    IntuitionBase = OpenLibrary("intuition.library", 0);
    if (IntuitionBase == NULL)
        {
        printf("intuition library open failed\n");
        exit(0);
        }

    Scr = (struct Screen *) OpenScreen (&NewScr);

    if (Scr == NULL)
        {
        printf("Couldn't open new screen\n");
        CloseLibrary(GfxBase);
        CloseLibrary(IntuitionBase);
        exit(0);
        }

    NewWdw.Screen = Scr;
    if ((window = OpenWindow(&NewWdw)) == NULL)
        {
        printf ("open window failed\n");
        CloseScreen (Scr);
        CloseLibrary(IntuitionBase);
        CloseLibrary(GfxBase);
        exit(0);
        }
    rast = window->RPort;
    }
```

```
/**************************************************************/

      wait_for_window_close ()  /* Wait for window close */

      { struct IntuiMessage *message;

      while (true)
           {
           while ((message=(struct IntuiMessage *) GetMsg
                                  (window->UserPort)) == NULL);
           class = message->Class;
           ReplyMsg(message);

           if (class==CLOSEWINDOW) break;
           }

      if (window != NULL)
           {
           CloseWindow (window);
           }

      if (Scr != NULL)
           {
           CloseScreen (Scr);
           }

      if (GfxBase != NULL)
           {
           CloseLibrary (GfxBase);
           }

      if (IntuitionBase != NULL)
           {
           CloseLibrary (IntuitionBase);
           }
      }
```

34 : The Atari ST

The C compiler for Atari ST micros (see acknowledgements), supports a full range of standard functions plus many more for manipulating the special features on the ST machines. The C programmer also has the benefit of a powerful and attractive programming environment which runs under the control of the mouse/window operating manager.

Running C under TOS

The Atari ST machines work under their own operating system TOS, running the GEM mouse-and-window environment. The C compiler and the editor programs are run by clicking icons or directory lists with the mouse. Program parameters are entered through 'dialogue boxes' which prompt the user for a response.

The machine boots up into the desktop manager, from which the user clicks and drags icons in order to operate the compiler and editor. The operation of the compiler is described quite fully in its manual. A program is created using the editor supplied. The compiler is executed and the linker is then used to link the compiler's code to ST object code libraries. The linker uses an extremely versatile command file method of operation, providing a very flexible programming environment.

Special Features

The Atari is a non multi-tasking machine and so it can support single keypress I/O in a simple way. This means that a program learns about every press of the keyboard the instant it happens. This makes it much easier to write friendly, typing based programs, or to respond to keyboard presses as well as mouse activities.

The ST supports an extra 'get character' function for this immediate I/O which is called:

```
getch
```

This function is almost identical to getchar except that it is 'connected' directly to the keyboard. Characters enter the keyboard buffer immediately and the user does not have to press RETURN in order to receive characters. The key character which is pressed on the keyboard does not appear on the screen if getch is called. The same facility commonly is supported in BASIC interpreters under the name:

```
GET
```

getch might be accompanied by getche, which works identically, but echoes the typed character to the screen in addition to receiving the input. Examples of the use of these functions are:

```
char ch;

ch = getch();   /* wait for 1 keypress */
ch = getche(); /* wait for 1 keypress */
```

In the second case, the typed character is seen on the screen when it is typed.

Examples

```
main ()

{
printf ("Press any key\n");
getch;
}

main ()

{    char ch;
printf ("Choose menu option A/B/C\n");

while (true)
     {
     switch (ch = getch())
          {
          case 'A' : printf ("A\n");
          case 'B' : printf ("B\n");
          case 'C' : printf ("C\n");
          }
     }
}
```

Special support is given to programmers who need to access the deeper levels of TOS, and the built-in operating system functions. In addition, the Atari's powerful graphics routines can be manipulated in a simple way through standard library functions, provided by the compiler development system.

Graphics and the GEM Environment

The ST compiler has a comprehensive set of graphics routines for line drawing, flood filling, drawing pie charts, circles, ellipses and plenty more besides. The GEM window system is fully supported, with functions to open and close windows, access to different screen fonts, fill-patterns and complete mouse control.

GEM uses the 'standard graphics' approach to windows. Before a program can make use of the GEM libraries, it must 'open a work station', which is actually a graphics driver library. This 'workstation' acts as a kind of 'pseudo-device' which the user can write commands to for rendering graphics under GEM.

Line 'A' Routines

The basic set of graphics primitives on the Atari is known collectively as the line 'A' routines. These routines represent the most efficient way of drawing on the ST. It is not necessary to open a workstation for them, as they are below the level of GEM – GEM calls them, in fact, for its own use.

The GEM VDI

A higher-level alternative to the line 'A' routines is to use the GEM VDI. The GEM system requires a 'graphics device driver' called a 'workstation' to be opened before it can be used. A program which uses the GEM routines is less efficient than one which uses the raw line 'A' routines, but has the advantage of being independent of the machine running it.

In order to understand the GEM environment, some terminology needs to be clarified.

Workstation A graphics device driver. There is a separate driver for every output device such as the screen, printer, pen-plotter. The device is chosen by setting parameters in the open workstation function.

Virtual Workstation

There is only one display screen in reality; in practice, you could imagine there being several, each behaving in different way and acting together to make up the total effect. A virtual workstation is a graphics driver with its own personal set of parameters about the way it works. Any real workstation can have several virtual ones attached to it.

Handle Every workstation has its own 'handle' by which the graphics routines talk to it. This is just a label to distinguish between different drivers.

Polyline A polyline is a shape made by joining up a set of points with straight lines. The name is an amalagamation of polygon and line. GEM uses polylines instead of normal primitive graphics commands. The user specifies an array of co-ordinate pairs which are to be joined up, as a parameter to the polyline draw function.

Window A window is a rectangular region of the screen display into which graphics are drawn. A window needs to be opened before it can be used, under the control of a particular workstation.

To open a virtual workstation (to operate under the desktop), the user calls the function:

```
WORD handle;
WORD user_settings[11];
WORD return_info[57];

v_opnvwk(user_settings,&handle,return_info);
```

The function is supplied with some parameters in the form of an 11-

element array, which the programmer must fill in. A program supplies it with the handle of the current 'real' workstation, and it returns a handle which is used to address and operate the virtual workstation plus a 57-element array of return data about the workstation's attributes! This return data need not concern programmers at this level. A program needs only to supply an array for the return values to be stored in – the values don't need to be used after that in simple programs. The user must, on the other hand, supply the complete 11-element array of parameters. This provides the workstation with details of screen colours, width and height of device and so on. The exact details of this need not conern the beginner – a general purpose static array may be contructed and initialised ready for simple programs, as follows:

```
static WORD user_settings[] =

        {
        1,
        1,
        1,
        1,
        1,
        1,
        1,
        1,
        1,
        1,
        2
        };
```

Include this as a 'plug in part' in programs which need to use very simple graphics.

There are many commands which can be addressed to the workstation. Here are just a few:

vsl_color(handle,colour)

This sets the graphics colour of lines drawn on the screen by the workstation specified. Colour is a value of Atari-defined type WORD:

```
WORD colour;
```

which takes a machine dependent value from zero up to the maximum number of colours on the machine, minus one. For example:

```
#define noofcols    32
```

states that the computer can support 32 colours. The colour values are then from zero to 31.

v_pline(handle,nopairs,coordpairs

This function draws a polyline, specified by an array of co-ordinate points. The polyline is drawn by the workstation specified by 'handle'. 'Nopairs' is the same as the number of points which make up the polyline. Coordpairs is an array of pairs. For example:

```
static WORD coordpairs =

    {
    10,10,                    /* Arranged x,y */
    20,10,
    10,20,
    20,20
    };

WORD nopairs = 4;

v_pline(handle,nopairs,coordpairs);
```

Area Filling

GEM permits two kinds of flood filling:

1) The user specifies a polyline which is then closed and filled with a particular colour by joining the last and first point together

2) The user specifies a contour line of a particular colour which is the boundary of the fill area

v_fillarea (handle,count,coords)

This function fills a 'multiply connected' polyline. The line may cross itself any number of times. The parameters are the same as those for the polyline command.

v_contourfill(handle,x,y,colour);

This function causes a closed boundary to be filled with the colour specified, by the workstation addressed under 'handle'. The user's workstation decides the colour and the pattern of the area to be filled.

v_recfl(handle,rectangle);

This function draws a filled rectangle under the workstation specified by handle. The rectangle is specified by an array of four co-ordinates:

```
static WORD rectangle[] =
     {
     top_left_x,top_left_y,
     bottom_right_x,bottom_right_y
     };
```

Listing 34.1. Atari graphics demo.

The example below is a simple illustration of how to draw simple graphics displays with the functions just listed.

```
/************************************************************/
/*                                                          */
/* Atari Graphics Demo                                      */
/*                                                          */
/************************************************************/
     /* Compile with -n option for long indentifiers */

     #include <portab.h>
     #include <gemlib.h>

/************************************************************/
/* Define some global data storage                          */
/************************************************************/

     WORD return_info[57];
     static WORD user_settings[11] =
          {
          1,
          1,
          1,
          1,
          1,
          1,
          1,
          1,
          1,
```

```
                1,
                2
                };

/************************************************************/
/* LEVEL 0                                                  */
/************************************************************/

        main ()

        {    WORD GetWorkStation(),handle;

        handle = GetWorkStation();
        GraphicsDemo (handle);
        CloseWorkstation(handle);
        }

/************************************************************/
/* LEVEL 1                                                  */
/************************************************************/

        WORD GetWorkStation ()

        {    WORD handle, d;

        appl_init();
        handle = graf_handle(&d,&d,&d,&d); /* give dummy values */
        v_opnvwk (user_settings,&handle,return_info);
        return (handle);
        }

/************************************************************/

        CloseWorkstation (handle)

        WORD handle;

        {
        getch();                  /* wait for a key to be pressed */
        v_clsvwk(handle);
        }

/************************************************************/

        GraphicsDemo (handle)
        WORD handle;

        {    static WORD coordpairs[] =
                {
                10,10,       /* Polyline coords Arranged x,y */
                20,10,
                10,20,
```

```
            20,20
            };

    static WORD rectangle[] =
            {
            500,500,
            600,400
            };

    WORD nopairs = 4;
    v_pline(handle,nopairs,coordpairs);  /* Draw polyline */
    v_fillarea(handle,nopairs,coordpairs);/* Flood fill    */
    vr_recfl(handle,rectangle);         /* Filled rectangle */
    }
```

35 :The Archimedes

The Archimedes supports a full implementation of ANSI C standard, very comprehensively so for its many internal facilities for sound, graphics and windowing. The special C support libraries are straightforward to use and provide a powerful extension to the full complement of standard library functions. C is an ideal partner for the Archimedes, providing speed, power and a state of the art programming environment.

Running C

In order to write programs effectively, you have to be able to type commands into a MOS CLI. CLI stands for Command Line Interpreter. A CLI is a program which interprets a command language, as discussed in Chapter Four, and provides the user with a relatively low-level interface to the computer. This is essential for programming, as all the programmer's tools exist at this level.

The C compiler is invoked by executing the program CC on the compiler disc. For example:

```
CC program_name <options>
```

The effect of invoking the compiler is to take a source program and to convert it into suitable object code. A separate linker is used to resolve references to library functions provided by the implementation. The naming convention of the files produced by the compiler is slightly unusual, due to the operating system's method of directory handling (see next section).

System Peculiarities

The Archimedes runs the ADFS filing system under which sub-directory file-paths are denoted by a full stop. This means that filenames can't be represented in the standard way with a 'dot extension' under ADFS. The reverse system is used, so that a traditional filename:

```
myprog.c
```

must be represented by:

```
c.myprog
```

Similarly header files:

```
stdio.h
```

are stored as:

```
h.stdio
```

by the local filing system. In order to cope with the ANSI standard representations of header files, such as 'stdio.h' and 'ctype.h', the compiler performs the conversion to local operating system format at compile time. You don't have to worry about calling the header files by their local ADFS names, but you can use the standard representations, with dot extensions afterwards, as used in this book.

Operating System Support

The standard operating system on the Archimedes is called Arthur. It is a non multi-tasking, command-driven operating system, which supports a wide variety of operations. A special library of commands called Arthurlib is endorsed by the compiler which allows the programmer access to the Arthur operating system in C programs. Users who are familiar with previous Acorn computers will recognise the similarity between the C functions listed below and their predecessors in the BASIC/assembler world.

Operating system comands can be passed to the Archimedes CLI by the function, system(). The purpose of system() is to pass a line of text directly to the command line interpreter of the computer. In other words, it imitates typing in a command to the CLI. The form of this function is:

```
int system (), returnvalue;
char *string;
returnvalue = system (string);
```

The return value is minus one if the operation failed, and zero otherwise. For example:

```
system ("cat");

if (system("CDIR fred") == -1)                    /* 2 */
    {
    printf ("Can't execute command");
    }
system ("run Myprog");                            /* 3 */
```

system allows a program user access to the operating system without leaving an application program.

Support is also provided for the standard operating system calls of the Acorn operating system, such as OSBYTE and OSWORD. The functions provided for handling these calls to operating system make use of special struct type variables to pass parameter values to them. The functions act and return a special struct type error message indicating whether or not an operation succeeded.

osbyte
osword
osfile
osargs
osfind

Friendly Text I/O

The standard Archimedes is a non multi-tasking machine and so it can support single keypress I/O in a simple way. This means that a program can learn about every keypress the instant it occurs. This makes it much easier to write friendly, typing-based programs.

The Archimedes supports an extra 'get character' function for this immediate I/O, which is called:

```
get() or getch()
```

These functions are almost identical to getchar except that they are 'connected' directly to the keyboard – characters enter the keyboard buffer immediately and you don't have to press RETURN in order to receive characters. The key character which is pressed on the keyboard does not appear on the screen if get() is called. The same facility is commonly supported in BASIC interpreters under the name:

```
GET
```

get and getch might be accompanied by getche which works identically, but echoes the typed character to the screen in addition to receiving the input. Examples of the use of these functions are:

```
char ch;
ch = (char)get();
ch = getch();   /* wait for 1 keypress */
ch = getche();  /* wait for 1 keypress */
```

In the first case the type of data returned is 'int', so the value must be cast into character form for normal usage. In the third case, the typed character is seen on the screen when it is typed.

Examples:

```
main ()

{
printf ("Press any key\n");
get();
}

void main ()

{    char ch;
printf ("Choose menu option A/B/C\n");

while (true)
     {
     switch (ch = (char)get())
          {
          case 'A' : printf ("A");
          case 'B' : printf ("B");
          case 'C' : printf ("C");
          }
     }
}
```

Sound

The sound facilities of the Archimedes are dealt with by a set of functions contained in the Arthurlib library. The Archimedes supports stereo sound in up to eight channels, which are manipulated in the traditional Acorn way, with some new additions. You must #include <arthur.h> in order to use these functions.

sound_on()

This function switches the sound system on so that the functions listed next can take effect.

sound_off()

This function shuts down the sound system.

voices(number)

The user can select the number of sound channels required as some power of two up to eight – 1,2,4 or 8.

stereo(int,int)

This function allows programmers to 'pan' sounds left and right in the stereo field of the sound system.

sound(channel,amplitude,pitch,duration,synch)

This function actually issues a sound from the sound output. Its parameters have the following meanings:

channel	a channel number from one to eight (see voices())
amplitude	the loudness of the sound -15 to zero
pitch	values from zero to 255
duration	the length of the sound–minus one to 254

synch this is a value which indicates whether the sound is to be played at the same time as another sound, or after it. A value of minus two implies that sounds will follow one after the other.

Listing 35.1. ARM jingle.

```
/*******************************************************/
/*                                                     */
/* ARM jingle                                          */
/*                                                     */
/*******************************************************/

        #include <arthur.h>

/*******************************************************/

        void main ()

        {
        sound_on();
        voices(1);
        jingle();
        sound_off();
        }

/********************************************************/

        jingle ()              /* instead of CTRL G beep ! */

        {
        sound (1,-15,100,1,-2);
        sound (1,-15,200,1,-2);
        sound (1,-15,150,1,-2);
        sound (1,-15,250,1,-2);
        sound (1,-15,100,1,-2);
        sound (1,-15,159,1,-2);
        }
                                 /* end */
```

Graphics

The Archimede's rich set of graphics and windowing routines can be accessed from C. The functions include primitives for rendering simple line-drawn graphics and for more complex imagery. The commands bear a sharp resemblance to the traditional BASIC routines as originally conceived by Acorn. A selection of the simplest of the line-drawing routines is listed below. These functions are located in the library

Authurlib. You must #include <arthur.h> in order to make use of these functions.

All of the parameters to the functions below are of datatype 'int'. For example:

```
int x,y,radius,col;
```

circle(x,y,radius)

This function uses the graphics routines to draw a circle whose centre lies at the co-ordinates (x,y), with radius as specified in the paramter list. Usage:

```
int x = 200;
int y = 300;
int radius = 50;

circle (100,100,30);
circle (x,y,radius);
```

clg

This valueless function clears the imagery from the current graphics window by filling the entire area with the background colour.

cls

This valueless function clears everything in the current text window, by filling the window with the current text background colour. Usage:

```
cls();
```

colour(col)

This valueless function sets the colour of graphics text as printed in a text or graphics window. Usage:

```
int col = 3;
colour (2);
colour (col);
```

draw(x,y)

This valueless function draws a solid line from the current graphics position to the position specified in the parameter list. Usage:

```
int x = 10, y = 514;
draw (200,412);
draw (x,y);
```

fill(x,y)

This valueless function flood-fills an area of the graphics window with the current graphics colour. The co-ordinates supplied are the co-ordinates of any place inside the area to be filled. The fill routines work up to boundaries in the current graphics colour. Usage:

```
int x = 400, y = 500;
fill (20,30);
fill (x,y);
```

gcol(mode,col)

This valueless function sets the current graphics colour and rendering mode. The modes are as for the BASIC command GCOL. Usage:

```
int mode = 0, col= 3;
gcol (0,3);
gcol (mode,col);
```

plot(k,x,y)

This valueless function plots and draws points and lines. It is the route to all of the pixel-drawing functions. The value of k specifies the plot mode (solid/dotted lines and so on). See the BASIC manual for details of the k numbers. Usage:

```
int k = 85, x = 100, y = 100;
plot (69,500,500);
plot (4,10,10);
plot (5,20,20);
plot (k,x,y);
```

rectanglefill(leftx,bottomy,width,height)

This valueless function plots and fills a rectangle in the current graphics colour. The user specifies the co-ordinates of the bottom left-hand corner of the rectangle and its width and height. Usage:

```
int leftx = 100, bottomy = 100;
int width = 200, height = 100;

rectanglefill(leftx,bottomy,width,height);
rectanglefill(0,0,20,20);
```

Listing 35.2. Archimedes graphics demo.

```
/*****************************************************/
/*                                                   */
/* Graphics Demo ARM                                 */
/*                                                   */
/*****************************************************/

        #include <arthur.h>

/*****************************************************/

        void main ()

        {    int discard;

        mode (1);

        gcol(0,1);
        move (20,20);
        draw (200,200);

        gcol (0,2);
        rectanglefill(200,200,100,100);

        gcol (0,3);
        circle (300,300,200);

        floodfill (300,300);

        discard = get();               /* Wait for key press */
        }
```

36 : PCs

C is an excellent language for programming PCs and MS-DOS computers. It has the necessary flexibility to work on projects of all levels, and there are superb C compilers available for these machines.

Running C

When switched on, a PC usually 'boots up' into a CLI (command line interpreter) straight away from the system disc. In the CLI environment the screen prompt will look something like:

```
A>
```

or alternatively:

```
C>
```

displaying the default drive. The command line interpreter allows the user to type in MS-DOS commands such as:

```
dir
mkdir  Cdevelop
```

or to run programs by typing their names. Most compilers work from the CLI directly – the user types a command in order to compile a program. A batch file is usually used to execute the different phases of the compiler in one typing operation such as:

```
cc  program
```

Some newer compilers offer a more substantial operating environment than the traditional CLI, with windows and mouse operations controlling a whole development environment of compiler, editor and debugger.

MS-DOS has a special naming convention for files. This convention is subtly different from that used by some other operating systems. The convention for C related files is:

filename.C	is a C source file
filename.EXE	is an executable file (not filename.x)
filename.BAT	is a 'batch' file which is used to execute whole 'batches' or groups of MS-DOS commands in a single user operation.

Filenames can be up to eight letters long, plus a dot extension as previously mentioned. When files have been named with the dot extension, they are not necessarily referred to with their full 'dotted' names. Files also look different in their directory, once they have been named with a file extension. When the user types:

```
dir
```

to find out what is on a disc, the filenames and their dot extensions are listed in a separate column:

FILENAME.C	becomes	FILENAME C
FILENAME.EXE	becomes	FILENAME EXE
FILENAME.BAT	becomes	FILENAME BAT

The C source files should always be called by the name filename.c, but the executable code which a compiler produces is run by typing a filename with or without its '.EXE' extension.

Although MS-DOS contains a text editor called EDIT, which can be used to edit program files, most compilers will come as a package with their own development editors. Some of these editors might have comprehensive debugging utilities incorporated into them.

MS-DOS and Facilities

The PC has a number of distinctive features. The obvious feature is that it runs MS-DOS or PC-DOS, an industry standard operating system. The basic hardware on a PC is often skeletal, so few compilers commit themselves to supporting graphics or operations which require special hardware, like mice and so on. Special extension packages can usually be purchased to deal with machine extras. This uncertainty about hardware means that the main thrust of basic PC compiler programming has to be textual.

Friendly Text I/O

The PC is a non multi-tasking machine and so it can support single keypress I/O in a simple way. This means that a program can learn about every press of the keyboard at the instant it happens. This makes it much easier to write friendly, typing based programs.

The PC supports an extra 'get character' function for this immediate I/O which is called:

```
getch()
```

This function is almost identical to getchar except that it is 'connected' directly to the keyboard – characters enter the keyboard buffer immediately – the user does not have to press RETURN in order to receive characters. The key character which is pressed on the keyboard does not appear on the screen if getch is called. The same facility is commonly supported in BASIC interpreters.This function is almost identical to getchar except that it is 'connected' directly to the keyboard – characters enter the keyboard buffer immediately – the user does not have to press RETURN in order to receive characters. The key character which is pressed on the keyboard does not appear on the screen if getch is called. The same facility is commonly supported in BASIC interpreters under the name:

```
GET
```

getch might be accompanied by getche() which works identically, but echoes the typed character to the screen in addition to receiving the input. Examples of the use of these functions are:

```
char ch;

ch = getch();  /* wait for 1 keypress */
ch = getche(); /* wait for 1 keypress */
```

In the second case, the typed character is seen on the screen when it is typed in.

Examples

```
main ()

{
printf ("Press any key\n");
getch;
}

main ()

{ char ch;

printf ("Choose menu option A/B/C\n");

while (true)
      {
      switch (ch = getch())
            {
            case 'A' : printf ("A");
            case 'B' : printf ("B");
            case 'C' : printf ("C");
            }
      }
}
```

Special Support

Special support is given to programmers who need to access the deeper levels of DOS and the built in operating system functions. The facilities available are compiler dependent, and to some extent PC model dependent. Some compilers support a full range of DOS and BIOS calls while others provide limited support. Readers should check individual compiler manuals to determine exactly what is supported.

Sound

One such facility is a 'sound' call which generates tones from the PC's internal loudspeaker. The sound functions are:

```
void sound_tone(cycles,uptime,downtime);
void sound_beep(frequency);
void sound_click();
```

All the function parameters are int types.

Sound_click simply makes a click sound from the loudspeaker. Sound_beep makes a tone of fixed length of the frequency given (1000 is a typical frequency value). Sound_tone allows the programmer to specify the pitch and duration of noises generated by the internal speaker. Cycles is the number of full cycles of the square wave-form which is output, so this specifies the duration of the sound. A small value is a quick click and a long value is a long tone. Uptime and downtime define the pitch of the sound. They are times so they vary the opposite way to pitch or frequency. The longer these values are, the lower the pitch and vice versa. Zero values result in uncontrolled effects.

This example provides a routine to go into an output toolkit. There is nothing more annoying than a program which beeps at the user with the same irritating tone everytime he/she does something wrong. The function jingle provides a friendlier sound.

Listing 36.1. A PC jingle.

```
/**************************************************/
/*                                                */
/* Jingle : sound example                         */
/*                                                */
/**************************************************/

      main ()

      {
      jingle ();
      }

/**************************************************/

      jingle ()

      {
      sound_tone (50,1000,10);
      sound_tone (50,400,10);
      sound_tone (50,600,10);
      sound_tone (50,900,10);
      sound_tone (50,90,10);
```

```
sound_tone (50,10,50);
}

    /* end */
```

MS-DOS Support

Another extremely useful function which can be found in C compilers is system. The purpose of system is to pass a line of text directly to the command line interpreter of the computer. In other words, it imitates typing in a command to the CLI. The form of this function is:

```
int system (), returnvalue;
char *string;

returnvalue = system (string);
```

The return value is minus one if the operation failed, and zero otherwise. For example:

```
system ("dir");                                    /* 1 */

if (system("mkdir fred") == -1)                    /* 2 */
   {
   printf ("Can't execute command");
   }

system ("Myprog.EXE");                             /* 3 */
```

system could be be used to allow a program user access to the operating system without leaving an application program.

Child Processes

Child processes are new programs which can be called and run during the course of some other program, without having to terminate the calling program. Child processes are a way of controlling a group of related programs from one manager. For example, a C editor could call up its C compiler as a child process, to compile a program without ever having to leave the editor. The compiled program could also be run under the auspices of the editor, as a child process. Another example, a menu manager, could select a given program from a menu of several, without having to abandon control. Child processes are not multi-tasking. They do not run at the same time as one another, they are simply a transfer of control to a new place.

One program is suspended while another one runs and then control returns to the original spot in the original program. Child processes give the programmer a tool with which to write more structured software. As a program naturally branches out, it can be split, not only into functions, but into separate programs, running under the guidance of a manager.

A program is said to 'spawn' a child process, so command functions dealing with the execution control are named:

```
int spawnl (mode,pathname,arg0,arg1,...argn, NULL);
int spawnlp (mode,filename,arg0,arg1,...argn, NULL);
int spawnv (mode,pathname,argv);
int spawnvp (mode,filename,argv);

int mode;
char *pathname, *filename;
char *arg0, *arg1,....                /* strings */
char *argv[];                         /* Array of strings */
```

These four functions work similarly. The programmer might wish to call a program which accepts parameters or 'arguments'. This is accommodated by the child process functions. The first two functions operate with a list of parameters, ending in a NULL byte. The second two use initialised arrays of parameters which must end with NULL entries.

The mode integer is irrelevant at present but is included for future compatibility. Pathname is a string which gives a full file specification for the program which is to be loaded. This includes the appropriate directory. Filename is simply a program name, with the directory path omitted.

```
#define mode 0

result = spawnl (mode,"A:branch\prog.EXE",NULL);
result = spawnlp (mode,"prog.EXE","1","param2",NULL);

static char argv[] =
    {
    "",          /* see text */
    "1",
    "param",
```

```
        NULL
        };

    result = spawnv (mode,"C:prog.EXE",argv);
    result = spawnvp (mode,"prog.EXE",argv);
```

The first element of the argument array (argv[0]) is ignored. The final element must be NULL to mark its end.

A child program can be aborted at any time by calling abort or exit(0). Control then returns to the caller.

Similar command functions may also exist under names beginning with
'exec':

```
    execl()
    execlp()
    execv()
    execvp()
```

These functions load a new program to replace the old one completely. Control does not return to the original program.

Final Note: Program Style

Even though many compilers don't provide immediate support for graphics and the more elaborate operations available, there is still room for these things in PC programs. Programmers are advised to have expansion and upgrade in mind and to design programs accordingly. Functions for graphics can still be incorporated into programs in the form of empty functions, to be filled in at a later date:

```
    draw_graphics ()

        {
        }
```

By adopting a practice like this, it becomes a simple matter to develop and expand programs in the future.

37 : BBC Master

C is available for the BBC microcomputers, the Acorn Master 128 and the Master Compact. It is a full implementation of Kernighan and Ritchie C with many of the accepted standard library functions.

Running C from the CLI

When switched on, Acorn computers boot up into the default language of the machine, which is normally BBC BASIC. The BASIC language allows commands to be passed to the operating system through the operating system Command Line Interpreter (CLI), by prefixing statements with a star character '*'. The C compiler has to be loaded into Sideways RAM, or second processor memory by inserting the disc and typing:

```
*EXEC SETUP
```

and pressing the BREAK key:

```
*C
*MOUNT
SETPATH $
```

then enters the C language CLI and leaves the machine ready for use. A program is compiled by the following sequence:

```
COMPILE program
LINK program
```

The C language package contains an excellent screen editor for preparing program source files (which is provided as standard on the Master 128).

System Peculiarites

Master computers running ADFS use the full stop ('dot') character for accessing sub-directories. This means that filenames cannot be represented in the standard way with a dot extension under ADFS. The reverse system is used, so that a traditional filename:

```
myprog.c
```

must be represented by:

```
c.myprog
```

Similarly, header files:

```
stdio.h
```

must be written as:

```
h.stdio
```

Limitations

The C language provided by this compiler does not approach ANSI standard C, but 'Kernighan and Ritchie' standard C. This means there are several features described in previous chapters which are not supported by this compiler.

1) Maths library. Although the header file 'h.math' is included in the header directory, no maths object code library is included, so none of the special maths functions of Chapter 21 are supported.

2) Structures may not be used as parameters and functions may *not* return a struct type. Functions which need to hand structures between functions must use pointers to structures as parameters only.

3) The data types: enum, volatile, const are not supported.

Listing 37.1. Sample C program for BBC Master.

The example shows how a simple C program looks under BBC MasterC.

```
/************************************************************/
/*                                                          */
/* BBC Master C                                             */
/*                                                          */
/************************************************************/

      #include <h.stdio>
      #include <h.ctype>

/*************************************************************/

      main ()

      {    char ch;
      do
           {
           ch = getchar();
           }
      while (isalpha(ch));
      }
                              /* end */
```

Special MOS Support

The following commands can be used to interface directly to the Acorn machine operating system (MOS) for access to user machine code routines and standard operating system calls such as OSBYTE and OSWORD. Some knowledge of 6502 machine code is assumed.

return = call(address,A,X,Y, param1,param2...);

This function is like the BASIC function, USR. It hands control over to a user machine code routine, located at the address supplied in the parameter list, and the values of A, X and Y are used to initialise the accumulator and index registers respectively. Any values provided after these are assumed to be parameters to the program. All parameters are of int type. The return value is of long int type.

The user's machine code program is entered with the variable:

```
_iacc
```

being equal to the address of the first parameter. Parameters are located on the stack. They are pushed on backwards, so that param1 is on top of param2 and so on. After your routine has been executed, the function returns with a long integer value:

```
long int return;
```

which is made up of four bytes arranged (as with the BASIC USR function) in the form AXYP. The value of the P register, for example, is then found by writing:

```
int P;
P = (return && 0xFF);
```

oscall(ptr,address,A,X,Y)

A variation on the call() function is supplied in oscall(). This routine calls a machine code user routine at 'address', supplying the A,X,Y registers with the values in the parameter list, and a pointer to a structure which contains the return information. For example:

```
struct _osret return;
oscall (&return, OSBYTE, 7,7,0);
```

The _osret structure is defined in the operating system header file 'h.osdefs'. The oscall function tests for system errors (handled in the usual way with BRK). The error member of the return structure is set to the value 'true' if an error occurred, and 'false' otherwise. This allows control to return to the calling C program intact, and informs the calling program of any errors which were incurred during the execution of the user routine. For instance:

```
/* true is anything except zero */
/* false is zero */

if (return.error)
     {
     printf ("Program returned with an error");
     }
```

system(string)

system passes a string of text to the operating system's command line interpreter. This allows programs to communicate directly with the

operating system, without leaving control of a C program.
For example:

```
system ("CAT");
```

is equivalent to the user typing *CAT on a command line.

Errors

Errors are flagged by the global variables errno and _sysmsg[], which contain the error number and error string respectively. Error number is an integer and _sysmsg is a pointer to a character array:

```
printf ("Error %d is: %s",errno,_sysmsg);
```

Graphics

No immediate support is given to graphics by this C compiler, but Acorn micros offer easy access to graphics routines in the form of control sequences, making it a simple matter to create a user graphics library.

The plot command could be implemented by the following:

```
plot (k,x,y)

int k,x,y;

{    char ck,lx,mx,ly,my;
ck = (char)(k && 0xFF);
lx = (char)(x % 0xFF);
mx = (char)(x / 0xFF);
ly = (char)(y % 0xFF);
my = (char)(y / 0xFF);
printf ("\x19 %c %c %c %c %c",ck,lx,mx,ly,my);
}
```

k is the plot mode and x and y are the screen co-ordinates. lx and mx are respectively the least significant byte and the most significant byte of the two-byte integer, x. Similarly, ly and my are the least significant byte and most significant byte of y. The code above is equivalent to the following BASIC procedure:

```
DEF PROCplot (k,x,y);

ck = k AND &FF
lx = x MOD &FF
mx = x DIV &FF
ly = y MOD &FF
my = y DIV &FF
VDU 25,ck,lx,mx,ly,my
ENDPROC
```

or even more simply:

```
PLOT k,x,y
```

The example shows how the main graphics functions can be implemented in C using printf(). The graphics routines have been made into a library file called 'h.graphics' (stored in the H directory), so that they may be included in any program.

Listing 37.2. Graphics demo and header file.

```
/**********************************************************/
/*                                                        */
/* Graphics Demo                                          */
/*                                                        */
/**********************************************************/

        #include <h.graphics>

        main ()

        {
        mode (2);
        gcol (0,1);
        RectFill (0,0,200,200);
        gcol (0,2);
        move (200,200);
        draw (0,0);
        pixel (300,300);
        }
```

Graphics Header File

```
/**********************************************************/
/*                                                        */
/* GRAPHICS HEADER FILE FOR BBC MASTER : h.graphics       */
/*                                                        */
/**********************************************************/
          /* Toolkit of graphics routines */

     #ifndef stdout

          #include <h.stdio>

     #endif
/**********************************************************/

     plot (k,x,y)

     int k,x,y;

     {    char ck,lx,mx,ly,my;

     ck = (char)(k && 0xFF);
     lx = (char)(x % 0xFF);
     mx = (char)(x / 0xFF);
     ly = (char)(y % 0xFF);
     my = (char)(y / 0xFF);
     printf ("\x19 %c %c %c %c %c",ck,lx,mx,ly,my);
     }

/**********************************************************/

     mode (k)
     int k;
     {
     printf ("\x16 %c",(char)(k && 0xFF));
     }

/**********************************************************/

     gcol (a,b)
     int a,b;
     {
     printf ("\x12 %c %c",(char)(a && 0xFF),(char)(b && 0xFF));
     }

/**********************************************************/
```

```
     #define move(x,y)        plot (4,x,y)
     #define draw(x,y)        plot (5,x,y)
     #define pixel(x,y)       plot (69,x,y)
     #define triangle(x,y)    plot (85,x,y)

/**********************************************************/

     RectFill (x1,y1,x2,y2)              /* Filled rectangle */
     {
     move (x1,y1);
     move (x2,y1);
     triangle (x2,y2);
     move (x1,y1);
     triangle (x1,y2);
     }
                                /* end */
```

The file 'graphics' should be saved under the 'h' directory so the compiler can locate it.

A : Style Notes

Levels, Zones and Toolkits

A computer program is like a tree, branching out, becoming ever more complex. A program starts from a certain place, called the main program, and branches out into subroutines, which in turn branch into more subroutines and so on. This creates a structure which has a number of levels:

```
Level 0              main ()
                      /  \
Level 1         sub1()  sub2()
                 /  \    /  \
Level 3          ..  ..  ..  ..
```

A convenient way of grouping functions in a C program is in levels like these. A program then consists of one main procedure at LEVEL 0, which branches out into a new level called LEVEL 1. LEVEL 1 contains all the procedures which are used in LEVEL 0. All the procedures used in LEVEL 1 are found in LEVEL 2 and so on until there are no more procedures left. It is not possible for programs written in C with a normal screen editor to look exactly like this structure diagram, but they can retain the essential features. The structure diagram can be squashed sideways so that the levels are preserved and the functions are listed, one after the other, inside their respective levels. This shows, at least, the status of every procedure in the tree and means that procedures can be found very easily. Any procedure which is called in LEVEL 1 would be found in LEVEL 2 and conversely any procedure defined in LEVEL 2 would only have been called in LEVEL 1.

What happens to procedures which are used throughout all the levels, such as special printing routines or graphics routines to draw certain shapes? The key to this lies in the re-usability of these routines. They are routines of a very general nature, which behave as basic tools for the main procedures. This motivates their inclusion in a special level, or set of levels called toolkits. A good reason for doing this is that toolkit routines are a type of routines which come to be needed again and again, in many different programs perhaps, and can subsequently be isolated and re-used. Toolkits automatically result in routine libraries, some of which hold details relating to particular computers only. Programs constructed in this way are highly portable, since it should only be necessary to replace a toolkit when carrying a program over to another system.

Nesting

When statements or loops are nested, they are indented for every loop so that the extent of nesting clear. A strict policy is important here too, to keep programs clear. In all the programs in this book the method:

```
for (n=1; n <= 10; n++)
    {
    while ( a < b )
        {
        printf ("...");
        printf ("...");
        }
    printf ("....");
    }
```

is used in preference to:

```
for ( n=1; n <= 10; n++)
    {        while (a < b) {
        printf ("....");printf ("..."); }  }
```

B : Compiler Variations

This appendix may be ignored by readers who have never used C before and are using only one compiler. It outlines the way compilers differ.

C has undergone various stages of development and improvement. One notable development was the creation of a new super C language called C++ by Bjarne Stroustrup, which means C incremented, in 'selve spraaket'! Newer versions of the C compiler tend to support more lavish operations than older ones, and in particular possess two new pre-defined data-types, called void and enum, const and volatile, which have been imported from C++. The following list items summarises the possible differences between a modern compiler and an older one. This book assumes that all of the new features are allowed by its compiler. Details of how to use these constructs are given in the relevant chapter.

New Data Types

void	This implies no value at all and is used for returning from functions without passing a value
enum	Enumerated or abstract types. This gives C facilities a bit like the abstract types of Pascal, though C's version of these is more concrete and user-controllable and so more 'primitive'
const	For naming constant expressions
volatile	For data which can be altered by agencies outside a program

Aggregate Assignment

An 'aggregate' data type is a 'structure' union or enum. These types are ways of holding several items of data in a single 'package' for convenience. They are not like arrays, however. Older compilers placed severe restrictions upon what could be done with structures and unions.

Essentially, the only things that could be done were to obtain the address of an aggregate type variable and to assign and read the values of the data spaces within. Only the locations of aggregates could be passed as parameters to functions. Modern compilers lift these restrictions and make aggregate types worth their weight in silicon. It is now possible to do the following:

1) Assign structures and unions of identical type to one another as a single unit

2) whole structures and unions can be passed as value parameters. This means that the receiving function makes a copy of the aggregate which is used until the end of that function

3) Functions can return whole aggregates by value. This is in contrast to ISO Pascal too

Miscellaneous

The $ symbol may, or may not, be allowed in identifiers. Check your manual for details.

Some implementations do not allow assignments to be made when declaring variables. For example, int i = 0;

The storage class 'register' may not be supported on some systems, since it is a machine dependent feature.

C : Conversions

Character Conversion Table

Decimal	Octal	Hex	Character
0	0	0	CTRL-@
1	1	1	CTRL-A
2	2	2	CTRL-B
3	3	3	CTRL-C
4	4	4	CTRL-D
5	5	5	CTRL-E
6	6	6	CTRL-F
7	7	7	CTRL-G
8	10	8	CTRL-H
9	11	9	CTRL-I
10	12	A	CTRL-J
11	13	B	CTRL-K
12	14	C	CTRL-L
13	15	D	CTRL-M
14	16	E	CTRL-N
15	17	F	CTRL-O
16	20	10	CTRL-P
17	21	11	CTRL-Q
18	22	12	CTRL-R
19	23	13	CTRL-S
20	24	14	CTRL-T
21	25	15	CTRL-U
22	26	16	CTRL-V
23	27	17	CTRL-W
24	30	18	CTRL-X
25	31	19	CTRL-Y
26	32	1A	CTRL-Z
27	33	1B	CTRL-[
28	34	1C	CTRL-\

Decimal	Octal	Hex	Character
29	35	1D	CTRL-]
30	36	1E	CTRL-^
31	37	1F	CTRL-_
32	40	20	
33	41	21	!
34	42	22	"
35	43	23	#
36	44	24	$
37	45	25	%
38	46	26	&
39	47	27	'
40	50	28	(
41	51	29	)
42	52	2A	*
43	53	2B	+
44	54	2C	,
45	55	2D	-
46	56	2E	.
47	57	2F	/
48	60	30	0
49	61	31	1
50	62	32	2
51	63	33	3
52	64	34	4
53	65	35	5
54	66	36	6
55	67	37	7
56	70	38	8
57	71	39	9
58	72	3A	:
59	73	3B	;
60	74	3C	<
61	75	3D	=
62	76	3E	>
63	77	3F	?
64	10	40	@
65	101	41	A
66	102	42	B
67	103	43	C

Decimal	Octal	Hex	Character
68	104	44	D
69	105	45	E
70	106	46	F
71	107	47	G
72	110	48	H
73	111	49	I
74	112	4A	J
75	113	4B	K
76	114	4C	L
77	115	4D	M
78	116	4E	N
79	117	4F	O
80	120	50	P
81	121	51	Q
82	122	52	R
83	123	53	S
84	124	54	T
85	125	55	U
86	126	56	V
87	127	57	W
88	130	58	X
89	131	59	Y
90	132	5A	Z
91	133	5B	[
92	134	5C	\
93	135	5D	]
94	136	5E	^
95	137	5F	_
96	140	60	`
97	141	61	a
98	142	62	b
99	143	63	c
100	144	64	d
101	145	65	e
102	146	66	f
103	147	67	g
104	150	68	h
105	151	69	i
106	152	6A	j

Decimal	Octal	Hex	Character
107	153	6B	k
108	154	6C	l
109	155	6D	m
110	156	6E	n
111	157	6F	o
112	160	70	p
113	161	71	q
114	162	72	r
115	163	73	s
116	164	74	t
117	165	75	u
118	166	76	v
119	167	77	w
120	170	78	x
121	171	79	y
122	172	7A	z
123	173	7B	{
124	174	7C	|
125	175	7D	}
126	176	7E	~
127	177	7F	DEL

D : Answers to Questions

Chapter 1

1) A tool which translates high-level language into machine language

2) By typing the name of an executable file

3) By typing something like 'cc filename'

4) No!

5) Compiler errors and runtime errors

Chapter 3

1) printf ("Wow big deal");

2) printf ("22");

3) printf ("The 3 wise men");
   printf ("The %d wise men",3);

4) Most facilities are held in libraries

Chapter 4

1) To provide a basic set of facilities to the user

2) The filename used by a computer to reference a device

3) accounts.c

4) accounts.x (or perhaps accounts.EXE)

5) By typing the name in 4

Chapter 5

1) #include <filename> or #include 'filename'

2) stdio.h

3) No. Only macro names can be used if the header file is not included

4) Header file

Chapter 7

1) A group of statements enclosed by curly braces { }

2) Comments, pre-processor commands, functions, declarations, variables, statements. This is a matter of opinion, of course!

3) Not necessarily. It starts wherever main() is

4) It signifies the end of a block, the return of control to somethng else

5) The semi-colon (;)

Chapter 8

1) The compiler thinks the rest of the program is all one comment!

Chapter 9

1)

```
function (a,b)

int a,b;

{
return (a*b);
}
```

2) No

3) The value is discarded

4) The result is garbage

5) By using 'return'

Chapter 10

1) A name for some variable, function or macro

2) a,c,f

3) int i,j;

4) double is twice the length of float and can hold significantly larger values

5) int can have values + or -. Unsigned can only be + and can hold slightly larger + values than int

6) I = 67;

7) int

8) At the function definition and in the calling function

9) printf ("%d",(int)23.1256);

10) No

Chapter 11

1) With variable parameters or with return()

2) Where a function is defined, after its name: For example:

function (...)

<-- here

```
{
}
```

3) Yes

4) No, and it is illegal

5) * means 'the contents of' and & means 'the address of'

6) No

Chapter 12

1) A global variable can be accessed by any part of a program

2) A local variable can only be accessed by a select part of a program

3) Local variables cannot leak out. Nothing outside them can reach local variables

4) Variable parameters do. Value parameters use their own local copies, so they do not

5)

```
int i,j;

main ()

{ float x,y;
another(x,y);
}

another(x,y)
float x,y;
{
}
```

There are six storage spaces altogether

Chapter 13

1) #define birthday 19

2) #include <math.h>

3) false

4) false

Chapter 14

1) A variable which holds the address of another variable

2) With a * character. For example, int *i

3) Any type at all!

4) doubleptr = (double *)chptr

5) Because number has not been initialised. This expression initialises the place that number points to, not number itself. (See main text)

Chapter 15

printf

1)

```
#include <stdio.h>

main ()
{
printf (“%2e”,6.23);
}
```

2) This depends on individual compilers

3) a. No conversion string
b. Conversion string without matching value
c. Probably nothing
d. Conversion string without matching value

scanf

1) space, newline or tab

5) true.

Low-level I/O

1) The statement is possible provided putchar() is not implemented as a macro. It copies the input to the output: a simple way of writing on the screen. Note, however, that the output is buffered so characters may not be seen on the output for some time!

2) ch = getchar();
putchar (ch);

Chapter 16

1) The thing(s) an operator acts upon

2) printf ("%d",5 % 2);

3) rem = 5 % 2;

4) variable = 10 - -5;

5)

```
if (1 != 23)
     {
     printf ("Thank goodness for mathematics");
     }
```

Chapter 18

1) Three: while, do...while, for

2) while : at the start of each loop
do : at the end of each loop
for : at the start of each loop

3) do...while

4)

```
#include <stdio.h>
#define true 1

main ()

{ char ch;

while (true)
      {
      ch = getchar();
      putchar (ch);
      }
```

Chapter 19

1) The array identifier (without square brackets) is a pointer to the first element in the array

2) You pass the array identifier, without square brackets. No! Arrays are always variable parameters

3) double array[4][5];
Valid array bounds from array[0][0] to array[3][4]

Chapter 20

1) Arrays of characters. Pointers to arrays of characters

2) static char *strings[];
Could then initialise with braces { } and item list. (See main text)

3) See the Morse code example

Chapter 21

1) double

2) Probably true. This is implementation dependent. The actual types are double, long float and int

3) The length of a string (excluding NULL byte)

4) Joins two strings

5) Overflow, underflow, domain error, Loss of accuracy and division by zero

Chapter 22

1) ++, -- and any assignment or unary operator

2) It could make a program too difficult to read

3) No. The function would return before the value could be incremented

Chapter 23

1) FILE is defined by stdio.h. It is reserved only when this file is included. It is not a built in part of the language

2) FILE *fp;

3) False. They are meant for comparitive purposes only. It does not make sense to do arithmetic with enumerated data

4) Yes. It provides a generic pointer, that is one which can be assigned to any other pointer type

5) volatile

6) typedef double real;

7) True

Chapter 24

1) Nothing – only the way it is used. Yes, every variable is a bit pattern. It is normal to use integer or character types for bit patterns

2) Inclusive OR is true if all possiblilities are true simultaneously. Exclusive OR is false if all possibilites are true simultaneously

3) Some kind of flag message perhaps. A bit pattern for certain

4) a. 00000111 & 00000010 == 00000010 == 2
b. 00000001 & 00000001 == 00000001 == 1
c. 00001111 & 00000011 == 00000011 == 3
d. 00001111 & 00000111 == 00000111 == 7
e. 00001111 & 00000111 & 00000011 == 00000011 = 3

5) a. 00000001 | 00000010 == 00000011 == 3
b. 00000001 | 00000010 | 00000011 == 00000011 == 3

6) a. 1 & (~1) == 00000001 & 11111110 == 0
b. 23 & ~23 == 00011111 & 11100000 == 0
c. similarly 0: n & (NOT n) is always zero

Chapter 25

1) a. A string which labels a file
b. A variable of type *fp which points to a FILE structure
c. The number of a file "portal" in the I/O array

2) High-level filing performs translations to text. Low-level files untranslated bit data

3) fp = fopen ("filename","r");

4) fd = open ("filename",O_WRONLY);

6) fprintf ()

Chapter 26

1) A structure can hold several values at the same time. A union holds only one value at any one time

2) A part of a structure, or a possible occupant of a union

3) x.mem

4) ptr->mem

5) False

Chapter 27

1) A diagram which shows how structures are put together

2) With pointers

3) False. Pointers are used to reference variables and data structures are built in such a way as to require only one name for a whole structure

4) With pointers. ptr->member and so on

5) ptr=(struct Binary Tree *)malloc(sizeof(struct Binary Tree));

Chapter 28

1) A function which is defined in terms of itself

2) A data structure run by the C language for keeping track of function calls and for storing local data

3) A lot of memory is used as stack space

Chapter 31

1) Declarations are in the wrong place

2) Missing closing brace }

3) Missing semi-colon after closing brace };;

E : Programs Disc

A disc of programs is available from Dabs Press, containing all the programs listed in this book plus several others – over 50 in total including an adventure game, telephone bill utility, a window graphics program and an automatic cross-referencing index generator.

The programs are available on discs for the following micros:

Acorn Archimedes
Commodore Amiga
PCs (two discs)

In all instances, both the source and the compiled object code is provided thus allowing the original programs to be run immediately or edited to suit individual needs as may be required.

The disc comes supplied with it own manual which documents how to use the files on the disc, and gives more extensive user notes on running the extra programs. The cost is £9.95 inclusive for each version.

The programs disc is available directly from Dabs Press, and you will find a cut-out order form at the very end of this book which may be used if needed. Alternatively, please simply list details in a similar format on a sheet of paper. Cheques and postal orders should be made payable to 'Dabs Press' and sent to the address given.

Brief details of three of the extra programs are listed below.

Telephone Bill Program Utility

The telephone example is a complete application program utility, written in portable C, which can be used to keep accurate records of phone calls made by partners sharing a phone line, or network, and accurately calculate the bill for a quarter!

The program is menu driven and provides the following options:

1 : Edit Defaults
2 : Charge Sheet
3 : Print Log Sheet
4 : Bill Calculator
q : Quit

The program caters for local, long distance and international calls. Bills may be loaded, saved and edited required and printed out.

Adventure Game

The adventure game is a simple game designed to show how C can be used to write programs which are split up into many files. The source code of the game consists of eight separate files. The main file contains the logical program code for the game. The remaining files contain the data and ancillary definitions for the program. In principle, it should be possible to solve the game by reading the source code of the program.

Index Generator V1.2

Index Generator is a utility program which you to create formatted indices from your own source data. Raw index data, consisting of words/phrases and page numbers, are arranged in alphabetical order and the relevant page numbers are ordered and formatted on screen. Index Generator provides the option to cross reference entries in an index and to merge several files of index data into one.

The resulting formatted information may be saved as a formatted ASCII file, for merging with wordprocessor documents, or printed out. The current version of Index Generator generates the Dabs index format, as used in the accompanying book.

The formatted output of the program may be sent to an ASCII file for merging with documents, or may be viewed on the screen.

Data can be entered into the program in either of two ways. Perhaps the simplest way is to use a wordprocessor as a kind of scratch pad for making index notes. Alternatively, data can be entered is via the update editor provided by the program.

F : Dabhand Guides

Dabhand Guide Guides

The following Dabhand Guides and software packs will be published in 1988. Leaflets are available on all these products which go into considerably more detail than space here permits. Publication dates and contents are subject to change. All quoted prices are inclusive of VAT (on software, books are zero-rated), and postage and packing.

Also by Mark Burgess, author of C: A Dabhand Guide:

AmigaDOS: A Dabhand Guide

ISBN 1-870336-47-X
Publication : July 1988. 300 pages approx
Price: £14.95

The complete and comprehensive guide to AmigaDOS for the user of the Commodore Amiga. This book provides a unique perspective on the Amiga's powerful operating system in a way which will be welcomed by the beginner and experienced user alike. Rather than simply reiterating the Amiga manual, this book is a genuinely different approach to understanding and using the Amiga.

Just some of the topics covered include: filing with and without the workbench, the hierachical filing system, pathnames and device names, multi-tasking and its capabilities, The AmigaDOS screen editor, AmigaDOS commands, batch processing, error codes and descriptions, creating system discs, recovering damaged discs and using AmigaDOS with C.

Simply a *must* for all Amiga owners and users!

WordStar 1512: A Dabhand Guide
Including WordStar Express
by Bruce Smith

ISBN 1-870336-17-8
Publication : July 1988. 300 pages approx
Book: £12.95. Disc: 5.25in, £7.95; book and disc together, £17.95

A comprehensive tutorial and reference guide to WordStar 1512 and WordStar Express from one of the country's most prolific and top selling computer authors. Many thorny subjects are revealed in the authors own inimitable style – which makes tough subjects easy to understand. The many features of this book include rulers, margins, copy, move, delete, dot commands, page layout, spelling checker, mail-merge, using printers, RAM discs, and Boost.

Many screen dumps provide visual re-enforcement while the unique reference sections will ensure all the information you can every require is available instantly. See below for quotes from reviews of Bruce Smiths previous book on wordprocessing.

VIEW: A Dabhand Guide
by Bruce Smith

ISBN 1-870336-00-3
Publication : Available now. 248 pages
Book: £12.95. Disc: DFS 5.25in, £7.95 ADFS; 3.5in, £9.95. Book and disc together, £17.95 (ADFS £19.95)

This is the most comprehensive tutorial and reference guide written about using the VIEW wordprocessor. Both the beginner, and the more advanced user, will find it to be an invaluable companion whether writing a simple letter or undertaking a thesis. In addition, a suite of VIEW utility programs are provided, including: VIEW Manager, an easily extendable front end. Thorny subjects such as macros, page layout and printer drivers are revealed.

What the reviews said:
John Allen speaking on Radio London: '*It's very good...*'

Mike Williams, *Beebug* magazine June 1987: '*...much more to offer the competent VIEW user...practical and down-to-earth...for those who want a complete, thorough and readable guide to VIEW then Bruce Smith is your man.*'

Bill Penfold, *Acorn User* September 1987: '*This is the first computer book I've read in bed for pleasure rather than to cure insomnia.*'

ViewSheet and Viewstore: A Dabhand Guide
by Graham Bell

ISBN 1-870336-04-6
Publication : March 1988. 350 pages
Book: £12.95. Disc: DFS 5.25in, £7.95; ADFS 3.5in, £9.95. Book and disc together, £17.95 (ADFS £19.95)

Written by *Acorn User's* Graham Bell this book is a complete tutorial and reference guide for the Acornsoft ViewSheet spreadsheet and the ViewStore database manager. It is specifically written to appeal both to the beginner and to the more knowledgeable user, whether you wish to double-check your bank statement or run a million-pound business! Every aspect of setting up and using a database or spreadsheet is described in detail, and numerous examples are provided to guide you. There are also a number of utility programs to help you get more out of the VIEW family, including programs that join two databases together and help transfer spreadsheets into a wordprocessor.

Archimedes Assembly Language: A Dabhand Guide
By Mike Ginns

ISBN 1-870336-20-8
Publication: July 1988. 350 pages approx
Book : £14.95. 3.5" disc, £9.95. Book and disc together, £21.95

This book shows you how to get the most from the remarkable new Archimedes micro by programming directly in the machine's own language – machine code. This book covers all aspects of machine code/assembler programming for all Archimedes machines.

For those who are totally new to assembler programming, the book contains a beginner's section which takes the reader step by step through topics such as binary numbers, and logic operations.

To make the transition from BASIC to machine code as painless as possible, the book contains a section on implementing BASIC commands in machine code. All of the most useful BASIC statements are covered.

Archimedes Operating System: A Dabhand Guide
By Alex and Nick van Someren

ISBN: 1-870336-48-8
Available August 1988. 250 pages approx
Price: £14.95. 3.5in disc, £9.95. Book and disc together, £21.95

The book that is a must for every serious Archimedes owner. It describes how the Archimedes works and examines the ARTHUR operating system in microscopic detail, giving the programmer a real insight into getting the best from the Archimedes.

The book is intended for the serious machine code, or BASIC, programmer and includes sections on: the ARM instruction set, SWIs, graphics, Writing relocatable modules, vectors, compiled code, MEMC, VIDC, IOC and much more.

Alex and Nick have both worked for Acorn and Alex is a former Technical Editor of *Acorn User*. He has written several computer-related books.

Master 512: A Dabhand Guide
by Chris Snee

ISBN 1-870336-14-3
Publication: June 1988. 200 pages approx
Book: £14.95 Disc £7.95. Book and disc £19.95 (£21.95 3.5")

At last, the book that all Master 512 owners have been waiting for – and it has been worth it! This book contains just everything that you are likely to want to know about your Master 512, and could prove to be your most significant purchase serving as a tutorial and reference guide.

Here is a list of just some of the topics that are covered in the book: what you get on the discs, DOS Plus versions, explanation of the filing system, DOS Plus CLI commands (syntax, abbreviations and errors), transient commands, file types, reserved extentions, reserved words, I/O, the 512 memory map, how a PC works, 8086 registers, MS-DOS, 512 Tube, the 80186 monitor, differences between DOS Plus and MS-DOS, making software work on the 512, colour limitations, hard disc set-up, PC disc formats, software compatibility, public domain software…

Bumper Assembler Bundle
by Bruce Smith

Publication : Available Now
Two books, two discs and booklet, just £9.95

If programming in 6502 machine code is just wishful thinking, here is the chance for you to explore this fascinating subject with our Bumper Assembler Bundle. We are able to bring to you a five-part package of assembly language materials at less than a third of their normal price – all from the prolific keyboard of BBC expert, and former *Acorn User* Technical Editor, Bruce Smith. Here's a summary:

1. BBC Micro Assembly Language is an excellent 200-page introduction and tutorial guide to 6502 assembly language. Normal price is £7.95.

2. A DFS format disc packed with 60 (yes, sixty!) programs from the book BBC Micro Assembly Language.

3. BBC Micro Assembler Workshop. Its 160 pages contain programs such as a super fast machine code sort, and a machine code disassembler. Normal Price of this book is £6.95.

4. A DFS format disc packed with 30 programs from the book BBC Micro Assembler Workshop.

5. A booklet detailing all the new chip commands and innovations supplied with the Master 128 and Master Compact that have come to life since the above books were published.

All together this bundle would cost you over £30. We can offer it to you at an exclusive price of just £9.95 including p&p and VAT. An ADFS version of the two discs is also available at the same price.

Forthcoming Autumn Books for 1988

PCW 9512: A Dabhand Guide by John Atherton

ISBN 1-870336-50-X. Publication: Third quarter. 300 pages approx

WordPerfect: A Dabhand Guide by Bruce Smith

ISBN 1-870336-53-4. Publication: Fourth quarter. 350 pages approx

Supercalc 3.1: A Dabhand Guide by Dr A.A. Berk

Publication: Fourth quarter. 300 pages approx

PostScript: A Dabhand Guide by Paul Martin

ISBN 1-870336-54-2. Publication: Fourth quarter. 300 pages approx

Ability Plus: A Dabhand Guide by Geoff Cox

ISBN 1-870336-51-8 . Publication: Third quarter. 300 pages approx

Software from Dabs Press

FingerPrint by David Spencer for the BBC and Master Micros

Available Now! Disc & manual, DFS version, £9.95, ADFS version, £11.95

A unique single-step machine code tracing program allowing you to step through any machine code program. FingerPrint will even trace code situated in Sideways RAM/ROM – learn how BASIC works!

MOS Plus by David Spencer for BBC Master 128

Available Now! ROM, £12.9; Disc for Sideways RAM, £7.95 (3.5in, £9.95)

Provides ADFS *FORMAT, *VERIFY , *BACKUP, *CATALL and *EXALL in ROM and new * commands such as *FIND – which finds a file anywhere on an ADFS disc. A complete alarm system is present using the Master 128 alarm facility, as is an AMX mouse driver. The ROM also fixes the infamous DFS *CLOSE bug.

SideWriter by Mike Ginns for BBC and Master with Sideways RAM

Available Now! 5.25in DFS disc, £7.95, 3.5in ADFS disc, £9.95

A pop-up notepad which can be used from within any application from Sideways RAM. Simply press SHIFT-CTRL-TAB and your program is suspended, and you're in SideWriter ready to make a note. Press TAB and you're back with your application screen exactly as you left it. Notes taken in SideWriter can be saved to disc, transferred to a wordprocessor, or printed out.

Master Emulation ROM by David Spencer for BBC B/B+

ISBN 1-870336-23-2 Available Now
Software pack in ROM, £19.95 (disc for Sideways RAM, £14.95)

Provides model B and B+ owners with most of the features of the Master 128, such as the new * commands, the extended filing system operations including the temporary filing system, the *CONFIGURE system (using battery-backed Sideways RAM and/or a disc file), and if you have the hardware, Sideways or Shadow RAM. The only Master Operating System software not covered in this ROM, is the extended graphics software. Works with all popular SRAM boards.

HyperDriver by Robin Burton for BBC and Master Micros

Software pack in ROM, £29.95. Sideways RAM version, only £24.95

HyperDriver isn't just another printer ROM – it's the ultimate one. And if you have a printer, then HyperDriver will be the most significant purchase you can make. It's absurdly easy to use and provides you with many of the facilities missing from your current software including: on-screen preview, CRT graphics, NLQ font and user-definable macros to name but a few. No matter what you use your printer for, wordprocessing, spreadsheets, databases, programming you will have in excess of 80, yes 80!, * commands available for instant use from within applications such as VIEW, InterWord and so on. Thus, commands can be embedded *within* text, spreadsheets etc.

HyperDriver provides a full preview facilty so that you can see what will be printed on screen. The effects of all HyperDriver commands are displayed, for instance, italics, double height, bold, condensed, super and subscript, underlined and so on.

HyperDriver is fully Epson-compatible. HyperDriver's macro command facility allows you to add your own HyperDriver commands so that effects present on new realeases of printer, eg, NLQ, double height and so on, can be added with the minimum of fuss.

The HyperDriver pack contains a 16k EPROM for permanent internal fitting to the micro, and a Sideways RAM image on disc. The disc also contains sample programs and files for ease of use and reference. A full and comprehensive 100-page manual and reference card complete this value for money package

The inbuilt NLQ font allows printers that do not have an inbuilt NLQ font to produce text of this standard, and provides printers that do have the capability with an extra NLQ typeface. CRT graphics handling and an integral VIEW driver are included.

HyperDriver is supplied in ROM format The accompanying disc contains a Sideways RAM version of HyperDriver plus numerous examples. The comprehensive 100-page manual ensures that you get the most from the product.

Please note:

All future publications are in an advanced state of preparation. Content lists serve as a guide, but we reserve the right to alter and adapt them without notification. If you would like more information about Dabs Press, books and software, then drop us a line at 76 Gardner Road, Prestwich Manchester M25 7HU, and we'll despatch our latest Dabhand Guides Guide.

Glossary of Terms

ACTUAL PARAMETER: See argument.

ADDRESS: A number which tells the computer (or the programmer!), the exact location of a single byte of data in memory.

AGGREGATE: A cluster of variables which is given a single name. Each variable is called a member of the aggregate, and is accessed with '.member' or '->member'. The two aggregates supported by C are called struct(ures) and union(s).

ALGORITHM: The name given to a programme of tasks is an algorithm. This is the part of a program which does the manipulation. It does not concern the way in which data is stored.

ARGUMENT: A variable or a value (number) which is passed to a function. For instance if function(a,b) is a function, then this function takes two arguments – a and b.

ASCII: American Standard Code for Information Interchange. An ASCII code is the number which represents a given character in the memory of the computer.

ASSIGNMENT OPERATOR: The symbol = is the standard assignment operator. C also supports +=,-=,*=,/=,|= and so on. See relevant chapter on operators.

BIT: The most elementary unit of memory. A bit can only store the values one or zero.

BRACE: The symbols { and }.

BRACKET: The symbols (and).

BUFFER: A buffer is an area of memory set aside for data which is in the process of being either transmitted or received. A buffer allows characters to build up somewhere if they are being received faster than they can be used, or being generated faster than they can be transmitted.

BYTE: A convenient grouping of eight bits (corruption of 'By Eight'). The maximum unsigned value it can hold is 255. The minimum unsigned value is zero. The maximum signed value is 127, and the the minimum signed value is -128.

CODE: Often used to mean 'program code', or a piece of program written in C.

COMPILE TIME: This is the time during the execution of the compiler program, ie, when a source file is being translated into machine code.

COMPOUND STATEMENT: Wherever a C statement can be given in a program, a 'compound statement' can given instead. This is a group of statements surrounded by braces. For example:

```
{
printf ("...");
for (x = 0; x <= 1; x++);
}
```

CONTROL STRING: A string used in formatted input/output in order to specify the type of data which is being read or written. For example, '%d' would signal that an integer type is to be read or written. Control strings are mixed up with ordinary text and always begin with a '%' symbol. Illegal characters after the % are just printed.

CRASH: A computer is said to have 'crashed' when it runs wildly out of control or just 'dies' because of a faulty program or hardware failure. The usual cause of crashing is faulty programming. Don't be surprised if your computer crashes regularly when programming with C!

DENARY: Number base 10 – our normal counting base. This is in contrast to binary or hexadecimal. It is sometimes called decimal, but this can be confused with other uses of the word.

DIMENSION of an ARRAY: The number of storage places for one index of an array. So:

```
int array[6];
```

would declare an array of dimension six. Arrays with two indicies are called 'two-dimensional' but this is a slightly different meaning, just to add to the confusion. A two-dimensional array:

```
char array[8][9];
```

would be called an array with dimensions eight by nine.

DOS: Disc Operating System.

DYADIC OPERATOR: An operator which is 'infixed', ie, it operates between two objects like the multiplication symbol – a * b. See also unary operator.

EXECUTION TIME: The time during which the user's program is running.

EXECUTABLE FILE: A file which has been translated into machine code by a compiler. For example, program.x.

FALSE: Opposite of true. It is applied to tests and decisions where comparisons are made. For example, (a == 0) is FALSE, if the variable a is not equal to zero. In C, false has the integer value zero (0). See also true.

FIELD: A print field is a space into which something is written. Often a screen will be thought of as being divided up into fields or areas. Printf fields are defined in C using the % character in a control string.

FORMAL PARAMETER: A temporary variable into which arguments are copied. Formal parameters are the names of function arguments inside the function definition.

GARBAGE: Nonsense. Values which are spurious or random and do not have anything to do with a program, or don't have any meaning.

GLOBAL: This means that something is valid everywhere.

GLOBAL WHITE SPACE: A fancy name for the space which is outside, and in between, functions in a C program. For example, at the very top of the file, before the first main() function. This is where preprocessor symbols must be defined.

HEAP: Another name used to describe a stack. The distinction is only for convenience, give or take some minor differences. See stack.

HEXADECIMAL: Number base 16.

IDENTIFIER: Any name which a programmer invents to label a variable or function. It identifies a C object.

INDEX (of an array): A variable or a number which is used to access the different elements or pigeon holes in the array.

INFIXED OPERATOR: An operator which is fixed between two values, like the addition, multiplication operators and so on – 2 + 3, a * b.

INSIDE: A term used in this book to mean something which is enclosed by block braces { }. See outside.

I/O: Short for input/output.

LINKED LIST: A versatile kind of list which is made of data pieces and connections between the data. Each element knows which is the next element in the list because it has a record of the next item. A linked list is made up of pointers and structures in C.

LINKER: A phase of a compiler which ties up all the loose ends, such as functions which have been called but not defined, and incorporates standard library code into programs and so on.

LOCAL: This means that something is valid only within a limited area. It is the opposite of global.

LOCAL MANUAL: An expression meaning the reference manual for a particular system. It is local because it does not apply for all computers or programs.

LOCAL OPERATING SYSTEM: The operating system under which a program is running. It is local because it does not apply to all computers.

NESTING: Objects are said to be nested when they are arranged one inside the other. For instance block braces are nested:

```
{
....
     {
     ...
     }
...
}
```

Loops are often nested:

```
for (a = 1; a < 10; a++)
     {
     for (b = 1; b < 10; b++)
          {
          do_something ();
          }
     }
```

#include files can also nest if there are includes inside includes. A compiler might impose restrictions on how many times things can be nested.

LVALUES: Any object which can be on the left-hand side of an assignment operator. It is the name of a variable.

MEMORY MAP: A list of all the address locations of memory in the computer.

MEMORY MAPPED INPUT/OUTPUT: The registers of chips which make up a computer have to be addressable by the central processing unit (CPU), so they are often made into a part of the memory map of the computer. Some processors can communicate more directly with I/O, or contain their own I/O interfaces already.

OBJECT CODE: A file of machine code which is generated by a compiler. This is not usually executable, as it must be linked to standard library code in order to be complete.

OCTAL: Number base 8.

OPERAND: The object acted upon by an operator. See operator.

OPERATOR: An operator is something which takes one or more variables (called operands) and produces a new result from them. For example, &( ) is the address operator, it takes a single value (some variable), and its value is a pointer to that object. The + sign is also an operator (a binary or dyadic operator, because it has two operands). It takes two variables or numbers and produces a result which is the sum of the two.

OUTSIDE: A term used in this book which means not inside block braces { }. This is important in discussing the scope of things. See inside.

POINTER: The address or location of a storage area used in a program is called a pointer to the data. In C the operator &(variable) gives the address of an object, so that we can write:

```
pointer = &(object)
```

The * symbol is used to affect the contents of a data store when only a pointer to it is known:

```
*pointer = 5
```

would set the contents of object to be five. The above is equivalent to:

```
object = 5;
```

Note that C pointers are not the same for different kinds of data. A pointer to an integer is not the same as a pointer to a floating point number and so on. They can be converted with the cast operator ( ) however. (See relevant chapter for details.)

REGISTER: Usually thought of as being a memory location inside a computer processor, which is used by the processor for working on data. See Chapter 24: Low-level Operations.

RESERVED WORD: A word which C uses for a special purpose and so cannot be used as the name of a variable or function.

RETURN: A function is said to return a value if it hands back some value to the function which called it. In C there is no distinction between routines which return a value and those which do not. If no assignment is made in the calling function any return value is discarded.

RUN-TIME: The time during which a compiled program is being executed or 'run'. It is held in distinction to 'compile time'.

SCOPE: The part of a program in which a variable has meaning. When a local variable is declared inside block brackets { }, it is only valid inside those brackets and any reference to it outside will result in an error at compile time. However, any variables declared outside block brackets { } are allowed inside them too. If there is a clash of names, the either an error will be signalled or the local variable, ie, the one declared inside will take precedence. See Chapter 12 on scope.

SOURCE CODE: A text file which contains the written program. All the printed examples in this book are examples of source code.

STACK: A pile of information which is built up in a simple way. It owes its name to the familiar idea of a stack. The only operations that can be performed with a stack are to put a new item on the top or to take an item from the top. Each new item in a stack is called a 'stack frame'. A stack is commonly used by an operating system for storing 'local variables'. See also heap.

STATEMENT: Any complete group of words ending with a semi-colon is called a statement. For example, printf (".."); or for (x=0; x<=1; x++). See also compound statement.

STRUCTURE DIAGRAM: A diagram which solves a computer program. It shows the structure of the program by using a series of levels, zones and toolkits.

SUBROUTINE: In C, all subroutines are called 'functions'. A subroutine is a piece of program code which is called as a part of a more major program.

TEXT FILE: A file which contains only writing and numbers – letters of the alphabet, spaces, new lines and numbers.

TOKEN: A number which is used to stand in place of a word. A token is often found by a 'hashing' or numbering function.

TOOLKIT: A group of functions which work on a particular problem. A function in a toolkit will be used many times from many different places in a program.

TRUE: The result of the comparison (a == 0) is true only if the variable a is zero. In C 'true' has an integer value which is any number except zero (0).

UNARY OPERATOR: An operator which returns a result from a single object. For example, the increment operator c++, or the address operator & c. 'sizeof' is also thought of as being a unary operator because it operates on a typename rather than a value. It is a compile time operator, however and it might be argued that it is really a function.

VDU: Visual display unit. The monitor or screen of a computer.

WHITE SPACE CHARACTERS: Characters which are not generally seen in a program such as spaces and carriage returns. White space means they are the 'white on a sheet of paper' ie, where no characters have been typed. The white space of a program can be thought of as the blank sheet of paper on to which a program is written.

WIMP: Windows, icons, mice and pull-down menus. A type of operating system which uses windows with mouse control and menus. It is easier to use than a system where the user has to type every command.

WINDOW: A rectangular box on the screen of a computer which behaves like an independent screen in its own right. Some computers have only one window on their screen. Many window systems are often accompanied by WIMP environments.

ZONE: The main zone is the main program idea. Any other zone is an area of program which is necessary for it to work, but has no real relevance to the main idea. For instance it may be a long section to do with opening windows or setting up a system.

Index

Corrections - 2nd Edition 

Here is a list of the errors discovered in the book which should be corrected. For production reasons, we regret that it has not been possible to incorporate the changes in the text itself. The actual text to be changed is shown in **bold** type.

p.25	'struct' (line 5) is used as part of a declaration, and should be followed by a **'d'**.
p.28	**scanf("...",a)** should be **scanf("...",&a)**
p.35	**#include 'stdio.h'** should be **#include "stdio.h"**
p.89	Line 4: Change **'standard libraries'** to **'libraries of source code'**.
p.111	The table should be formatted. The middle column always contains %...f, and the | symbols mark the columns.
p.119	Throughout the whole of Figure 15.2, **'ln'** should be **'/n'**
p.209	Fig.20.1, insert **'/0'** in the bottom panel at the point marked by the arrow and legend 'zero byte end marker'.
p.242	The lines **ch++;** and **comparison--;** in the listing at the foot of the page should be transposed.
p.326	The **'S'** marker on the compass has been misplaced. It should of course be at the foot of the compass.
p.392	In the heading **'trappable'** is misspelt.
p.443	In the listing replace **floodfill(300,300);** with **fill(300,300);**
p.469	Chapter 5, 1) should read ...<filename> or **include "filename"** (double quotes).

Programs Disc

Please send me a programs disc to accompany C:A Dabhand Guide. I would like the

Acorn Archimedes	£9.95
Commodore Amiga	£9.95
IBM/Amstrad PC 5.25" (2 discs)	£9.95
IBM/Amstrad PC 3.5"	£9.95
BBC B/Master 5.25"	£7.95
BBC B/Master 3.5"	£9.95

version (Please tick as appropriate).

I enclose a cheque/official order no ....

or

My Access/Visa number is ....

Price includes VAT and postage in the UK. Foreign readers, please pay the same amount as there is no VAT, but additional postage costs.

Name..

Address..

....

....

....